JEWISH AND CHRISTIAN TEXTS IN CONTEXTS AND RELATED STUDIES

39

Executive Editor
James H. Charlesworth

Editorial Board
Motti Aviam, Michael Davis, Casey Elledge, Loren Johns,
Amy-Jill Levine, Lee McDonald, Lidia Novakovic, Gerbern Oegema,
Henry Rietz, Brent Strawn

Mosaic of Samson carrying the gate of Gaza from the Huqoq synagogue. Reproduced with permission of Jodi Magness; photo by Jim Haberman

SCRIPTURAL TALES RETOLD

The Inventiveness of Second Temple Jews

Erich S. Gruen

LONDON • NEW YORK • OXFORD • NEW DELHI • SYDNEY

T&T CLARK

Bloomsbury Publishing Plc, 50 Bedford Square, London, WC1B 3DP, UK
Bloomsbury Publishing Inc, 1359 Broadway, New York, NY 10018, USA
Bloomsbury Publishing Ireland, 29 Earlsfort Terrace, Dublin 2, D02 AY28, Ireland

BLOOMSBURY, T&T CLARK and the T&T Clark logo are trademarks of
Bloomsbury Publishing Plc

First published in Great Britain 2024
Paperback edition published 2026

Copyright © Erich S. Gruen, 2024

Erich S. Gruen has asserted his right under the Copyright, Designs and Patents Act, 1988,
to be identified as Author of this work.

All rights reserved. No part of this publication may be: i) reproduced or transmitted in any form, electronic or mechanical, including photocopying, recording or by means of any information storage or retrieval system without prior permission in writing from the publishers; or ii) used or reproduced in any way for the training, development or operation of artificial intelligence (AI) technologies, including generative AI technologies. The rights holders expressly reserve this publication from the text and data mining exception as per Article 4(3) of the Digital Single Market Directive (EU) 2019/790.

Bloomsbury Publishing Plc does not have any control over, or responsibility for, any third-party websites referred to or in this book. All internet addresses given in this book were correct at the time of going to press. The author and publisher regret any inconvenience caused if addresses have changed or sites have ceased to exist, but can accept no responsibility for any such changes.

A catalogue record for this book is available from the British Library.

A catalog record for this book is available from the Library of Congress.

ISBN: HB: 978-0-5677-1517-3
PB: 978-0-5677-1521-0
ePDF: 978-0-5677-1518-0
eBook: 978-0-5677-1520-3

Series: Jewish and Christian Texts in Contexts and Related Studies, volume 39

Typeset by RefineCatch Limited, Bungay, Suffolk

For product safety related questions contact productsafety@bloomsbury.com

To find out more about our authors and books visit www.bloomsbury.com
and sign up for our newsletters.

*FOR ANN,
NOW AND FOREVER*

CONTENTS

Acknowledgments	ix
INTRODUCTION	1
Chapter 1 THE TOWER OF BABEL	13
Chapter 2 ABRAHAM IN EGYPT	21
Chapter 3 SARAH AND HAGAR	25
Chapter 4 THE AQEDAH	31
Chapter 5 THE TESTAMENT OF ABRAHAM	39
Chapter 6 THE RAPE OF DINAH	43
Chapter 7 THE CONFLICTING CHARACTER OF JOSEPH	53
Chapter 8 TAMAR AND JUDAH	63
Chapter 9 MOSES AND GOD	71
Chapter 10 MOSES IN ETHIOPIA	75
Chapter 11 MOSES AS UNIVERSAL FIGURE	79
Chapter 12 BALAAM AND WAYWARD PROPHECY	83

Chapter 13
YAEL AND THE DEATH OF SISERA   95

Chapter 14
JEPHTHAH AND HIS DAUGHTER   101

Chapter 15
SAMSON AS SUPERHERO   107

Chapter 16
THE JUDEAN MONARCHY AND SAUL   115

Chapter 17
SOLOMON AND THE BUILDING OF THE TEMPLE   131

Chapter 18
THE TRAVAILS OF JOB   137

Chapter 19
THE ADDITIONS TO ESTHER   145

CONCLUSION   149

Bibliography   151
Primary Sources Index   161
Author Index   167
Subject Index   171

ACKNOWLEDGMENTS

Declaration of debts is always among the happiest of tasks for a writer. First and foremost, it means that the current work is complete (at least as conceived) and that the author can turn attention to other matters that have long been sidelined. But, equally important, it allows for public expression of sincere gratitude to those who have helped, wittingly or unwittingly, to stimulate, motivate, and indeed provoke this project. I owe much to colleagues and friends who read and commented on an earlier draft of this work and offered generous suggestions while not withholding trenchant criticisms. I am happy to single out especially René Bloch, Marc Brettler, Ron Hendel, Michael Satlow, Greg Sterling, and Ben Wright. I owe gratitude also to Jim Charlesworth who advocated publication of the manuscript in the distinguished series, *Jewish and Christian Texts in Contexts and Related Studies*, and to the supportive and accommodating editors at Bloomsbury, T&T Clark, Dominic Mattos and Katherine Jenkins. Over and above all, my wife Ann Hasse, my constant and beloved companion, has been present at the gestation and development of this project, has read the manuscript at least twice, improving it each time, has provided invaluable benefit as editor and proofreader, and, not least, has performed the selfless and thankless task of collaborating in the compilation of the indexes. She receives my deepest thanks here—and my enduring love.

INTRODUCTION

Biblical narratives retain a powerful hold on our imaginations. They have a resonance almost unmatched in literary, intellectual, and cultural history. Stories like that of the (near) sacrifice of Isaac, the conflict of Sarah and Hagar, Moses and the golden calf, Joseph in Egypt, David and Goliath, and the exploits of the superhero Samson helped to define a people in antiquity and carry a legacy through the centuries to the present day. The familiar tales hold a special significance, with enduring influence and authority, for they stem from sacred Scriptures.

Yet their sacrality did not entail inviolability. Indeed, they possess a surprisingly malleable character. Among the notable features of Second Temple Judaism (ca. 515 BCE to 70 CE) was the frequency with which these stories took on different shapes, sometimes expanded, sometimes reduced, sometimes embellished, sometimes muted, occasionally recast in other genres, or re-presented with new messages or alternative meanings, or even as altogether novel narratives. The variety of renderings that we possess may indeed be only a fraction of the writings that circulated in this period, drawing on scriptural material but advancing the insights of subsequent authors.

How should one understand this flurry of activity in the Second Temple era? Did these rewritings compromise the aura of holiness ascribed to the Scriptures? Did they diminish the authority of texts taken as expressions of the divine? Was there a recurrent agenda or objective in these efforts to apply new slants to traditional tales?

On the face of it, the sanctity of scriptural material ought to have discouraged tampering with the text. Indeed, we possess testimony that declares Jewish awe at the solemnity of the sacred word. An event of momentous importance occurred some time in the 3rd century BCE. The Hebrew Bible, or at least the Pentateuch, the Five Books of Moses, we are told, was translated into Greek. As the famous story in the *Letter of Aristeas* has it, Jewish sages from Jerusalem visited Alexandria, at the behest of King Ptolemy II, who wanted a Greek version of the Bible for the great library in Alexandria. Greek was, after all, the lingua franca of much of the eastern Mediterranean. Greek was the prevailing language of the ruling classes, the courts, the soldiery, the bureaucrats, and the intelligentsia of the eastern

Mediterranean ever since the conquests of Alexander the Great and his successors. It was also the prevailing language of the Jews everywhere in the diaspora. And the vast majority of the Jews in the Hellenistic and Roman periods did live in the diaspora. Just a small minority dwelled in Palestine, and even there Greek had penetrated, at least among the cultivated and the upper echelons.

According to the narrative in the *Letter of Aristeas*, the Jewish bi-lingual scholars collaborated carefully, compared translations, discussed and refined the wording, and eventually reached a consensus on a version acceptable to all. When it was presented to the priests, elders, and entire body of Jews in Alexandria, it received, we are told, a great ovation. And, more importantly, the leaders of the Jewish community pronounced the translation accurate in every respect, well and piously rendered, and not a word should be changed. Anyone who would venture to add or subtract a line would be placed under a curse. Thus, the work, it was determined, would be preserved intact and unsullied forever.[1]

The story is doubtless a fiction, concocted long after the fact.[2] Indeed, the great Jewish philosopher Philo of Alexandria in the mid-1st century CE, produced another and even more famous version of the story that embellished it further. He had the Jewish sages who translated the Bible do so individually and independently, indeed in seclusion from one another—and yet all of them produced exactly identical renditions, word for word, as if guided by an invisible hand.[3] Philo thus underscored the genuine solemnity of the process and its outcome, an emphasis on the absolute accuracy of the translation, the insistence that the Hebrew and Greek bibles were identical, and the deep reverence in which both must be held.

It is, of course, unthinkable that the fashioning of a viable Greek translation took place as a single event. The process must have occupied an extensive period of time, with a good deal of revising and rephrasing, and probably multiple versions before one of them gained authority, eventually to be known as the Septuagint.

Whatever the truth of the celebrated tales, however, a Greek rendition did eventually emerge, a matter of considerable significance. For Jews living in Alexandria and elsewhere in the diaspora, the Hebrew language, it appears, had

---

1. The famous story appears in the so-called *Letter of Aristeas*, composed by a Jewish intellectual, probably in the 2nd or early 1st century BCE, perhaps a century after the translation was accomplished. See, especially, *LetArist*. 308–311: ἐπεὶ καλῶς καὶ ὁσίως διηρμήνευται καὶ κατὰ πᾶν ἠκριβωμένως, καλῶς ἔχον ἐστίν, ἵνα διαμένῃ ταῦθ' οὕτως ἔχοντα, καὶ μὴ γένηται μηδεμία διασκευή. See the commentary of Wright (2015), 441–453.

2. Rajak (2009), 38–43, 51–55, argues for a mixture of fact and fiction in the *Letter of Aristeas*, emphasizing particularly the plausibility of Ptolemy II's promotion of the translation project. Cf. Honigman (2003), 136–139. For a sober summary of scholarship on the historicity of the tale, with a proper dose of skepticism, see Wright (2015), 6–15.

3. Philo, *Mos.* 2:38–40.

largely been lost.⁴ Hence the appearance of the Bible in Greek, the language with which they were most familiar and comfortable, constituted a major milestone.

The strong, unequivocal statements by our sources make clear that the new translation should be regarded as belonging in the same category as the Hebrew original—which, in their view, it duplicated precisely. The Greek Bible or, at the very least, the Pentateuch, was regularly characterized as "sacred," "holy," or "divine," in texts of the Second Temple period.⁵ Did the Septuagint then carry the same aura of sanctity that held for the Hebrew Pentateuch, allegedly composed by Moses himself, inspired by the hand of God? At least some Hellenistic Jews, who relied upon the Greek version, were eager to claim that it carried equal authority and commanded equal devotion. We need not doubt the devotion to the sacred writings. The Jews of the diaspora did wish to represent their scriptures as being on a par with and demanding the same awe and respect as that of their Hebrew precursor. But as for exact and unfailing accuracy, studies of the Septuagint have long ago shown that there are countless differences, discrepancies, modifications, and permutations between the Septuagint and the Hebrew Bible. Indeed many of the divergences to be found in the Septuagint may well have depended upon variants in the Hebrew precursors, for no fixed "Bible" existed at the time of the translation or translations.

With regard to close and reverential adherence to the original, the historian Josephus, in the late 1st century CE, went further still. At the outset of his twenty-volume work on *Jewish Antiquities* in Greek, the narrative of his nation from biblical times to his own day, he affirmed that he would set forth the entire ancient history of his people and the constitution of the state translated from the Hebrew writings themselves.⁶ He reiterates the commitment a few lines later, asserting quite explicitly that he promises neither to add nor to omit anything.⁷ Still later in his text, Josephus underscores the point that he has inserted nothing for the sake of embellishment that was not already there in Moses' own composition.⁸ The historian in his last work, the *Contra Apionem,* insists again that he, like all faithful

---

4. Bloch (2021), 261–278, makes a good case that Hebrew was by no means altogether lost in Alexandria, where the translation was (in all probability) made. But, as Bloch acknowledges, the slender evidence does not permit the conjecture of widespread bilingualism.

5. E.g., *Let Arist.* 3, 31, 313; Demetrius, *apud* Euseb. *PE*, 9:29.1, 9:29.15; 1 *Macc.* 3:48, 12:9; 2 *Macc.* 8:23; Philo, *Sobr.* 17; *Virt.* 95; *Mos.* 2:45; Jos. *Vita*, 418; *BJ*, 2:159; *AJ*, 12:113, 16:164. See Bremmer (2010), 336–347.

6. Jos. *AJ*, 1:5: μέλλει γὰρ περιέξειν ἅπασαν τὴν παρ' ἡμῖν ἀρχαιολογίαν καὶ τὴν διάταξιν τοῦ πολιτεύματος ἐκ τῶν Ἑβραϊκῶν μεθηρμηνευμένην γραμμάτων. On the rendering of μεθηρμηνευμένην as "translated," see the lengthy note by Feldman (2000), 3–4.

7. Jos. *AJ*, 1:17: ἐπηγγειλάμην οὐδὲν προσθεὶς οὐδ' αὖ παραλιπών. See also 10:218; cf. 2:347, 9:208, 14:1, 20:261; *CAp.* 1:42.

8. Jos. *AJ*, 4:196.

Jews, approaches the sacred writings in such a way that no one would be so bold as to add, remove, or change a thing; every Jew from the day of his birth inherently considers them as the decrees of God.[9] This theme derives its force from the injunction that the Lord imposed upon the children of Israel, according to the Book of Deuteronomy, before they entered the promised land. He instructed them to obey his commands unstintingly, to add nothing to them, and to subtract nothing.[10]

Josephus, however, plainly did not adhere to his own precepts. Very far from it. Not only did he depart considerably from a mere reproduction of the biblical text, offering in general a paraphrase rather than a literal translation of the Hebrew Bible (or the Septuagint). He also omitted numerous portions of the received text, dropping a number of somewhat embarrassing stories, such as that of Jacob's deception of Isaac in Genesis or the construction of the Golden Calf in Exodus; he inserted several episodes not found in the Bible, like Moses' wedding to an Ethiopian princess; and he often reduced the role of God and of miracles in the biblical narrative, perhaps to put greater stress on human agency.[11] So, how could Josephus possibly get away with claiming scrupulous faithfulness to the text? How does one reconcile the *claim* of absolute adherence to the Scriptures with the *fact* of considerable discrepancy between the biblical text and the historian's reconstruction? And what does this tell us about attitudes toward the Scriptures among Jewish writers who sought to revamp them?

Discomfort with this discordance has generated numerous efforts to get around the problem. It has been suggested, for example, that perhaps Josephus, at least in his own mind, did not really alter the text but just applied new readings to it that left the meaning intact. Or by stressing the authorship of Moses Josephus could dodge any infringement of God's word by claiming the right to modify the words of a human being. Or, on another theory, the historian could make such sweeping statements with impunity, since readers, in the absence of bound manuscripts, indexes, or research assistants, let alone search engines, would simply be unable or unwilling to challenge his claims on exactitude. The efforts to resolve this glaring problem are thus many and ingenious.[12]

---

9. Jos. CAp. 1:42: οὔτε προσθεῖναί τις οὐδὲν οὔτε ἀφελεῖν αὐτῶν οὔτε μεταθεῖναι τετόλμηκεν, πᾶσι δὲ σύμφυτόν ἐστιν εὐθὺς ἐκ τῆς πρώτης γενέσεως Ἰουδαίοις τὸ νομίζειν αὐτὰ θεοῦ δόγματα.

10. Deut. 4:2, 12:32. A similar pronouncement at the end of Rev. 22:18-19.

11. See the examples collected by Feldman (1998b), 37–39; *idem* (2000), 7.

12. A valuable summary of opinions, with their principal proponents, may be found in Feldman (1998b), 39–44; *idem* (2000), 7–8; see also Sterling (1992), 252–256; Barclay (2007), 31; Inowlocki (2005), 50–51. A notable parallel to Josephus' statements occurs in Dionysius of Halicarnassus' claim that early Greek historians, in drawing on non-Greek sources of other peoples, added nothing and subtracted nothing; Dion. Hal. *On Thucydides*, 5:331: μήτε προστιθέντες αὐταῖς τι μήτε ἀφαιροῦντες. See the commentary of Pritchett (1975), 54. Cf. Attridge (1976), 59.

Yet Josephus' language about adding or subtracting nothing is pointed and firm. He reiterated this position several times, and could hardly have taken it lightly. He was surely not seeking to deceive a knowledgeable Jewish readership who would see immediately that Josephus' history was no mere replica of the original. Nor is it likely that he would deliberately mislead his gentile readers, for they would not care one way or the other whether he was faithful to the Hebrew original. Was he deceiving himself? Not very probable. There are enough instances of calculated omissions (like the golden calf episode) to make clear that Josephus knew exactly what he was doing.

One cannot get around the fact that the historian (and his readers) understood this notion of exactitude rather differently from our customary usage. Yes, the sacred Scriptures were inviolable. But those who reproduced them in other languages, other genres, or from other perspectives were not thereby precluded from altering, adapting, or departing from the original whose sacrosanctity was, in their view at least, uncompromised by alternative versions. The authors of such versions evidently did not see them as substituting for or supplanting their model. The latter remained untouched and intact.

Readers of Josephus who were familiar with the Hebrew or Greek bibles would not have been misled by his pronouncements. The fact is that rewritings of Scripture were deeply embedded in Jewish culture. The Bible itself, as we have it, contains its own internal revisions. One thinks immediately of the 'Book of the Covenant,' the Mosaic regulations that followed directly upon the Ten Commandments in Exodus, as recast and expanded by Deuteronomy, or the two books of Chronicles which offered their own retelling of material to be found in the books of Samuel-Kings.[13]

Indeed, a veritable industry of reframing and retelling biblical stories long preceded Josephus. Numerous Jewish writers operated with tales familiar to us from the Scriptures, and then manipulated them at will. Nothing indicates that this activity challenged the authority of the Scriptures. Change or reworking evidently did not diminish the sacred aura ascribed to those writings.

New versions of the familiar tales emerged early in Hebrew and Aramaic. One need mention only the *Book of Jubilees* composed in Hebrew, probably in the 2nd century BCE, although extant now largely in its Ethiopic version, and comprising a rewrite of the Book of Genesis and part of the Book of Exodus.[14] The author of *Jubilees*, in fact, claims divine sanction for his own work. He asserts at the outset that his text was delivered by God to an angel who provided it to Moses on Mt. Sinai.[15] He thus asserts absolute authority, on a level with, even as a replica of,

---

13. Exod. 20:22-23, 20:33; Deut. 12–26. Among innumerable discussions, see Fishbane (1985), especially 231–277. On the Chronicler, see Fishbane (1985), 380–403. Cf., more recently, Zakovitch (2012), 27–63.

14. See now the indispensable commentary by VanderKam (2018), with extensive bibliography.

15. *Jub.* 1:27-29, 2:1.

the scriptural precursor. Yet the text itself is far from a duplicate. Little in it even pretends to offer precise correspondence to the Hebrew Bible.

Further, among the discoveries of the Dead Sea Scrolls is the so-called *Genesis Apocryphon*, composed in Aramaic. It exists only in fragments. But the extant portions offer a retelling of the Noah story and traditions on Abraham, with considerable reshaping, both additions and subtractions, and other departures from the Hebrew Bible, for it evidently drew on sources well beyond that account.[16]

The availability of the Bible in Greek, however, spawned a whole spate of altogether new versions of biblical tales, composed by Hellenistic Jews, but diverging, sometimes slightly, often quite drastically, from the Hebrew and Greek Bibles. The variety of scriptural writings in Greek that took different shape, with different resonance, in the hands of subsequent creative writers was quite remarkable. Too many of them, unfortunately, survive only in fragments, their works collected by an assiduous polymath named Alexander Polyhistor, a Greek intellectual from Miletos in the 1st century BCE, whose own compilation is available only in fragments.[17] But we owe him a lot. Many Jewish writers and indeed Polyhistor himself would have disappeared into the void were it not for the Church Father Eusebius and, to a lesser degree, Clement of Alexandria. As so often, we are in the debt of Christian theologians, with their own special motives, for this slender link to important Jewish writers who were ignored or scorned by the rabbis.

To take just a single example: the historian Eupolemos, who composed a work in Greek entitled "On the Kings in Judaea," probably in the 2nd century BCE.[18] Eupolemos plainly felt no restrictions that obliged him to stick to the familiar (to us) text of the Septuagint. He depicts Moses, interestingly enough, as the first wise man and the first to give the alphabet to the Jews, who then passed it on to the Phoenicians, and from them it came to the Greeks. He mentions Moses as lawgiver only as an afterthought. For Eupolemos, Moses is the font of the cultural evolution of both the Near East and Hellas.[19] And the author takes even greater liberties with the scriptural material. He boasts of King David's victories that go well beyond any biblical warrant, having him subjugate Assyrians, push into Asia Minor, rout the Phoenicians, clash with the Nabataeans, and conduct international relations with Egypt.[20] It is remarkable that amidst all the peoples and lands with whom Eupolemos has David clash, the one missing is precisely the one which is the

---

16. The edition by Fitzmyer (1971) remains invaluable. See also Alexander (1988), 104–107; Crawford (2008), 105–129.

17. The fullest study of Polyhistor remains Freudenthal (1874/5).

18. See the text and translation of Eupolemos' fragments, with commentary, in Holladay (1989), II, 93–156.

19. Clem. Alex. *Strom.* 1:23:153:4; Euseb. *PE,* 9:25:4-9:26:1.

20. Euseb. *PE,* 9:30.3-4.

centerpiece of the biblical story: the Philistines. The historian is clearly calling attention to his own originality.

Eupolemos is equally idiosyncratic in recording the deeds of Solomon. On his account, after the building of the Temple, organized and dictated by king Solomon, with the assistance of craftsmen and laborers from Phoenicia and Egypt, the king sent a handsome gift to the Phoenician monarch: nothing less than a golden column to be set up at Tyre in the temple of Zeus.[21] No scriptural basis exists for this. Moderns have found the passage puzzling and unacceptable. How could a Jewish historian credit Solomon, whose piety and magnanimity had been responsible for the First Temple in Jerusalem, with setting up a gold pillar in Tyre to honor the chief god of the Phoenicians?[22] Eupolemos himself, however, evidently saw no inconsistency or contradiction here. Solomon emerges as both a dedicated devotee of Yahweh and as patron of foreign princes and benefactor of their cults. Nor is there reason to believe that such a portrait would be marginalized as heterodox opinion.

Numerous other examples could be offered. This study seeks to illustrate the free adaptation of biblical narratives by Jewish writers, historians, poets, dramatists, philosophers, and novelists that can be found throughout the Hellenistic and Roman periods. That feature held for revised tales of even the most revered figures, the patriarchs and Moses, whose lives and achievements were integral to the scriptural record.

The widespread character of this practice has given rise to a larger question. How exactly does one characterize the nature and meaning of these efforts to provide new texts that departed from or revised biblical traditions? The question has spawned a raft of scholarly publications devoted to defining a presumed genre of literature, namely the "rewritten Bible." And various proposals emerged to identify which works qualify under that rubric and which not. It has generated a vibrant scholarly debate.[23]

---

21. Euseb. *PE*, 9:34:18.
22. E.g. Wacholder (1974), 217–223; Mendels (1987), 131–143.
23. The term was evidently coined by Vermes (1961), 95. Numerous efforts have been made to define a genre or to identify the texts that would fit into that concocted category. It goes without saying that no such pigeon-hole ever receives mention in antiquity. Among attempts to provide a frame and to assemble works that can be set within it, see, in general, the survey of Nickelsburg (1984), 89–156; further, Harrington (1986), 239–247; Alexander (1988), 99–121; Halpern-Amaru (1994), 4–5; Najman (2003), 7–8; Crawford (2008), 2–15; Zahn (2010), 323–336; Kugel (2012), 3–23; Campbell (2014), 49–81; Petersen (2014), 13–48. A selective summary of some contributions by Machiela (2010), 308–320. Bernstein (2005), 169–196, ostensibly questions the value of the category but struggles at length to define criteria, more narrow than loose, that would include some texts and exclude others. See also Zahn (2012), 271–288, and *eadem* (2020), 56–73, with additional bibliography. She does reckon rewritten Bibles as a genre, but with a flexible and nuanced understanding. On the issue of genre in Hellenistic Jewish literature more broadly, see now Adams (2020), esp. 174–181, on rewritten scripture and 244–249, on Josephus' *Antiquities*.

The very concept, however, is problematic. Was there ever such a genre at all? The fact that moderns have struggled, largely in vain, to find a definition or even a label that encompasses the range of texts that might come under that heading attests to the difficulty of the endeavor, and should raise questions about its usefulness. Each scholar who has taken a stab at it has produced a somewhat different list of items that might fall within the boundaries of the description. It is worth stressing that the category, whether one calls it "rewritten Bible," "rewritten Scriptures," or "rewritten scriptural texts," all of which have been applied to this phenomenon, is a strictly modern concoction. The ancients possessed no such classification. Nor is there any reason to believe that they grouped under a single heading texts of the variety represented by diverse adaptations of scriptural material—let alone that they considered themselves as contributing to a particular genre with a distinctive tag. For some scholars, troubled by the problematic character of discerning an identifiable category, it seemed preferable to postulate a "process" or a "textual strategy" rather than a genre.[24] But the astonishing range and diversity of these writings resist any uniform description or definition. The application of labels detracts from appreciation of any individual composition and its particular flavor.

Yet a further complication exists. Can there be such a thing as a "rewritten Bible," however loosely defined, at a time when the canonical Bible did not yet exist?[25] Use of the phrase suggests the existence of an agreed upon canon which could be expanded, abridged, or recast. But fluidity and malleability prevailed in the Second Temple period, rather than a firm and fixed "Bible." Discovery of the Dead Sea Scrolls, with multiple variants of biblical material, made the fact incontrovertible. Indeed, the very search for an "original" text from which others derived or departed, an Ur-text or archetype, a Vorlage that lay behind subsequent renditions is itself highly problematic and a source of much scholarly discussion. Widespread agreement among scholars of biblical textual criticism now holds that pluriformity prevailed almost from the outset and that any boundary between the "original" and "reception" is blurred at best.[26]

The absence of a definitive text that constituted a prototype meant that a range of compositions could lay claim to their own standing. Indeed, in a period when the authority of individual writings was itself unclear, at least some of the "rewritten texts" may well have carried as much stature as those on which they based their

---

24. So, already, Harrington (1986), 239–243. Cf. Machiela (2010), 313; Campbell (2014), 64–65; Petersen (2014), 29.

25. The question is rightly posed by Crawford (2008), 3–7. So also Petersen (2014), 25.

26. A large literature exists on the subject. See, e.g., the recent surveys of scholarship in Tov (2002), 155–190; Breed (2014), 15–51; Nati (2022), 1–18, 25–37. The controversial thesis of Satlow (2014) argues that the authoritative character of the Bible was itself fluid, shifting, and multifaceted prior to the later 3rd century CE or even beyond, when it was shaped by Church Fathers and the rabbis.

compositions.[27] Furthermore, there were certainly other, now lost, sources on which later authors drew that did not eventually make it into the canon, but may well have been regarded as comparably definitive at the time. The legends and tales that inspired those compositions need not and almost certainly did not confine themselves to writings that we now characterize as Scriptures. A rich range of antecedents, no longer extant, must have existed and simply elude our grasp.[28] All of this demands caution in the use of terminology like "biblical" or even "scriptural," and impedes any simple dichotomy of model and remodel. As a matter of convenience and convention, I employ terms like "Bible" and "Scriptures." But they must be understood as serviceable vocabulary, not as implying that a firm and uniform text had gained ubiquitous acceptance in the Second Temple era.

That being said, however, it would be wise not go too far in the direction of limitless mutability. Something like an accepted body of Scriptures did exist in the time of Ben Sira's grandson in the 2nd century BCE, which he divided into law, prophets, and writings. And Josephus attests a comparable division when he speaks of the five books of Moses, another thirteen volumes by prophets, and four more consisting of hymns and moral advice. This is not the place to discuss the interminable problem of the canon, its form, and the date (if there were an identifiable one) when it came into being.[29] But a collection of sacred writings was plainly acknowledged in this era, as is demonstrated by the translation into Greek of at least the Pentateuch in 3rd century Alexandria, even if, as is now widely recognized, they did not congeal into anything like a fixed entity for a considerable time thereafter. In view of the circulation of numerous traditions and narratives of wide variety regarding scriptural figures and events, there may not have been a clear and consistent sense of what counted as authoritative texts. But a body of material with considerable overlap with what we now possess plainly existed for the revised and altered versions that obviously drew upon them, and anticipated audiences who knew them well enough to appreciate divergences from them.

A notable fact needs emphasis. The plethora of Jewish writers who produced variants on antecedent texts did not, it seems, generate any resistance or anxieties about departures from their precursors. This obviously bears on the question of what might have been considered sacred texts or what constituted authoritative writings in the Second Temple. The fact that numerous Jewish compositions existed that depended to some degree on what we know as the Scriptures, but played freely with preceding traditions, carries real significance. Creativity and imagination obviously had substantial scope. And none of the variant versions was

---

27. Cf. Zahn (2010), 330–331; *eadem* (2012), 282–286.

28. Mroczek (2015), 2–5, 31–33, makes the point persuasively. See also *eadem* (2016), 118–120. Cf. Simkovich (2018), 221–222.

29. The relevant texts are Sira, *Prol.* and Jos. *CAp.* 1:37-41. See the useful collection of essays by McDonald and Sanders (2002). Note especially, the contribution of Mason, 110–127, who questions Josephus' relevance for this purpose.

branded as tampering with the word of God. The idea of scriptural sanctity does not appear to have acted as a deterrent to new renderings. The fact that variants circulated as far back as we can trace them should render that phenomenon unsurprising.

The practice of producing variants itself, however, evokes a fascinating question. Why did they do it? Many biblical stories known to Second Temple Jews hold great charm, appeal, intrigue, stimulation, and provocation. Why should anyone feel the need to recast them in different forms and genres, to provide alternative versions, to recapitulate them with variant renderings of characters or outcomes, to supply additional components, to erase some portions, or to expand the tales with a broader compass?

On this question two general explanations have found favor. One sees these re-doings as a matter of exegesis. The authors, on that view, sought to fill in gaps, to address incongruities, to explain away embarrassing features, to interpret difficult passages and render them accessible, or to articulate a hidden meaning that lies beneath the surface.[30] The alternative approach finds the retellings to be an effort to respond to hostile criticisms of Jews, to bring a better appreciation of the Jewish experience to Greek and Roman readers, and to refashion traditional tales to make them more palatable to gentile audiences.[31] On this understanding, they are forms of apologia.

These explanations, in my view, fail to provide full satisfaction. With regard to the first, exegesis, as we normally understand it, like midrash or Talmudic dissections of problems in the received texts, occurs only very rarely in the multiple retellings. Allegorical interpretations, as applied by the great Alexandrian philosopher Philo, do occur regularly in his work, but this stands quite apart from the vast bulk of our extant retellings. To be sure, the notion of exegesis can carry a broader sense. It can signify an indirect commentary, inexplicit but conveyed within the new narratives as alternative understanding. Some of the retold tales do indeed have such a character, as we shall see. But to make exegesis the driving force behind this phenomenon fails to account for the effect, the allure, and the integrity of most of the new stories.

As for the second explanation, that of seeing the changes as apologia, this begs a very large question, namely the notion that Hellenistic and Roman Jews were anxious about their reception by gentile readers and thus needed to reassure real or imagined critics. In fact, very few retold tales show signs of such a purpose. Did

---

30. The most influential writer with this approach is James Kugel. See, especially, Kugel (1990), 264–268; *idem* (1998), 1–6, 14–30; *idem* (2012), 9–23. Cf. Alexander (1988), 117: "The intention of the texts is to produce an interpretative reading of Scripture;" Bernstein (2005), 177: "I believe that all rewritten Bible is biblical interpretation." This view is shared, in modified fashion, by Zahn (2010), 329–331: "implicit interpretation"; *eadem* (2020), 206–211. See also Najman (2003), 43–50. But cf. the remarks of Mroczek (2016), 119–120.

31. See, preeminently, Feldman (1998b), 132–162. Cf. Schürer (1986), 472.

the authors really expect to have much of a pagan readership? How many pagan readers were likely to plow through, for example, the repository of scriptural stories contained in the first ten books of Josephus' *Antiquities*? And how many would care whether some Israelites in distant antiquity did or did not worship a golden calf, an episode that Josephus conspicuously omitted? It is certainly true, as we shall see, that some biblical episodes or behaviors by biblical figures could cause discomfort for readers and spur later writers to repress, alter, or massage them. Jews troubled by questionable features of their nation's past might welcome such revisions. But they did not expect to present a better image to appease gentiles.

One might look more profitably at a comparable phenomenon: the Greek respect and near reverence for the ancient myths enshrined in the works of Homer and Hesiod. The legends held a firm place in the self-consciousness of the Greeks and their sense of national identity. But, however powerful a hold the Homeric poems and the Hesiodic theogony had on the Hellenes' vision of themselves, those works gave rise to plentiful reuse of characters and recasting of legends in a diversity of genres that brought them renewed life. No one would claim that Greek drama, hymns, or lyric poetry compromised Homer's integrity by setting his gods and heroes on stage or utilizing them to convey moral pronouncements or national values. The reverse holds. The Second Temple period in the Jewish experience encompasses the Hellenistic period in Greek history. And the latter employed a wealth of literary forms, like epic poetry, pastoral, hymns, and mimes that revivified ancient Hellenic myths, giving them new shape and new meanings, even occasionally subjecting them to parody and mockery. But none of them diminished the power and authority of ancient myth. The nature and thrust of retold scriptural stories should be seen in that light—not so much as mutual influence as parallel processes that provide mutual illumination.

Most of the scholarship on the subject of scriptural retellings leaves out of account or downplays an element of high significance: creativity and imagination. Many of the writings have no obvious agenda, apart from an exhibition of the author's personal take on the story, his inventiveness, his cleverness, or just his desire to provide entertainment. Those features need to be given their due. Jewish writings in the Hellenistic and Roman periods had a life of their own.[32]

This work does not pretend to conduct a comprehensive survey of the retelling of scriptural tales. It constitutes a more modest foray into illustrative examples of notable and enduring narratives that captured the attention of subsequent writers who reproduced them to their own taste and with their own flair. They provide an entrance into this vibrant practice and an opportunity to consider its relationship to holy writ.

In this study I confine myself to the Second Temple period and make no effort to pursue the stories as commented upon by the rabbis with their very different approaches, methods, and goals. And the focus rests upon narrative rather than

---

32. See the important study by Wills (1995), although he does not focus on the recasting of biblical tales. See also Wills (2011), 141–165. Cf. Gruen (2002), 182–212; (2016), 79–94.

legal matters, the haggadic rather than the halakhic. The former lends itself most readily to the creative instincts of the re-tellers. The structure of the book is simple and straightforward. In most cases it offers a summary of each tale as it appears in the Masoretic version. It proceeds in each instance to explore the novelties and revisions applied by later writers and to suggest reasons and aims that might have motivated the adaptations. This does not, of course, imply that each of the re-tellers used as springboard what we now possess as the Masoretic text. Those writing in Greek, for the most part, relied upon the Septuagint which, although it generally followed the course of the Hebrew original, frequently departed from it in both small and large ways that may have influenced the form or substance of the new versions. Moreover, some revised tales, when they abandon the standard text but share certain frames or features with one another, may well have been inspired by traditions available to them but no longer at our disposal. We cannot always be confident that the changes that we detect represent sheer creativity rather than a dialogue between the creator and a received tradition to which we no longer have access.

These caveats impose hesitation in comparing what we presume to be an original with a subsequent re-creation. Indeed this study provides a few examples of writings that have little foothold in the Scriptures, but reproduce biblical characters in flights of fancy with a life of their own, like the *Testament of Abraham*, *Joseph and Aseneth*, and the stories of Moses in Ethiopia. Such texts disclose quite decisively that their authors paid lip-service to familiar forerunners but took pride in their own unrestricted inventions.

My choice of which stories to include is largely determined by those that provoked Second Temple writers to produce new versions, thus shedding light on the reasons for their novelties, their methods, and their expectations. It swiftly becomes clear that no uniform or consistent objective dictated the variations. Each writer applied his own imaginative reconstruction to each story, character, or episode, sometimes with substantial additions that altered the nature of the source text and produced an altogether new saga. Even this selective assemblage of reworked or converted narratives, however, reveals the plethora of approaches and modes utilized by imaginative, ingenious, and occasionally whimsical improvisers. They prompt us all the more pointedly to ask why such endeavors were undertaken and what implications they had for the authority of scriptural texts.

Chapter 1

THE TOWER OF BABEL

The construction and destruction of the infamous Tower of Babel constituted a tale of extensive resonance through the ages. It appears early in the Book of Genesis. After the narrative of the Flood and the recounting of Noah's lineage, their clans, and their lands, the text supplies yet another dark record of humankind's sinful behavior leading to calamity.

At this time, says Genesis, the whole earth had but one language and a single set of words. But human beings sought something more: a settlement where they could build a city with a tower that could extend to the heavens, and supply a name for themselves, so as to avoid a splintering of the people. The aim apparently was to establish a unified entity and a collective identity. God, however, upon inspecting this development, felt deep dissatisfaction. The peoples of the earth already had a single language. If they seek to entrench their corporate character further, what might they not do in the future? The Lord now determined to put an end to the venture. He confounded their tongues, so that they could no longer understand one another and thus had to abandon the building project. He then scattered the people all over the earth, with their diverse languages, leaving the city to be called, appropriately, Babel. Such is the Genesis account.[1] It gives no reason for God's displeasure, nor does it explain why the people were dispersed or why the multiplicity of languages should serve as suitable punishment.

The tale sparked the interests of various later scribblers who evidently also found it puzzling and thus cast it in their own frames. The *Book of Jubilees*, originally composed in Hebrew probably in the 2nd century BCE, is extant now most fully in an Ethiopic translation. The surviving text encompasses Genesis and part of Exodus. Among other things, its author took on the task of rendering the tale of the Tower intelligible.[2] He begins directly by confronting the central question that was simply ignored by Genesis: why was the Lord so hostile to the builders of the structure? He introduces the segment with the statement that

---

1. Gen. 11:1-9.
2. On the composition and date of *Jubilees*, see the thorough discussion of the texts and valuable summary of scholarship by VanderKam (2018), 1-38.

humankind has become evil as exemplified by the wicked plan to construct a city and tower. What made this a depraved act? Genesis says only that the builders aimed at a structure whose top would reach the heavens. That is conventional imagery and rhetoric to describe lofty edifices.[3] It did not itself imply that the builders aimed to climb it to gain access to the heavens themselves. *Jubilees*, however, declares that the perpetrators intended to use the tower to ascend to heaven, a prime example of their wickedness.[4] This provides grounds for God's reaction as a check on the overweening arrogance of men who sought to compete with the divine. The author thus provides a form of gloss on God's warning in the Bible that if men could get away with this, there is nothing they won't do.[5] For *Jubilees*, the issue is one of hubris, a challenge to divine authority that brought the wrath of God. The biblical author has God muddle their language, a single tongue now made multiple, so that they could not communicate, a scenario rather at odds with his own prior narrative that spoke of the lineage of Noah, the numerous nations already scattered with diverse languages.[6] Those who took on the mission of building the tower, according to Genesis, did so because they feared being scattered over the earth.[7] But what reason did they have to fear, and how would the building of the tall structure preempt a prospective dispersal?[8] The scenario is thus all the more puzzling. *Jubilees* supplies a more coherent narrative. By stressing their immorality from the outset, the text has them aim to ascend to heaven, with no anticipation of a scattering, and gives the Lord sound reason for frustrating their plan. Whereas Genesis speaks of a single language that unites humanity, the author of *Jubilees*, more logically, refers to plural languages that featured the motley groups. God confused their tongues so that they could not collaborate in completing their task. The dispersal followed as punishment, and the various languages now became unintelligible to one another, bringing about the divisiveness of the nations. And God put a fitting end to the episode by having a great wind topple the tower to its destruction.[9] The story thus makes more sense.

The destruction of the great tower had resonance also for the author of the Third Sibylline Oracle. The extant collection of Sibylline sayings, ostensibly modeled on the utterances of the Greek prophetess, is actually a compilation and literary fabrication by Jewish and Christian authors mostly in Homeric hexameters, ranging in date from the 2nd century BCE to the 7th century CE.[10] The Third Sibyl

---

3. Deut. 1:28. See von Rad (1961), 144–145.
4. *Jub.* 10:18-19.
5. *Jub.* 10:22; cf. Gen. 11:5.
6. Gen. 10.
7. Gen. 11:4.
8. Cf. Kugel (1998), 228.
9. *Jub.* 10:22-26. Cf. VanderKam (2018), 414–415.
10. See, in general, the comprehensive survey by Parke (1988). Brief summaries by Collins (1983), 317-324; Goodman (1986), 617-627, Gruen (2016b); and, most valuable, Lightfoot (2007), 3–23.

constitutes a composite concoction, much of which, however, dates from the 2nd and 1st centuries BCE.[11] The conglomerate verses, most of them forecasting the doom of various nations, include an oracle addressing the implications of the tower and its collapse. The Sibyl adopts Genesis' claim that the peoples of the earth all shared the same language, but, like *Jubilees*, identifies the transgression of the offending nation as that of aspiring to climb the tower to the starry sky.[12] She sees this explicitly as the motive for God's ferocious reaction. He instructed the winds to hurl down the great tower, and also to engender strife among mortals. The Lord achieved that object by splintering their languages and thereby produced a plethora of divided kingdoms.[13] The transmitter (or fabricator) of the oracle thereby provided a motive, comparable to that in *Jubilees*, that had the Lord exhibit his wrathful power by causing men to rue their effort to breach the gap between the human and the divine. The shattering of a misused and abused unity resulted in eternal divisions and divisiveness. In this abbreviated form, the Third Sibyl parallels the strictures of *Jubilees* and gives the Lord's reactions a raison d'etre.

The strands of the story were picked up elsewhere. They suggest efforts by ancient re-tellers to identify the villains of the piece. The segment of Genesis just preceding the tale of the tower, its discussion of the multiple descendants of Noah, supplies an intriguing notice. It draws brief attention to one of those descendants, Nimrod, named as a mighty hunter, indeed the first mighty man on earth. Further, it locates him in the land of Shinar, which encompassed, among other places, the city of Babylon.[14] The Septuagint translation here rouses interest and provokes speculation. In describing Nimrod, it renders "mighty man" as "giant," and "mighty hunter" as "giant hunter."[15] And the reference to "Babylon" as part of his kingdom could evoke "Babel." The Hellenistic Jewish writer usually reckoned as Pseudo-Eupolemos in the scholarship seems to have seized upon these hints and produced (or reproduced) a version that pulled some threads together.[16] The pertinent fragment of his work has Abraham trace his ancestors back to the giants, locates

---

11. On the dates and circumstances of the material in the Third Sibyl, much of it disputed, see the influential works of Collins (1974), 21–71; *idem* (2000), 83–87; *idem* (2005), 82–98; cf. Goodman (1987), 632–641. Other voices in Nikiprowetzky (1971); Gruen (1998), 269–291; Buitenwerf (2003), esp. 124–134, 370–381; Bacchi (2020), esp. 2–26, 56–85.

12. 3 *Sib.* 99-100: ὁμόφωνοι δ' ἦσαν ἅπαντες καὶ βούλοντ' ἀναβῆν' εἰς οὐρανὸν ἀστερόεντα.

13. 3 *Sib.* 101-107. Cf. 11 *Sib.* 6-13.

14. Gen. 10:8-10. On the figure of Nimrod generally in Jewish tradition, see van der Toorn and van der Horst (1990), 1–29.

15. Gen. 10:8-9 (Sept.): γίγας κυνηγὸς.

16. On "Pseudo-Eupolemos," if indeed he is different from Eupolemos (a matter not relevant here), see the fragments collected, with commentary and notes, by Holladay (1983), 157–177.

them in Babylon, and has them destroyed by the gods because of their evil ways, an evident allusion to the battle of gods and giants in Greek mythology, here located in Babylon. The author's intriguing syncretism then becomes more precise. He has a single giant, Belus, survive the contest and make his home in Babylon, where he built a tower and dwelled in it.[17] A separate fragment of Pseudo-Eupolemos apparently fills out the tale. He credits the giants in general with building the great tower, which was then felled by God, who scattered the giants over the earth.[18] This plainly reflects a version of the tower of Babel tale. It may suggest an identification of the biblical Nimrod with the Belus of the Hellenistic author and thus single out a particular villain, a mighty giant who authorized a giant tower that provoked the Lord's righteous wrath culminating in the fall of the tower and the scattering of the giants.[19] Whether this signals a piecing together of diverse traditions by Pseudo-Eupolemos or his adaptation of a prior inventive reconstruction, the pieces themselves indicate diverse efforts either to flesh out or to sharpen the focus of the compressed biblical narrative.

The role of Nimrod evidently took on expanded proportions in subsequent retellings. By the time the tale reached the historian Josephus in the late 1st century CE, Nimrod had become the key figure. He also served to underscore the wickedness emblematized by construction of the tower that justified the retaliation by God. What Genesis had left unsaid now took central stage. Josephus pins the blame firmly on the *hubris* of Nimrod, a man of physical power and authority, who persuaded the populace that their happiness stemmed not from any divine support, but solely from their own virtue (*arête*). He proceeded to transform his control of affairs into a personal tyranny, affirming that only if the people took matters into their own hands could they rid themselves of fear of God. This provided the springboard for the building of the tower.[20] Human arrogance thus gave rationale for the Lord's reaction. Yet there is more to it than that. Josephus sets the events in a broader context than merely the failings of humanity and the justifiable reaction of the divine. The historian deftly blends the flood legend with that of the tower. He introduces the Nimrod narrative by adding a nuance that helps to account for humankind's disaffection with the divinity. Their recalcitrance was due not only to *hubris* but to their suspicions about God's malicious intentions in scattering the folk, thus to make them more vulnerable to assault.[21] This striking insertion anticipates the tower episode and the dispersal of nations. By placing it as prelude to the narrative, Josephus implicates God himself in the origins of human depravity. He has Nimrod justify the resistance to God's will as a matter of revenge for the devastation of the flood. The building of the tower, therefore, aimed to create a

---

17. Ps-Eupolemos in Eusebius, *PE*, 9:18:2.
18. Ps-Eupolemos in Eusebius, *PE*, 9:17:2-3.
19. See the tempting reconstruction by Kugel (1998), 232.
20. Jos. *AJ*, 1:113-114.
21. Jos. *AJ*, 1:112.

structure tall enough to keep humans safe from the waters that had destroyed their forefathers.[22] It was, in short, a security measure and an exaction of revenge, not just a matter of heedless defiance.

Nimrod had touched a nerve. The populace deemed it slavery to yield to the dictates of God, and thus proceeded with vigor and speed to put the massive tower in place.[23] Josephus (or his source) had thus added a twist to the story, a dimension that suggested shared responsibility for the debacle. The historian also gave his interpretation greater weight by calling upon corroborating sources. He cites Hestiaios, a Phoenician writer, for the region in which these events transpired, and a variety of other non-Jewish historians on whom he drew as providing authority for his account in general.[24] And he brings to bear also the Sibylline Oracles, by quoting the passage that we have already noted.[25] Josephus thereby claimed a sound basis for his more complex analysis of a story that went beyond a human challenge to divine power. It raised a subtle question about legitimacy in the exercise of that divine power.

Another author, the so-called Pseudo-Philo (Ps-Philo), also weighed in on this tradition. His *Liber Antiquitatum Biblicarum* (*LAB*), "The Book of Biblical Antiquities," is extant now only in a Latin translation but derives from a Hebrew original, subsequently rendered in Greek, probably from the 1st or 2nd century CE. It constitutes a retelling of the Scriptures that covers events from the time of Adam to the brink of king David's reign.[26] *LAB*, like Josephus, offers the preliminary notice that the people who gathered in Babylon already anticipated their dispersal and subsequent conflicts among themselves. The erection of the tower, therefore, constituted a means of unity, a solidarity that would hold the nation together and delay the fragmentation. The goal was to establish a tower that would reach the heavens and afford the builders renown.[27] In the next segment, perhaps following a separate tradition, Ps-Philo drops the notion that God already contemplated the dispersal of the people, and ascribes the initiative for the tower to the malignant aims of the people themselves. They saw it not as a means to preserve unity but as a bulwark for their power and a guarantee of their long-term endurance.[28] Nothing is said here about innate evil among the populace or how the plan reflects

---

22. Jos. *AJ*, 1:114.
23. Jos. *AJ*, 1:115. Cf. Feldman (2000), 41.
24. Jos. *AJ*, 1:107, 119.
25. Jos. *AJ*, 1:118.
26. The learned work on this author with text, translation, and extensive commentary, by Jacobson (1996), is indispensable.
27. *LAB*, 6:1.
28. *LAB*, 7:1. I pass over here the conflation of the tower tale with that of Abraham and the fiery furnace; *LAB* 6:3-12, 7:4. For possible explanations of this combination, see Jacobson (1996), 380–381. The discussion of Murphy (1993), 41–50, focuses almost solely on the Abraham portion of the narrative.

malevolent schemes. Nimrod goes altogether unmentioned.[29] *LAB* makes no connection with the flood legend. God's distress, as in Genesis, arises simply from the fact that humankind seeks to maintain uniformity, entrenched by a single language.

Ps-Philo fails to supply grounds for God's displeasure, a failure already in the Genesis account. He eschews explanations such as the people's desire to reach the heavens and thus challenge divine ascendancy or a wish to thwart any future flood. The text, like Genesis itself, says only that God wished to act now, for if humankind were not restrained at this juncture, nothing could halt even more ambitious and unpredictable schemes that they might concoct.[30] That serves as sole motive for the Lord's extreme measure of fracturing their languages, estranging them from one another, and, an even more severe penalty not otherwise attested, assigning them to wretched abodes like nests and caves where they will dwell like beasts of the field.[31] That outburst seems superfluous and excessively harsh, perhaps also drawn from another tradition. For Ps-Philo immediately reverts to the Genesis account that simply reports the splitting up of languages and the mutual unintelligibility that brought the building project to an end, followed by scattering over the earth.[32] The author thus sticks fairly closely to the biblical original. He does not endeavor to accord a nefarious purpose to constructing the tower nor an explanation for the fierce reaction of God. The question of why he should be hostile to the idea of humankind coming together as a unity remains as baffling for *LAB* as for Genesis. But the author does take one stab at imagining the divine disposition. Despite the vitriol leveled at the tower builders, God stayed his hand, as he did with the great flood, and left the land of Israel intact. He had it in mind, of course, as a dwelling place for his favorite Abraham and the seed of the patriarch.[33] Ps-Philo left well enough alone. He did not further scrutinize human or divine motivation.

Philo, the great Jewish philosopher from Alexandria, took the confusion of the tongues as inspiration for an entire treatise on the subject. He quotes the biblical passage about the erection of the tower and God's muddling of languages at the outset of his work *De Confusione Linguarum* (*On the Confusion of Tongues*). But, unlike other ancient references to the narrative, Philo employs it for polemical purposes. He reacts sharply to those who criticized the Books of Moses for retailing the same types of myths that Jews decry when they are propounded by Gentiles. He cites their mockery of a structure that can reach into the heavens, a fallacious fable comparable to the Hellenic myth of piling Ossa and Pelion upon Olympus in vain effort to supply a road to heaven. The critics, according to Philo, deliver the

---

29. He is mentioned elsewhere in passing, but not in connection with the tower tale; *LAB*, 4:7, 6:14.
30. *LAB*, 7:2.
31. *LAB*, 7:3. On this text, see the comments of Jacobson (1996), 376–380.
32. *LAB*, 7:5.
33. *LAB*, 7:4.

same censure of the fiction that has the confusion of tongues brought about as a cure for men's and nations' inflicting of evil upon one another. Hence, in their view, the Pentateuch is as filled with mythology as Hellenic poetry.[34] Philo roundly rejects the cavils as a categorical error. Critics simply fail to understand that these narratives must be understood allegorically.[35] Having made the point, Philo uses the remainder of the treatise to present a host of instances not meant to be taken literally but of great ethical significance when understood allegorically.[36] He is not interested in parsing the tale or substituting for it. He eschews any grappling with problems raised by the text, but limits himself to rising above them through allegory.

The divergent endeavors to recast the tale of the Tower offer a useful window on how ancient Jews could mold and remold a story that raised tortured problems and spurred tortured responses. Some addressed the problematic character of the text by offering a rationale for God's action as a lesson for human arrogance; others sought to give greater coherence to the Genesis narrative; still others scrapped much of the tale and substituted another that singled out a particular villain or combined it with traditions from other cultures, whether Israelite or non-Israelite; yet others rewrote the original and supplied more widespread offenses without resolving the roots of divine displeasure; and Philo deployed the legend to legitimize his own methodology and resist the claims of gentile caricatures of Hebrew mythology. The serviceability and the manifold malleability of the original emerge unmistakably. This example serves as a harbinger of numerous comparable retellings.

---

34. Philo, *Conf. Ling.* 1–13. On the polemical character of the treatise, perhaps more apparent than real, see Bloch (2019), 119–124.

35. Philo, *Conf. Ling.* 14–15.

36. Philo makes brief references to the tale of the tower and the confusion of tongues in Genesis later in the treatise, but does not touch on the issues explored here; *Conf. Ling.* 150–158. 168, 196. He makes one mention of Nimrod as an opponent of God elsewhere; *Quaest. Gen.* 2:82.

Chapter 2

ABRAHAM IN EGYPT

A famous narrative in the Bible sets the patriarch Abraham in a rather less than positive light. Here is the story. A famine took place in the land of Canaan, so Abraham took his wife Sarai (Sarah) and went down to Egypt. But he suddenly had a very troubling concern. Sarah was an exceedingly beautiful woman, so much so that Pharaoh was likely to want her for his own, and would thus probably kill her husband first in order to wed Sarah himself. So, Abraham, foreseeing this, concocted a scheme whereby Sarah would pretend to be his sister rather than his wife, and thus Abraham could escape death. Now, this seemed to work like a charm for a time. Pharaoh was indeed smitten by Sarah, did take her into the royal palace to live with him as his wife, and paid off Abraham, ostensibly her brother, with lavish gifts of sheep, oxen, camels, donkeys, and slaves. Abraham thus seemed to have gotten away with it, enjoyed wealth and luxury at the hands of Pharaoh, simply for the price of giving his wife away. Abraham may have been content with this, but the Lord was not. Divine punishment rained down from heaven in the form of mighty plagues afflicting Pharaoh and his people because the king had taken to himself the wife of another. Pharaoh at least got the point. He immediately returned Sarah to Abraham, but not before rebuking the patriarch for telling him that she was his sister rather than his wife, and thus bringing pestilence and disaster upon Egypt. He then sent Abraham back to Canaan, with his wife, and with all his possessions.[1]

Such is the narrative in the Book of Genesis.[2] Abraham certainly does not come off very well in the story. It is noteworthy that subsequent renditions make different attempts to clean up the record. In the *Book of Jubilees* Pharaoh simply takes Sarah by force, and the Lord, as a consequence, blasts him with plagues. Nothing is said about any deception on the part of Abraham. The battered Pharaoh lets Sarah go under duress and showers Abraham with wealth and possessions—but after the

---

1. Gen. 12:10-20.
2. Variants on this version occur already in Genesis itself; 20:1-18, 26:6-11 (the latter with regard to Isaac). In one version, Abraham claims that Sarah and he are indeed siblings, though with different fathers; Gen. 20:12. Cf. Philo, *Quaest. Gen.* 4:68.

fact, not as the result of any arrangement with the patriarch.³ A sharp diversion from the biblical account.

The *Genesis Apocryphon*, an Aramaic text discovered among the Dead Sea Scrolls, has a different twist on the tale. The author presents Sarah as the most dazzling of creatures, alluring, seductive, and irresistible, even lingering over the details of her appearance, including the shape of her thighs, the whiteness of her skin, and the grace of her breasts. This is almost soft-porn. Of course, Pharaoh could not help himself and took her as his wife. To assure success he attempted to kill Abraham. And here comes the twist. Sarah stepped in and claimed to be Abraham's sister, thus dissuading the king from killing him. Abraham is a purely passive character, no schemer to save his skin. He can only weep and pray to God for help. And God designed an ingenious punishment. Mere plagues were too good for the wicked king. The Lord did worse. He tortured Pharaoh by making him impotent, so that, though he was living for two years with the gorgeous temptress Sarah, he could not have sex with her. Only then did the plagues intensify, Pharaoh returned Sarah to Abraham, now revealed as her husband, and sent the two of them on their way with lavish gifts.⁴ On this version, Abraham, while not a particularly forceful character, is at least an innocent one. Sarah (with the help of God) is the manipulator. And the story has some bite to it.⁵

A much briefer version appears in the fragments of a Hellenistic-Jewish author usually designated as Pseudo-Eupolemos and preserved by the Church historian Eusebius. He radically abbreviates the biblical anecdote, leaving out most of it. But he gets the core. And he is less eager than the others to exculpate Abraham. Pseudo-Eupolemos has Pharaoh take Sarah in marriage after Abraham had introduced her as his sister. As in the *Genesis Apocryphon*, the king is unable to have intercourse with his new bride, and also suffers from a pestilence that ravages his household. When he learns from his seers that the reason is his unlawful marriage to Sarah, he swiftly restores her to her husband.⁶ That is the stripped-down version. The text alludes indirectly to Abraham's deception but makes no issue of it.

Philo of Alexandria, the philosopher, by contrast, in his retelling of the episode, pins all the blame on Pharaoh. The king, swept away by Sarah's beauty, paid no heed to decency or the laws of hospitality, just snatched her from her husband, forcing Abraham and Sarah both to pray for rescue from God. The merciful Lord, of course, heard their pleas, wracked the king with plagues and pain, and inflicted similar punishments on all his household before he could lay a hand on Sarah, thus preserving her virtue intact and the sanctity of her marriage from which would

---

3. *Jub.* 13:13-15. Cf. van Ruiten (2012), 73–80.

4. *Gen. Apoc.* col. XX1.1-33. See the text, translation, and commentary in Fitzmeyer (1971).

5. The recapitulation of the *Gen. Apoc.* version by van Ruiten (2012), 109–112, misses most of this. So also, with different emphases, Crawford (2008), 116–126; Docherty (2019), 67.

6. Euseb. *PE*, 9:17.6-7.

issue the children of Israel.[7] Not a hint of any wrongdoing by the patriarch, only piety and righteousness. Philo certainly knew the biblical story. But he gave it his own spin.

The historian Josephus was a bit truer to the biblical text.[8] He does acknowledge that Abraham pretended to be Sarah's brother in order to preserve his own life. But certain changes suggest that he was not altogether comfortable with the story. Abraham receives an added dimension of some significance in the historian's hands. His trip to Egypt was not simply to find food but to inquire of Egyptian priests about their religion, even to consider adoption of their beliefs if they could persuade him. The voyage was thus an intellectual as well as a practical one. Josephus acknowledges that Abraham pretended to be Sarah's brother in order to preserve his own life, but, unlike the biblical author, he makes sure to say that God intervened right away, triggered an outbreak of timely pestilence and disease, and thwarted the criminal passion of the wicked king—just when he was about to lay hands on Sarah. God therefore preserved her chastity. Also unlike the Bible, Josephus has Pharaoh provide Abraham with abundant wealth only after restoring Sarah, and not as part of a bargain. And he elaborates further on Abraham's discussions with the priests, exhibiting the patriarch's superiority in their theological debates and his earning of their admiration through his intellectual prowess and learning. Indeed he proved responsible for introducing Egypt to the sciences of mathematics and astronomy.[9] And he makes sure to conclude the tale by saying that Abraham's reputation for virtue scaled even greater heights.[10] It is hard to see much justification for that verdict in Genesis. Josephus plainly did not feel bound by that narrative. He conveyed the essence of the biblical version but took pains to leave the reader with a fuller picture of the patriarch and one that would deliver a most positive impression—however forced and unwarranted. The

---

7. Philo, *Abr.* 92-98. On Philo's treatment of Abraham generally, see now Adams (2019), 75-92.

8. It is neither possible nor desirable to register the numerous treatments that have endeavored to offer an overall assessment of Josephus' methods, goals, and unifying themes. Valuable surveys, among many, can be found in Holladay (1977), 67-79; Bilde (1988), 123-171; Feldman (1998b), 214-217; Mason, in Feldman (2000), xiii-xvi, xxii-xxxv. The argument for apologetic aims recurs regularly in the literature: note, especially, Attridge (1976), 43-66; Cohen (1979), 114-169; Sterling (1992), 226-310.

9. Josephus was not the first to make Abraham a provider of knowledge to the Egyptians. Hellenistic Jewish writers like Artapanos and Ps. Eupolemus ascribed to him the teaching of astrology to Egyptians; Euseb. *PE*, 9:17:8, 9:18:1. On the preservation of Sarah's chastity, other writers too sought to give assurances; see Kugel (1998), 272-273.

10. Jos. *AJ*, 1:161-168. See 1:165: τήν τε ἀρετὴν αὐτῷ καὶ τὴν ἐπ' αὐτῇ δόξαν ἐντεῦθεν ἐπιφανεστέραν συνέβη γενέσθαι. Cf. the notes of Feldman (2000), 60-64. On the depiction of Sarah, an interesting study in itself, see most recently McDonald (2020), 40-46, 97-103, 193-200.

historian transformed the critical tale into an encomium. The dubious actions of Abraham gave way to laudation and elevation. The freedom that Josephus felt in revising the original is striking.

As this résumé of different renditions makes clear, none of the authors felt any obligation to duplicate the biblical account. All of them preferred in one form or another to shield Abraham from the negative portrait in Genesis, but each did it in his own way, whether adding erotic elements, shifting the initiative to Sarah, or increasing the villainy of Pharaoh. The Jewish authors of the variations on this theme obviously felt free to reshape or amend the tale to their own tastes and purposes.

Chapter 3

SARAH AND HAGAR

Sarah too had her flaws, a potential embarrassment for the sympathetic readers of the Scriptures. Genesis delivers the familiar narration of Sarah's distraught childlessness, the summoning of Hagar, and the consequences for the perpetuation of Abraham's legacy. Sarah's attitude and behavior, as represented in Genesis, may well have caused some misgivings among Jews who cherished the record of their origins.

The biblical account represents Sarah as lamenting her inability to produce offspring for Abraham, an affliction she ascribes to God. The solution comes on her own initiative. She offers up her Egyptian slave-girl Hagar to serve as surrogate mother, urging Abraham to take Hagar as his wife and to impregnate her. Abraham duly complied and Hagar duly conceived. But Sarah suddenly wondered whether this had been a good idea after all. Hagar had been successful where Sarah had failed, and the slave-girl could now look down upon her former mistress. Sarah reacted with fury and leveled it against Abraham. She railed at him and held him accountable for the insults suffered at Hagar's hands. She even appealed to God to pass judgment, as if in a judicial dispute between Abraham and his wife.[1] The compliant Abraham yielded without hesitation. He told Sarah that she could work her will on Hagar. And so she did. Sarah tormented the slave-girl and drove her into flight. The harried woman found herself in the wilderness, where an angel of the Lord reassured her that by returning to Sarah and submitting to her, she will eventually benefit through the multiplication of offspring too countless to number. The divine figure forecasts the birth of her son Ishmael, as ordained by the Lord, a son who will be akin to a wild ass and whose hand will be against all, and all against him. The astonished Hagar wonders aloud whether she has actually seen the Lord and survived. The angelic prophecy is fulfilled: Hagar gives birth to Ishmael, first-born of the patriarch Abraham.[2]

---

1. Gen. 16:1-5. In the view of von Rad (1961), 186–187, Sarah appealed to legal precedent, for Hagar was now the property of Abraham, who had to be held accountable for her actions. But Sarah's outburst and passion hardly depended on any legalities.

2. Gen. 16:6-12. This need not be an altogether negative description. Ishmael represents the rugged, nomadic, and self-sufficient figure who rejects convention and defiantly builds his own society.

This memorable episode does not reflect especially well upon Sarah and gives little stature to Abraham. Sarah conceives the scheme to have her servant be the receptacle for Abraham's seed. But she abruptly burst with indignation and distemper when Hagar took pride in her conception, and turned her into a desperate fugitive, while at the same time denouncing and pinning ultimate blame on Abraham. The patriarch emerges as a weak and unsympathetic character, meekly complying with Sarah's wishes, first for a fertile bed-partner and then for her subsequent angry dismissal. Hagar gets a more sympathetic treatment. She may have gone too far in contrasting her swift conception with Sarah's infertility, thus provoking her banishment, but the appearance of the angel and the promise of a glorious future as reward for her suffering put her back in divine graces. She certainly comes off better than the founding father and mother.

Sarah's misdemeanors did not stop there. When the Lord sent word that she would indeed give birth, Sarah, now in advanced old age, laughed inwardly at the absurdity of the prospect. That roused the indignation of God, who took umbrage at the fact that Sarah could imagine anything to be beyond God's divine powers. Sarah swiftly backtracked, gripped by fear, and mendaciously denied that she had ever laughed. God, of course, saw right through the attempted deception: "Yes, you did laugh."[3] A decisive rebuke.

The sequel, of course, brought the birth of Isaac, an event also marked by Sarah's laughter, although of an evidently different sort.[4] More significantly, for our purposes, it provided background for renewing the strained relations between Sarah and Hagar. On the day of Isaac's weaning, Sarah was offended by Ishmael's laughter, and immediately insisted that Abraham banish both the slave-girl and her son, lest Ishmael compete with Isaac for the patriarch's inheritance. Abraham was taken aback, quite unhappy with the idea of his son being sent into exile. But the Lord intervened, counseling Abraham to curb his displeasure and to act on Sarah's wishes. He promises that the line would be perpetuated through Isaac but that Ishmael too will be the founder of a nation. Abraham followed the divine orders, providing some sustenance to Hagar and Ishmael, but sending them out once more to the wilderness. This time again, when matters seemed desperate, God came to the rescue, sending a messenger, soothing Hagar's fears, sustaining their lives, and forecasting Ishmael's destiny as progenitor of a great nation. The young man came to maturity in the wilderness, adapted successfully to his surroundings, and even became an expert bowman.[5]

---

3. Gen. 18:10-15. Abraham too had earlier laughed at this prospect but suffered no rebuke from the Lord; Gen. 17:17.

4. Gen. 21:1-7. This is not the place to investigate the not altogether obvious role played by laughter in this episode. Cf. von Rad (1961), 226–227. On Sarah's laughter, see also Philo, *Abr.* 112, 206, who explains it away.

5. Gen. 21:8-20.

Sarah once more is the darker figure in this tale. She was quick to take offense, even on trivial grounds, and insisted on drastic, unmerited, measures. Abraham was yet again relatively passive, even though he did express displeasure, and went along with the expulsion, mollified by the divine promise of a happy ending for his progeny.

This scriptural story evidently caused misgivings among some of the faithful.[6] The saga presented a harsh and unfeeling Israelite mistress, a victimized and (largely) innocent Egyptian servant, and a meek patriarch incapable of initiating action. Unsurprisingly, later renditions sought to supply different impressions.

The author of *Jubilees* made perhaps the most blatant change in the narrative. He followed the scriptural script faithfully with regard to Sarah's childlessness, her complaint that God willed it so, her offer of Hagar to Abraham as a wife to produce an heir, his readiness to cooperate, and the birth of his son Ishmael. But *Jubilees* completely left out the crucial passages about estrangement and conflict. The text pointedly and conspicuously omits any allusion to Sarah's perception of a slight by Hagar, her outrage at the slave-girl, her denunciation of Abraham, her effort to have Yahweh adjudicate, her harassment of the young woman, the banishment into the wilderness, and the arrival of the angel to reassure Hagar of a glorious future. The omission of this whole segment, bracketed by close correspondence with the surrounding passages, can hardly be accidental.[7] The author, deeply concerned for the reputation of his nation in its earliest history, preferred to overlook the shadier aspects. The characters take on an altogether different aspect with those deletions. Gone are Sarah's ferocity and disagreeableness (not to mention her challenge to God), Abraham's wimpishness, Hagar's slight, her victimization by Sarah, and her bolstering by Yahweh's agent.[8] The version in *Jubilees* suggests only harmony and collaboration among the forbears of the nation. This may be a worthy effort, but it robs the story of its powerful tensions, friction, and drama.

The episode of Sarah's laughter at the very idea of her pregnancy was also an embarrassment. As depicted in Genesis, it generated scorn and reprimand by Yahweh, who wondered why she would doubt that anything was beyond God's capacity. Worse still, she tried to cover up the blunder by denying that she had giggled at the notion, thus drawing Yahweh's sharp retort, "oh yes you did." The episode evidently had purchase. The author of *Jubilees* found it awkward but could

---

6. The portrayal of Hagar by various Second Temple sources is usefully surveyed now by Heinsch (2022), 56–120, although his emphasis is largely upon her depiction as a foreigner and ethnically inferior.

7. *Jub.* 14:21-24, parallels Genesis, 16:1-16, but notably drops all of Gen. 16:5-14, thus leaving an altogether different impression of the principals. The idea that the author may simply be using a different *Vorlage* is unlikely; see van Ruiten (2012), 127–130. VanderKam's comment (2018), 504, that "the author felt no need to include these sections," is surprisingly bland and unhelpful.

8. Cf. van Ruiten (2012), 132–134.

not sweep it altogether under the rug. He did the next best thing. He included Sarah's laughter when she heard the news that she would carry a child, but he has her rebuked not by God but by the angelic visitors who delivered the annunciation. The mendacious denial does not receive refutation by Yahweh, and Sarah is spared divine humiliation. God plays no part in the exchange.[9]

Jubilees supplies a near facsimile of the Genesis narrative of Hagar's second expulsion to the wilderness, this time with Ishmael, now a teenager, and its outcome. The author adds a few details and provides a slightly longer version but makes no significant changes.[10] He eschews any effort here to whitewash Sarah, elevate Abraham, or soften the victimization of Hagar. Indeed, one small addition even points in the other direction. The text has Sarah motivated by jealousy of Ishmael, a comment not in the original.[11] This may simply be inference from the original, rather than an effort to accentuate any fault of Sarah's. The basic thrust of the segment, however, is to account for Sarah's behavior in terms of an overriding principle, namely that of assuring the perpetuation of Abraham's line, the vast progeny that the Lord had promised him. When she failed to produce issue, she had turned to a substitute to fulfill the promise. But her expectation of being mother of the flock returned with the birth of Isaac. The author of *Jubilees* embellishes slightly but importantly on the scene that saw Sarah turn on Hagar at the celebration of Isaac's weaning. The Bible sets it at the point when Ishmael laughed (perhaps in mockery?), a sufficient trigger for Sarah's deep resentment. *Jubilees* offers a fuller description: Sarah saw Ishmael playing and dancing with joy and Abraham expressing great pleasure, the occasion on which her jealousy surfaced and she insisted on the exiling of both mother and son, lest Ishmael share the inheritance of Isaac.[12] That underscores what is already indicated in the Bible: the legacy of Abraham, as guaranteed by God, should issue from his Israelite wife, not from an Egyptian servant. Although *Jubilee*'s version does not eradicate Sarah's excessive harshness, it sets it more firmly in the context of the larger goal for the future of Israel.

Josephus too felt a need to retell the tale of Sarah and Hagar—and he too with an eye to setting the matriarch in a better light. Judicious omissions or additions would do the trick. The historian softens the blow for Sarah wherever he can.

Genesis had Sarah conceive the idea of having Abraham bed Hagar in order to produce an heir, after she had given up on her own powers to perform that deed. Josephus gives God the initiative on this move, thus to make it part of a larger

---

9. *Jub.* 16:1-2. This is more than just the author's stripping the Genesis text of all its frills, as van Ruiten (2012), 173. It leaves Sarah unharmed by divine wrath.

10. See the handy juxtaposition of the two texts by van Ruiten (2012), 196–199.

11. *Jub.* 17:4. On other aspects of the text here, see the commentary of VanderKam (2018), 551–560, with bibliography.

12. *Jub.* 17:4; cf. Gen. 21:8-11.

divine plan to which Sarah contributed.[13] The fraught encounter between Sarah and Hagar after the latter had conceived takes on a very different flavor in Josephus' hands. For the biblical author, Sarah reacted with outrage and ferocity at a perceived slight. Josephus, by contrast, has Hagar act with insolence and arrogance toward Sarah, adopting the aura of a queen, and behaving as though hegemony would pass to her (as yet unborn) son. The historian reinforces his interpretation by omitting Sarah's indignant reprimand of Abraham, her audacious summoning of God as arbitrator, and her harassment of Hagar that drove her to flight. Instead, he has the slave-girl choose exile of her own accord and seek divine assistance.[14] The angel who answers Hagar's plea in the wilderness not only orders her to return to her mistress but pins the blame squarely on her for thoughtlessness and willfulness.[15] Sarah is thus no longer the real villain.

Josephus similarly turns about the episode of Sarah's laughter. Her scornful mockery of the idea of conception at her age, God's castigation of her, the dissembling denial, and the divine refutation all disappear in Josephus' account. Sarah simply smiles.[16] The revision is transparent. Josephus' silence puts Sarah in the clear.

Josephus' handling of Hagar's second departure for the wilderness is more problematic and presents greater difficulty of interpretation. He sets the stage in Sarah's favor by maintaining that she welcomed the birth of Ishmael and showed him great affection in his early years, as if he were her own son, a deliberate addition to the Bible. And his explanation for her turnabout is not ascribed to jealousy, resentment, or anxiety about a shared inheritance. He offers a more satisfying explanation: fear that the older boy, now a teenager, might do Isaac injury after their father passed away.[17] What follows carries additional novelties. When Sarah pressed Abraham to send both Hagar and Ishmael away, the patriarch initially resisted, regarding it as excessively cruel to expel an infant with a mother who had no means of livelihood. He subsequently relented when he realized that this was part of God's plan.[18] Josephus' depiction of Ishmael as a helpless infant is quite striking, since the youngster was, in fact, a teenager at the time, as Josephus himself had signaled just above by setting the event after the birth of Isaac. Just how to account for this is not readily at hand. But Josephus may well be seeking to highlight Abraham's compassion and to make him a more sympathetic figure than the one who simply acts at Sarah's behest.[19] The historian's version thus offers

---

13. *Jos. AJ,* 1:187; cf. Gen. 16:1-2.
14. *Jos. AJ,* 1:188; cf. Gen. 16:4-6.
15. *Jos. AJ,* 1:188-189; cf. Gen. 16:6-9.
16. *Jos. AJ,* 1:198, 1:213; cf. Gen. 18:10-15. See Feldman (2000), 75, 81.
17. *Jos. AJ,* 1:214-215.
18. *Jos. AJ,* 1:216-217.
19. Cf. Feldman (2000), 82. These matters are passed over by Heinsch's discussion (2022), 106–116; cf. also van der Lans (2010), 185–199.

rehabilitation of patriarch and matriarch, even if somewhat at the temporary expense of the Egyptian handmaiden. The story ends happily, as it did in Genesis, with God promising great nations for both sons, Sarah evidently mollified, Hagar a successful progenitor, and Abraham a more rounded figure. Josephus thus indulges his readers with a more edifying rendition than the darker Genesis version of the origins of Israel.

Improvements on Genesis may also have motivated two other Jewish writers if one can judge from their very brief allusions. Philo of Alexandria transforms the "laughter" scene into a most positive and uplifting event. When the annunciation of Sarah's pregnancy comes from God, Abraham collapses with laughter as an expression of joy, and Sarah follows suit, asserting that the laughter constitutes a paean of delight to the Lord for the blessing of procreation.[20] Pseudo-Philo reduces the whole narrative of Sarah and Hagar to the barest of bare bones. In his truncated summary, Sarah was sterile, could not conceive, Abraham then took Hagar, his servant, and she produced Ishmael, who then generated twelve sons.[21] No hint of any complications or controversy.

This tale of rivalry, jealousy, punishment, and vindication in Genesis addressed a pivotal moment: the origin of the nation. Genesis presented the principals warts and all. *Jubilees* and the *Antiquities* of Josephus, each in its own way, through deletions or reinterpretations, left the founders of Israel with a more agreeable aura. Bold omissions softened Sarah's character, dubious actions are ascribed to Hagar, and turns in the tale become part of a divine plan. All of this gave a more satisfying image of the nation's founders, and a better story for the faithful—but it came at the expense of a compelling drama. The re-tellers were prepared to pay that price.

---

20. Philo, *Leg. All.* 217–219, with, of course, an allegorical understanding. On Philo's transformation of Hagar for allegorical purposes, see Heinsch (2022), 90–106. It has little to do with the biblical narrative.

21. *LAB*, 8:1.

Chapter 4

THE AQEDAH

No episode in the Hebrew Bible has greater resonance or more moving force than the Aqedah, the binding of Isaac. Its dramatic power rings through the ages in written word and visual imagery. The excruciating trial that the Lord imposed upon his beloved Abraham remains indelible. Writers who created new versions of scriptural tales could not escape it.

The story occupies a single chapter in Genesis. It is swiftly told. God determined to put Abraham to the test. He called upon him to take his cherished son Isaac to the land of Moriah and offer him up as a sacrifice.[1] Abraham obeyed the command without hesitation and without a word. He took Isaac, carrying split wood, and himself with fire and the ominous knife for the offering, to the mountain as bidden by the divine directive.[2] The puzzled lad stopped on the journey and asked his father why there was no lamb for the sacrifice. The patriarch reassured his son that God would provide the lamb as victim. When they reached the place that God had designated, Abraham built an altar, set out the wood, bound Isaac, and laid him upon the wood.[3] Just as he stretched out his hand with the knife to perform the fatal deed, however, an angel of the Lord called out Abraham by name and bade him to cease and desist with the sacrifice. The divine emissary declared that Abraham's very willingness to slay his son at God's order sufficed to establish his unequivocal devotion to the Lord.[4] Fortuitously, indeed miraculously, Abraham suddenly spied a ram caught by its horns in a thicket; it served as substitute for Isaac as a sacrificial victim, and the lad went free. The angel declared God's satisfaction that Abraham did not shrink even from yielding up his only son on divine instruction, and he conveyed the Lord's blessing for the infinite multiplication of Abraham's seed that would people all the nations of the earth.[5]

---

    1. Gen. 22:1-2. Isaac was not, of course, the only son, Ishmael having been born several years before. But the text stresses Isaac's singular status as son of Sarah and chief heir to Abraham's legacy.
    2. Gen. 22:3-6.
    3. Gen. 22:7-9.
    4. Gen. 22:10-12.
    5. Gen. 22:13-18.

The story is spare and stately.⁶ Although the buildup and the outcome stir emotion and grip the reader, the author refrains from comment. No word is wasted. The reasons why God sought to inflict such a task on Abraham gain no explanation. And the actions of both father and son receive no accounting. Abraham acts without question or hesitation, let alone agonizing. Isaac may have resisted; otherwise, why the binding? But the author of the drama gives him no lines—apart from the query about what is going on. Abraham, in effect, deceives him by saying that God will supply the lamb for the slaughter. The episode concludes only with the reaffirmation of Abraham's unflinching dedication to God and of Yahweh's commitment to his descendants. Abraham had passed the test. The author leaves it at that.

The *Book of Jubilees* clearly finds that picture disquieting.⁷ Genesis had God simply decide to test Abraham out of the blue, with no preliminaries and no motive. The author of *Jubilees* decided to provide a backdrop—and to offer some justification for Yahweh's action. He introduced a new character to trigger the episode. Mastema had appeared earlier in the text, more than once, and would appear again afterward, a demonic figure, "chief of the spirits," as he is termed, each time as a villainous personage.⁸ In *Jubilees*' version of the Aqedah tale he takes center stage. It is Mastema's idea, not God's, to put Abraham to the test. As the text has it, word was out in heaven that Abraham was faithful to Yahweh in all matters, however difficult, and was beloved of the Lord. Mastema disputed the idea and challenged Yahweh to prove it by directing Abraham to make Isaac, his dearest son, a sacrificial victim.⁹ God readily accepted the challenge. He knew very well that Abraham had successfully surmounted such divinely imposed trials in the past: famine in the land, the seizure of his wife by Pharaoh, and the exile of Hagar and Ishmael. So God was perfectly comfortable with this new scenario and with the demands made by the demonic Mastema.¹⁰ This framing of the episode sets it in a context altogether different from the Genesis narrative. The initiative and the challenge come from the head of the evil spirits, a close parallel to the role of Satan in prodding God to demonstrate Job's loyalty by afflicting him with the most horrific experiences. For *Jubilees*, therefore, God does have a motive, no mere

---

6. Discussions of the *Aqedah*, of course, are legion. See, e.g., von Rad (1961), 232–249; Daly (1977), 45–75; Davies and Chilton (1978), 514–546; and see the excellent collection of articles by Noort and Tigchelaar (2002).

7. On the version in *Jubilees*, see the commentary by VanderKam (2018), 551–582, with bibliography. Cf. also the comments of Kugel (2012), 166–171.

8. *Jub.* 10:8, 11:5, 11:11, 48:2, 48:9, 48:12, 48:15. On the role of Mastema in *Jubilees* generally, see VanderKam (2017), 1350–1360. Mastema also appears as the Prince of Malevolence and a prod to God for the sacrifice of Isaac in a fragmentary text from Qumran; 4Q225, col. I. On that text, see Garcia Martinez (2002), 44–57.

9. *Jub.* 17:15-16.

10. *Jub.* 17:17-18.

whim. He reacted to the unfounded skepticism of the demon and made sure to exhibit Abraham's devotion in the most dramatic fashion.

That frame having been established, the author of *Jubilees* proceeds to follow the scriptural account with regard to Abraham's journey to the mountain, the construction of the altar, binding of Isaac, even the scene of Abraham's brandishing the knife to commit the sacrifice.[11] Whereas Genesis at this point has the voice of an angel come from heaven with the divine message that Abraham had proved himself and should put down his weapon, *Jubilees* provides a more dramatic confrontation. The angel arrives in person and sets himself directly in front of Abraham—and in front of Mastema. The voice from heaven calling a halt to the proceedings was that of the Lord himself. And the upshot was to shame the wicked Mastema.[12] The author also beefs up the spare blessing of Abraham's line by God in Genesis through a second divine speech elaborating upon the benefaction.[13] *Jubilees'* rendition, therefore, while honoring the original in sticking closely to its narrative, introduced elements that gave it a rationale, intensified the drama, and turned the imposition of a divine command into a combat between the divinity and his demonic adversary.

Polemic prompted Philo's treatment of the *Aqedah*. Like the author of *Jubilees*, he preferred a fuller version of the story, providing more details like the virtues of Isaac, both physical beauty and greatness of soul, the depth of Abraham's feelings for his beloved son, and the unflinching and pious reaction of the patriarch to the command of God—a rather more vivid presentation of the story than Genesis' stark narrative.[14] But improvement on the Bible was not Philo's principal motivation. He presents the context of the composition as one of harsh polemic. Critics of Jewish pride in the story chose to minimize its significance. They argue, so Philo alleges, that Abraham's willingness to sacrifice his son was no big deal. They pointed to many other examples of people in different cultures who sacrifice their children to the gods in the interests of their nations' welfare, citing both Greek and non-Greek peoples, not to mention the gymnosophists of India who toss their elderly onto funeral pyres, and women who hurl themselves on the pyres after deceased husbands. Abraham had no monopoly on this practice and deserves no special credit.[15] Philo takes up the cudgels with a rhetorical rejoinder. Other peoples, he observes, may have performed such deeds under fear or compulsion or in search of honor and fame, but no such motivation prompted Abraham and no imminent national disasters required drastic appeals to the divinity.[16] Moreover, so

---

11. *Jub.* 18:1-8.
12. *Jub.* 18:9-12.
13. *Jub.* 18:13-16.
14. Philo, *Abr.* 167–177.
15. Philo, *Abr.* 178–183.
16. Philo, *Abr.* 184–190. On Philo and critical allegorists, cf. the discussion of Hay (1979–80), 41–75.

Philo insisted, Abraham's deed (or willingness to perform the deed) stands out starkly from all ostensible parallels for human sacrifice. It was a practice alien to Hebrews. Abraham's voluntary submission to Yahweh on this score thus becomes all the more extraordinary and inexpressibly laudable.[17]

Philo plainly felt the force of the Aqedah. His reproduction of the story was a meaningful act, a reassertion of the very core of the faith, the unequivocal trust in the Lord as patron and protector of his flock, regardless of circumstance or consequence. That does not, however, prevent the philosopher from drawing out more vibrantly than the biblical source the sterling character of Isaac, the deep love and tenderness of his father which made his steadfastness all the more compelling, and the enduring power of the tale as enshrined in the sacred books themselves. And he goes still further to utilize the episode as a prime exhibit to refute the crabbed criticisms of those who would minimize its significance and who misunderstand the grandeur of his people.

Josephus also regarded the spare account in the Bible as inadequate to express the depth and power of this emblematic event. His additions heightened sensitivities and gave expression to the emotions evoked by the episode.[18] Abraham, Isaac, and indeed God take on dimensions and evince feelings only barely hinted at in the scriptural text. The latter opens abruptly with God simply calling on Abraham to ready Isaac for the sacrifice. Josephus introduces the episode by underscoring the deep-seated relationship between father and son, a tie cemented by the fact that Isaac had been a long awaited and late-coming child of his father's old age. The devotion of his parents was all the stronger because the boy was the very model of virtue, of filial dutifulness, and of zealous commitment to God. Abraham's fondness for his son knew no bounds; he set his own happiness on the expectation that Isaac would survive him intact when he departed from life.[19] When God enters the scene to announce the trial of piety that he would impose upon the patriarch, he puts it in the context of numerous benefits that he had accorded to Abraham over the years, including the birth of Isaac. The injunction to make this sacrifice thus takes its place amidst a surrounding array of divine favors,

---

17. Philo, *Abr.* 193, 196.

18. On Josephus' narrative here, see Franxman (1979), 156–162; Feldman (1998b), 266–285. Feldman's comparison of the *Aqedah* with the sacrifice of Iphigeneia, especially as found in Euripides' *Iphigeneia in Aulis*, however, presses the case a bit too far. There are as many contrasts as parallels. And the idea that Josephus' retelling of the episode is a "supreme example of Hellenization" is hardly warranted. His version is readily understood without recourse to Euripides. The issue of a sacrifice of a child was not unknown in Hebrew traditions, as witness the tale of Jephthah and his daughter. Feldman's notes on this segment of Josephus' *Antiquities* (2000), 84–94, are nevertheless essential reading for references to rabbinic material and classical sources. On the Iphigeneia story and the issue of human sacrifice in Greece, see Bremmer (2002), 21–43.

19. *Jos. AJ,* 1:222-223. On this, see the note of Feldman (2000), 84.

a sign that this test arises out of benevolence, not distrust or doubt.[20] The event, so Josephus suggests, therefore carries a more profound meaning than just a test alone. But the historian leaves ambiguous just what relationship holds between God's generosity and his directive to Abraham to offer up his son. Josephus expands the story but renders the divine motive even more obscure.

The Bible has Abraham dutifully and unhesitatingly acquiesce. Josephus felt the need for a fuller account. He gives Abraham no words, but does conjure up his thoughts: his compliance is not blind obedience but the firm belief that God's providence governs all and guarantees a proper outcome.[21] The historian inserts an item here not found elsewhere. He observes that Abraham hid from his wife and the rest of the household the purpose of his journey with Isaac.[22] That might, of course, have been inferred from silence in the original. But Josephus injects it explicitly to lend more drama to the tale. And not only that. He notes that Abraham's concealment here arose out of concern that he might otherwise be talked out of doing the deed![23] This striking remark, rarely commented upon, gives an important human dimension to Abraham, one that is absent in the Bible's representation of him as an unswerving adherent to God's will. The implication here is quite clear: Abraham's deception did not arise out of desire to spare Sarah and others the agony of anticipating the slaying of Isaac. Rather, Abraham was concerned about *his own weakness*. If he divulged his mission, the resistance of his wife and household might well induce him to abandon God's order. This insertion in the narrative applies a very different element to the character of Abraham. No unbending servant of the Lord, he is anxious about his susceptibility to abandonment of his obligation. If he falters, humane considerations might outweigh divine directives. He had to get on with the job.

A major question arises from the Genesis text. Isaac is purely passive, apart from his inquiry about the apparent absence of an animal victim. Yet Abraham resorts to binding him before the event. Would this not imply potential resistance that had to be prevented? Was Isaac then not a voluntary victim?[24] Josephus may have had some worries on this score. The idea of the father coercing an unwilling son to submit to slaughter would cast some doubt on both parties, not a message that the historian was comfortable in delivering. Josephus simply took the easy way out: he omitted the binding altogether. No Aqedah for him. Instead he composed a speech for Abraham that would allow him to soften the blow. The patriarch reminds Isaac that it was God who answered his prayers in bringing a child into the world in his old age, that he (Abraham) had spared no pains in

---

20. *Jos. AJ,* 1:224. Cf. Feldman (2000), 86–87.
21. *Jos. AJ.* 1:225. Feldman (2000), 87, sees this as embrace of Stoic doctrine.
22. *Jos. AJ,* 1:225.
23. *Jos. AJ,* 1:225: ἐκωλύετο γὰρ ἂν ὑπερετῆσαι τῷ θεῷ.
24. *Jubilees* also reports the binding without comment; 18:8. Philo merely has Abraham lay Isaac on the altar; *Abr.* 176.

raising him, and that he had no greater joy than the thought that Isaac would be heir to his legacy. But what God giveth he can take away. It was Yahweh who made it possible for Isaac to be born, and it is Yahweh who asks him back. Isaac entered the world at a most unusual time, and he will depart from it in a most unusual way. Nor would he disappear into nothingness. God will take Isaac's soul unto himself and make the lad a guardian and supporter of Abraham in his old age. Thus God himself would take the role that Isaac would have had as mainstay of the patriarch in his final years.[25]

Lest there be any doubt about Isaac's voluntary submission to his fate, Josephus erases it in the scene that followed. Isaac not only greeted his father's words with joy, but actually raced to the altar, declaring his eagerness to meet his end.[26] Isaac himself is accorded a speech, declaring that he ought not to have been born in the first place if he were to question the wishes of his father, let alone the will of God.[27] Josephus thus makes the lad a flesh and blood figure, no mere prop in the story. And he adds further to the drama by having God himself, not an angel, intervene to stay Abraham's hand, and indeed to deliver a speech of his own justifying his action. The Lord asserts that he orchestrated this event not because he was out for human blood, nor would he have provided Abraham with a son and then rob him of that blessing. He simply wished to put Abraham to the test. Now that he has proved his mettle, he will enjoy all the benefits of his piety including the multitude of nations who would be his legacy.[28]

Josephus thus filled out and expanded upon the slender account in Genesis. He created a scenario in which the characters took on human features, spoke for themselves, and intensified the drama rather than appearing as stock figures. In the end, however, the central question of why God felt the need to put Abraham to the test at all goes unanswered. The power of this compelling, signature event that went to the heart of the Israelites' relationship to their god was such that any attempt at explanation would be inadequate. Better not to make the attempt.

Ps-Philo, in his *Liber Antiquitatum Biblicarum,* whether following another tradition or taking his own initiative, also supplied a backstory to this troubled tale. As *Jubilees* invented a Satan-like figure to provoke God into imposing a test upon Abraham, so *LAB* conjures up angels who were jealous of God's favoritism toward Abraham and thereby prodded him to require his favorite to give up his son as proof of loyalty to divine command.[29] The author further enlivens the tale

---

25. *Jos. AJ,* 1:228-231. Cf. Feldman's remarks (2000), 90–91.

26. *Jos. AJ,* 1:232: ὥρμησεν επὶ τὸν βωμὸν καὶ τὴν σφαγήν. There may be a hint of Isaac's willingness in the fragmentary 4Q225, col. II, from the Dead Sea Scrolls. See García Martínez (2002), 32–33.

27. *Jos. AJ,* 1:232.

28. *Jos. AJ,* 1:233-235.

29. *LAB,* 32:1-2. On the mysterious *cultores militiarum*, mentioned as parallel to the angels, see the note of Jacobson (1996), 861–862. Other brief allusions to the *Aqedah* at *LAB,* 18:5, 40:2.

by inserting a dialogue between father and son, which has no counterpart in Genesis' brief and straightforward narrative. Abraham actually announces to Isaac his intent to turn him into a burnt offering, a sharp deviation from the biblical account which has him lie about the object of the sacrifice. This obviates and dispenses with Isaac's question about the missing lamb and makes him aware from the start of his impending fate. Isaac is thus an active player in the drama, no mere passive and unwitting participant. This shift, of course, also eradicates the binding itself. No need for it. Abraham explains his mission as delivering Isaac into the hands of the one who provided him in the first place.[30] And the lad does something more than simply accede to the sacrifice. He actually lectures to his father in order to clarify the significance of the deed. Isaac asks why he was not told that such a sacrifice would give him a secure life and immeasurable time. He takes pride in the fact that he was singled out for this sacrifice, for it will grant him a blessedness beyond that of all men and will extend through generations to come.[31] At the climax, as in Josephus' version, it is the Lord, not an angel, who enters the scene himself. It is his own voice from on high that deters Abraham from delivering the fatal blow. And the scenario that he had put into motion now comes full circle: he boasts that he has shut the mouths of those who maligned Abraham. The envious angels who had stirred God to create the episode had now been silenced.[32]

Grappling with the profound mystery of the *Aqedah* presented a severe challenge to revisionists.[33] The terrible task imposed on Abraham for no obvious reason and the stark brevity of the biblical tale which had both father and son as passive playthings of divine power left much in troubling obscurity. The versions of *Jubilees* and *LAB* at least attempted to supply some motivation to God, but the introduction of a demonic Mastema or envious angels were rather lame efforts to rationalize Yahweh's behavior—and indeed only served to diminish him. Philo and Josephus, by contrast, left the choice of such a fearful test unmotivated, leaving the enigma as it stood. That may have been the wiser course—and closer to the intent of the biblical author. The new renditions, evidently uncomfortable with the starkness of the biblical story, each in its own way, added some color and vividness,

---

30. *LAB*, 32:2: *in manus te trado qui donavit te mihi.*

31. *LAB*, 32:3. The text here is problematic and subject to different readings, but the gist seems clear. See the discussion by Jacobson (1996), 863–865. Murphy (1993), 145, oddly takes this as Isaac questioning the appropriateness of the sacrifice. It is true that in the subsequent passage (32:4), Abraham does bind Isaac (though only his feet). *LAB* follows the scriptural source here. But it makes little sense in the context, following upon Isaac's declaration of pride in his position as victim for the greater glory of the generations to come.

32. *LAB*, 32:4: *et clausi ora maledicentium semper adversus te.*

33. Other references to the Aqedah in Second Temple authors are brief and unelaborated, usually with reference to the event as a test for Abraham; *Judith*, 8:25-26; Ben Sira, 44:20; 1 *Macc.* 2:52; Philo Epicus in Euseb. *PE*, 9:20:1; *Wisdom of Solomon*, 10:5.

dialogue and human interchange, direct confrontation, increased intensity, a firmer grasp of the implications, heightened emotions, a greater emphasis on the benevolent feelings and actions that characterize relations with the deity—and the humanity of the participants.

Chapter 5

THE TESTAMENT OF ABRAHAM

The figure of Abraham not only sparked rewritings of biblical material. It could inspire compositions that had barely the slightest foothold in the Bible itself. Writers, it appears, were at liberty to concoct their own imaginative tales, even about the ultimate forefather. And they could do so with humor and mischief. The prime exhibit in this category is a fascinating and most peculiar text entitled the *Testament of Abraham*. It was composed probably in the 1st century BCE or the 1st century CE.[1] The narrative has virtually nothing to do with anything in the Bible. Abraham, to be sure, is presented as a man of preeminent righteousness, boundless hospitality, and graciousness. That does suit the picture of Abraham in Genesis. So, we have the right guy. But apart from that, the author took off on a flight of fancy without worrying about the fact that it lacked any biblical basis. No summary of this text can do it justice. But I will present a few highlights, stressing the comic aspects of the work, which pervade it from start to finish.

Whereas most of the post-biblical writings on Abraham, Sarah, and the visit to Egypt seek to rescue the patriarch's reputation by molding the biblical story to his advantage, the *Testament of Abraham* has an altogether different agenda. It turns the patriarch into a rather less than admirable character, and it sets him up as a foil in a series of farcical situations.[2] As a concocted fiction unmoored in any known biblical tradition, it provides the most striking instance of the license accorded to Jewish writers to create their own depictions of the forefathers.

---

1. On the date, see bibliography in Gruen (2002), 327, and the full discussion, with additional bibliography, in Allison (2003), 34–40.
2. Much of what follows summarizes the fuller treatment in Gruen (2002), 183–193, with stress on the humorous aspects of the text. That aspect is also well discussed by Ludlow (2002), *passim*, especially 28–47. See further Wills (1995), 249–256. The excellent commentary on the work by Allison (2003) endorses the idea of its pervasive comic character; e.g. 51–52. For Konstan (2015), 45–51, it is a "subversive biography" on the analogy of the Alexander Romance. I use the text of Recension A, the longer text, here. On the two recensions, see Allison (2003), 12–17.

The story takes place near the end of Abraham's life. He is nearly a millennium old. God decided that his time had come, and he asked the archangel Michael to break the news to Abraham that he was about to be gathered to his fathers. But Michael was not quite up to the task. Abraham wished to prolong his stay on earth, laid out a lavish banquet for Michael, with the result that the angel could not bear to carry out his assignment. He asked to be excused from the banquet on the pretext that he needed to relieve himself, and shot back up to heaven to consult with the Lord. God sent him back twice more with soothing words for Abraham to convince him to release his soul and to enjoy his well earned everlasting reward. But Abraham was simply not ready to go. He dawdled and delayed, making up excuses for staying on earth a little longer, leaving the angel dismayed and the Lord frustrated. Among other things, Abraham suggested that he take a final trip, namely one in which he would be escorted around the world to see every creature in it. The obliging God granted his wish and had Abraham taken everywhere on the globe in a carriage drawn by a heavenly host of cherubim, with a side trip to the seat of judgment where he could witness the fate of those souls who had been consigned to perdition. Now, at last, Michael could expect Abraham to relinquish his hold on life. But no. The patriarch announced again, "I'm not going."[3]

Poor Michael had to return once more to the Boss to ask for help because he could get nowhere with Abraham. God now released Michael from his job and turned to plan B. He sent his most effective messenger for this task: the dread specter, Death. The grim reaper appeared first in disguise, as God had ordered him, so as not to frighten Abraham, and requested that the patriarch follow him to heaven. But Abraham tried yet more delaying tactics, claiming that Death was not really who he claimed to be because he looked too nice and charming. Whereupon the specter stripped off his mask and exposed himself in all his ghastly gruesomeness. He gave Abraham the full treatment: seven fiery dragon-heads and fourteen additional faces, ranging from repulsive reptiles to a raging sea. So ferocious was the appearance and so terrifying the noise that all of Abraham's male and female servants, seven thousand of them, dropped dead on the spot. The patriarch now realized that he had gone too far; he asked Death to put his pleasant camouflage back on and join him in prayer to restore his innocent household staff to life. The double prayer worked. The Lord complied and Abraham seemed compliant.[4]

But not yet. The patriarch still scrambled for ways to defer his own fate, coming up with a half dozen more delaying tactics to postpone the inevitable. In the end, Death had to resort to subterfuge himself. When Abraham feigned exhaustion in order to rest and thus buy more time, Death asked him to clasp his right hand so that the patriarch could regain some strength. The trick worked. Abraham took the bait, and his soul forthwith stuck fast to the hand of Death. The patriarch had at

---

3. *TAbr.* 1–15.
4. *TAbr.* 16–18.

last been entrapped. Michael reappeared, as did a plethora of angels. Abraham got a splendid escort to paradise. So ends this remarkable work.[5]

The author, in his depiction of Abraham, obviously felt no constraint from the Bible. The humor in this text is deliberate and persistent, no mere marginal presence. It would go too far to characterize this work, as some have, as a parody of the pious Abraham. The patriarch's piety is not, in fact, satirized. Indeed, it earns him good will, favors, and countless concessions from God and his ministers. Abraham emerges rather as a master manipulator, exploiting his advantages with the divine, and prolonging his mortal existence again and again through a series of subterfuges. The author does not diminish Abraham's stature but gives him added dimensions—including the very human emotions of spleen, regret, and reluctance to die. And much of it is delivered tongue in cheek.

Nor is Abraham the only comic character in the piece. The image of the hapless archangel Michael who kept zooming back and forth between earth and heaven to seek counsel from the Lord, even offering the pretext of a need to urinate, but never fulfilled his task of persuading Abraham, was surely concocted to draw laughs. And Death too is subject to mockery. That fearsome creature, when summoned by God to finish the job on Abraham, turned to jelly in the presence of the Lord. He quivered and shivered, moaned and groaned, and panicked at the prospect of orders delivered by the Boss. This is plain parody. And the interchange between Abraham and Death operates at the level of comic caricature, with first the removal, then the restoration of the grim reaper's shining visage that cloaked the rot and horror of his real appearance and loathsome odors that felled thousands at a shot. This is overkill indeed. The topsy-turvy character of this interaction bears a strong affinity to farce. And the final reversal of expectations confirms it. On the patriarch's beseeching, Death joined forces with Abraham in prayer to bring back to life the very souls whom he had sent to sudden and premature perdition. If Death can restore life, we are indeed in bizarre wonderland.

The *Testament of Abraham,* whatever else it contains, has the characteristics of a light-hearted fantasy. The patriarch proved to be a maestro of the evasive action, adept at dissimulation, perhaps indeed of self-deception. His evasive tactics and multiple modes of dalliance provide more entertainment than instruction. Abraham is the artful dodger and inventive manufacturer of pretexts to prolong his earthly existence. He is a memorable character, unparalleled in this depiction. The text, replete with wit and whimsy, demonstrates most conspicuously that imaginative Jewish writers could create their own fictions with barely a nod to the scriptural word.

---

5. *TAbr.* 17–20.

Chapter 6

THE RAPE OF DINAH

A most troublesome tale surfaces in the midst of the Genesis narrative on the era of Jacob. The ravishing of Jacob's daughter Dinah deeply darkened the record. Not only the victimization of Dinah but the behavior of her brothers gave reason for profound dismay.

The story is brief but painful. Jacob came peacefully into the town of Shechem in the land of Canaan. On the spot where he pitched his tent he purchased the land from Hamor, the city's head man and father of Shechem, whose name matched the location. There followed a visit by Jacob's young daughter Dinah to the town to enjoy the company of the women who dwelled there. But the friendly encounter swiftly turned to a nightmare. Shechem seized the young girl and forced himself upon her. His feelings for her, however, went beyond mere momentary lust. Shechem found himself smitten, and asked his father to arrange a marriage with Dinah for him. The arrangements proved to go well beyond the union of Shechem and Dinah. Hamor approached Jacob, not only asking for his daughter in marriage to Shechem, but also proposing a wholesale set of weddings between the daughters of Israel and the men of Shechem, and vice-versa. He also generously offered the Israelites lands on which to settle and the dwellings that stood there. Shechem himself made a special plea to Jacob, essentially a request for his daughter's hand in marriage, and promised in return whatever price Jacob should name.[1]

The circumstances prompted a hasty show of harmony and good will from the Shechemites. They aimed to erase the stigma of the rape and to bring about concord and kinship between the nations. But it was not to be. The sons of Jacob were incensed by the defilement of their sister. They responded to the offers of Hamor and Shechem in a deceitful manner, says the text, claiming that the plans for uniting the two communities through marriage can only take place if all Shechemite males are circumcised; otherwise the arrangement is off.[2] The genial and accommodating Shechemites followed the wishes of their leaders and did indeed perform the painful act of slicing off their foreskins, a most generous show

---

1. Gen. 33:18-34:12.
2. Gen. 34:7, 34:13-17.

of compliance.³ But it played into the hands of Jacob's sons Simeon and Levi, who now carried out their dastardly scheme. While the Shechemite males were still suffering the effects of their self-inflicted surgeries, the two Israelites entered the city and massacred every one of them. They then took their sister out of the town and proceeded to plunder it unhindered. As if that were not enough, Simeon and Levi seized all the livestock, took the women and children captive, and looted everything that was valuable in the houses. Even Jacob was alarmed at these unbridled actions. The concern, however, came not because he was chagrined at the deceit and brutality, but because he worried about his own reputation and the fall-out from hostility roused among other peoples in the area who could retaliate against him and his household.⁴ The brothers' response was short and curt. They simply asserted that they could not tolerate their sister being treated like a whore.⁵

The grim story surely troubled Jews in the Hellenistic and Roman periods. The rape of the innocent Dinah may have been an abomination, but the bountiful making of amends by the Shechemites, the false deception by Jacob's sons, the appalling overkill perpetrated by them, and even the selfish and misplaced regrets by Jacob cast a dismal pall on the house of the patriarch.

The Genesis narrative could not easily be dismissed or discarded. But new and altered versions eventually surfaced. The need to modify was keen. A certain Theodotus, known to us only through fragments preserved in Alexander Polyhistor's 1st century BCE collection of Hellenistic Jewish authors and quoted by Eusebius, took up the task. Theodotus composed an epic poem in Homeric hexameters, dealing at least in part with the life of Jacob. His date and provenance are disputed, but general consensus has him as a Hellenized Jew of the 2nd century BCE.⁶ The excerpts include an extended portion on the Dinah episode. And they accord it a very different flavor.

Theodotus works within the original but molds it to his own purposes. He adds details like the description of Dinah, the occupations of Jacob's children, and the existence of a festival that drew Dinah to the city of Shechem. His initial comment on Hamor and Shechem characterizes them as stubborn, evidently an allusion to their determination to bring Dinah into their family.⁷ He introduces Dinah as

---

3. Gen. 34:18-24.

4. Gen. 34:25-30. In a later reference to Jacob on his deathbed, Genesis does have the patriarch denounce, even curse, Simeon and Levi for their ruthlessness and murderous fury; Gen. 49:5-7.

5. Gen. 34:31.

6. See the text in Lloyd-Jones and Parsons (1983), 360–365; Holladay (1989), II, 106–127, with translation and notes. On the dating, see the balanced discussion of Holladay (1989), II, 68–72, with notes. Whether Theodotus was Jewish or Samaritan need not here be argued. See bibliography in Pummer (1982), 17; Holladay (1989), II, 58–68; Gruen (1998), 123–124. On Theodotus as an epic poet, see now Adams (2020), 26–33, 41–43.

7. Euseb. *PE*, 9:22:2.

beautiful, shapely, and noble, perhaps to accentuate the vileness of Shechem's deed.[8] More significantly however, in the immediate aftermath of the rape and of Hamor's proposal not only to have Shechem wed Dinah but to merge the two peoples through mixed marriages, Theodotus focuses attention upon the issue of miscegenation. In the Genesis narrative the sons of Jacob introduce the applying of circumcision, but only to further their deceptive plot of weakening the Shechemite males and rendering them vulnerable to mass murder. Theodotus omits any hint of deception or nefarious plotting. The idea of circumcision comes from Jacob, not the sons, and it is set squarely in the context of Jewish identity. By circumcising themselves the Shechemites would in some sense become like Jews.[9] Jacob asserts as fundamental doctrine that Hebrews were prohibited from bringing home sons-in-law or daughters-in-law from elsewhere but must confine themselves to those of the same clan.[10] The point is amplified by reference to the circumcision of Abraham, which set a precedent unchanged throughout since it stemmed from the word of God.[11]

Theodotus goes further to distinguish the failures of Shechemites, their character, and inferior qualities. They are impious, they dishonor the high and low alike, they do not render justice or keep to the laws, but care only for deadly deeds.[12] By branding them thus, Theodotus sets the stage for the murderous deeds of Simeon and Levi, who disposed of Hamor and Shechem respectively—in graphic Homeric detail.[13] As representatives of this wicked clan they evidently had it coming. The author neither offers nor implies any negative judgment on the brothers' actions. The other brothers then enter the scene, pillage the city, take captives, and rescue Dinah.[14] An appropriate outcome for the wicked Shechemites, and a happy ending.

The biblical account, remarkably enough, makes no mention of God. The actions of Shechemites and Israelites alike are their own responsibility.[15] Theodotus' poem, by contrast, makes God a key agent, constituting a marked shift of responsibility. Simeon spurs his brother Levi into action by citing an oracle, in good Greek fashion, which delivered the word of God, asserting that Abraham's descendants would acquire rule over ten nations, a reference to the divine promise

---

8. Euseb. *PE*, 9:22:3-4.
9. Euseb. *PE*, 9:22:5: Ἰουδαίσαι.
10. Euseb. *PE*, 9:22:5: γενεῆς ... ὁμοίης. On the textual difficulties here, see Holladay (1989) II, 178.
11. Euseb. *PE*, 9:22:7.
12. Euseb. *PE*, 9:22:9b.
13. Euseb. *PE*, 9:22:10–11.
14. Euseb. 9:22:11.
15. Kugel (1998), 411–412, suggests the possibility that the line in *Gen.* 34:7, with regard to the rape, that "such a thing should not be done" is actually a divine pronouncement or might have been read as such.

in the covenant with the patriarch.[16] It was the Lord himself who put the idea of vengeance upon the Shechemites into the minds of Jacob's sons. And it was God who guided the disabling of the Shechemites.[17]

Theodotus' poem thus diverges notably from the message of the Scriptures. While acknowledging the brothers' indignation at the violation of their sister,[18] he puts the principle impetus elsewhere. The Lord's pronouncement prompted the bloody deed. The brothers simply carried out a divine judgment. The wicked character of the Shechemites provided justification. Theodotus drops any reference to the brothers' deception. The fact that the Shechemites were in a wounded state because of circumcision is omitted in the poem. So is the chagrin of Jacob when learning of the massacre. Indeed there was no real massacre. Apart from those whom the brothers encountered on the way, only Hamor and Shechem were killed. The other brothers engaged in plunder, but not butchery. Simeon and Levi, it seems, have nothing to answer for. The whole scenario takes on a new coloration. Retaliation for the ravishing of Dinah is subsumed in the larger context of maintaining a proper Jewish identity through resistance to a mingling with the wicked.[19]

The recounting of this episode in the *Book of Jubilees* represents yet another turn in the justification of the brothers' ferocity and violence.[20] The author gives voice to both of the purported motives for their deeds: rage at the violation of their sister and rejection of any adulteration of the clan by consorting with foreigners of depraved character. The text first stresses the abominable nature of the rape, adding the age of Dinah, just twelve years old, a defilement that stirred the passionate ire of Jacob as well as his sons. *Jubilees* states unabashedly that Jacob joined with his sons in a deceptive scheme against the Shechemites.[21] No effort here to hide or soften the duplicity, nor to exculpate Jacob. The rape alone seemed to legitimize the extreme reaction. Even the issue of circumcision goes unmentioned. Simeon and Levi simply entered the city by surprise, slaughtered in painful fashion every man they found, leaving no one alive because of the violation of Dinah.[22] This was not so much a defense of the brothers as a portrayal of their vengeance, even their treachery, as self-evident, fully to be expected, given the heinous crime that they were avenging. The author of *Jubilees* reinforces and expands upon the point at a

---

16. Euseb. *PE*, 9:22.8-9a; cf. Gen. 15:18-21.
17. Euseb. *PE*, 9:22:9b.
18. Euseb. *PE*, 9:22:8.
19. Feldman (2004), 271–275, acknowledges but oddly minimizes the changes, and passes over the issue of ethnicity and identity.
20. For an analysis of the *Jubilees* version, see Werman (1997), 1–22. See also the discussion of Endres (1987), 120–154.
21. On efforts to interpret "deceitfully" as "cleverly," see Kugel (1998), 408–409.
22. *Jub.* 30:2-4. Other calculations of Dinah's age have her even younger; see Endres (1987), 125–127; VanderKam (2018), 821–822.

broader level. "Nothing like this should ever be done again," says the text. The annihilation of the Shechemites was pursuant to a divine decree, for the defilement of an Israelite virgin is intolerable. The Lord himself had armed the avengers.[23]

That would seem to be the sufficient and satisfactory explanation. Yet the author of *Jubilees* glides immediately, without signposting it, into the second, rather different, legitimization of the deceit and brutality. He speaks here of the prohibition of intercourse with non-Israelites. If any Israelite should give daughter or sister to a gentile, he is to be executed by stoning and the girl by burning. The bans derive from biblical pronouncements against intermarriage, which would lead to idolatry.[24] Scorn for foreigners outside the Israelite nation represents a repeated theme for the author of *Jubilees*. The Dinah tale constitutes a prime example. For him, the Shechemites' offense consists of defilement of an even more grievous sort than the rape itself, for it casts shame on all of Israel and violates the eternal codes inscribed on the heavenly tablets themselves. The author goes on at some length in insisting upon the profanation that would ensue upon mixed marriages with gentiles, as proposed by the Shechemites, the impurity and contamination that the nation would suffer, and the inevitable divine punishment that would be rained upon them. Hence the killing of the Shechemites, even with the infliction of pain, according to *Jubilees*, is fully appropriate and a rendering of well-deserved justice.[25] The collective punishment, in this rewriting, is warranted only in small part by Shechem's crime and more profoundly by the move toward miscegenation, which rendered the whole community culpable. The author of *Jubilees* goes further in praise of the massacre by finding Levi's part in it as the meting out of righteous punishment that justified the elevation of his descendants to the Israelite priesthood itself.[26] One might note that the final lines of the Genesis narrative have the sons reassert defiantly that their ire was prompted by the fact that their sister was treated like a whore. *Jubilees* leaves that out. For the author, the central issue was not the defilement of Dinah but the potential defilement of the Hebrew people.

Theodotus and the author of *Jubilees* both confronted a biblical tale, which, on the face of it, suggested a ruthlessness and barbarity that reflected little credit upon the house of Israel. Each attempted to undo that impression—but in strikingly

---

23. *Jub.* 30:5-6.

24. *Jub.* 30:7-10. Cf. Exod. 34:16; Deut. 7:3-4a. See also Lev. 18 and 20, with Werman (1997), 11–15. VanderKam (2018), 826, rightly notes the confluence of exogamy and idolatry. Cf. also Kugel (1998), 425–427.

25. *Jub.* 30:11-17. On the issue of impurity, see VanderKam (2018), 832–833, and the works cited there.

26. *Jub.* 30:18-20, 23. The author's confidence in the righteousness of the brothers' aggression is indicated also by the fact that he includes the biblical notice of Jacob's unhappiness at the slaughtering at Shechem, *Jub.* 30:25, which Theodotus had omitted. But this concern, as Genesis also had it, arose from apprehensions about retaliation by neighboring gentiles, not about the rightness of the deeds.

different ways. Theodotus modified and reduced any guilt on the part of the brothers. He denied by omission the idea of calculated deceit, he reduced the dimension of the killings, he dropped the misgivings on Jacob's part, he stressed the wickedness of the Shechemites, and he placed principal responsibility for the event upon God. *Jubilees* approached the tale from another angle altogether. The text makes no effort to mitigate the savagery of the brothers' actions, nor to deny their deceptiveness, nor to spare Jacob, nor to stress divine intervention, nor even to exaggerate the wickedness of the Shechemites. The author takes the justification of the Israelites' actions for granted. The ravishing of Dinah simply demanded vengeance, and the attempt to blend the nations was a fundamental abomination, a violation of Israelite purity and special identity. It was not any evil deeds by Shechemites that authorized their annihilation but simply the idea of compromising the integral nature of the chosen people. The author's revising of Scripture was radical, but only (in his eyes) to bring out the inner meaning that spoke to the core of the nation.

The saga of Dinah's rape and its baneful consequences evidently gained wide circulation in the Second Temple era, mentioned with some frequency in the literature. The remarks and allusions that have survived, while relatively brief, offer some additional insights as to how the episode was perceived—and recast.

The *Testament of Levi* forms part of the assemblage, *Testaments of the Twelve Patriarchs*, originally composed in Hebrew and/or Aramaic and extant now in Greek translation. The collection purports to record the deathbed prophecies and ruminations of the twelve sons of Jacob, dating perhaps to the late 2nd or early 1st century BCE.[27] This treatise forms part of that collection.

The relevant portion concerns the divine promise to Levi of the priesthood, delivered to him by an angel in a dream. The vision directed him to avenge his sister Dinah by executing the sons of Hamor, an act fully backed by the messenger of God and inscribed on the heavenly tablets of the fathers.[28] Hence, the murder of Shechemites not only received divine sanction but justified the bestowal of the priesthood upon Levi and his descendants.[29]

This abbreviated version of the tale bypasses the issue of deception in inducing the Shechemites to undergo circumcision. Indeed the *Testament* departs intriguingly from the Genesis account in this regard. Whereas the Bible has all the sons of Jacob engaged in this deadly ruse, the *Testament* states that Levi actually

---

27. On the *Testaments*, see the commentaries by Charles (1908); Hollander and De Jonge (1985). See also the review of earlier scholarship by Slingerland (1977). On the date, still controversial, see Kugler (2001), 31–38; Kugel (2013), 1697–1700.

28. *TLevi*, 2:1-10, 5:1-4. That divine sanction buttressed the brothers' action appears also in *Jubilees*, 30:5; *Judith*, 9:24; *JosAs*, 23:13.

29. The extensive discussion by Kugel (1992), 1–34, is invaluable, but stresses too much the exegetical motivation in the Testament's departures from and additions to the Genesis text. See also the detailed treatment of *TLevi* on the rape of Dinah by Baarda (1992), 11–73.

opposed the imposition of that ritual upon the Shechemites, a stance nowhere else attested.[30] The author's purpose here, however, was not exculpation of Levi, divorcing him from the treacherous plot of wounding and weakening the enemy. Quite the contrary. As in *Jubilees*, the righteousness of the slaughter is unquestioned. For Levi, no ruse was needed. He urged its abandonment because of his fiery zeal to avenge his sister's defilement. That abominable deed sufficed to justify the murderous assault.[31] It simply reinforced the abominable character of the Shechemites and the many evils they had perpetrated upon the Hebrews from the time of Abraham.[32] The *Testament* does, however, disclose a division in the house of Jacob on the issue, and not merely a matter of strategy. It records the discomfiture of Jacob at the massacre, as in Genesis, although the author gives it a quite different meaning. Whereas Genesis, followed by *Jubilees*, has Jacob criticize the sons for potentially unleashing a backlash from neighbors against him, the *Testament* provides a more meaningful interpretation that distinguishes Jacob from his sons. The patriarch was aggrieved because the Shechemites had been killed *despite* having submitted to circumcision.[33] That revision of the story carries significance. Jacob's unhappiness should not be interpreted as pity or lament for Shechemite lives, but as something quite different. Circumcision had, in Jacob's eyes, turned the Shechemites into something like Israelites themselves. Hence their murder would dilute the very sense of distinctive Jewish identity that underlay the entire episode. Not that the *Testament* sided with Jacob on this score. The text proceeds to affirm the propriety of the massacre for it was God's decision, based on a history of Shechemite wickedness that included their efforts to ravish both Sarah and Rebecca, their persecution of Abraham, and their penchant for mistreating foreigners by seizing their wives.[34]

The *Testament of Levi* thus brings a somewhat different perspective to the troubling tale. The legitimacy of Levi's (and thus the Israelite) assault on Shechem is guaranteed from the outset by angelic authority and emblematized by the promise of Levi's priestly legacy. The sins of the Shechemites, punctuated by the violation of Dinah, merited extreme retaliation. The treatise is not defensive or apologetic. Like *Jubilees*, it takes the righteousness of the deed for granted. Yet it also alludes to some internal tension in the house of Jacob, an element not drawn from Genesis or from other extant retellings. That adds an extra dimension. By calling attention to Jacob's dissent on murdering the circumcised, the author

---

30. *TLevi*, 6:3. There is divergence in the manuscript tradition on Levi's stance here. That he opposed the circumcision, rather than advocated it, makes far better sense. See the persuasive arguments by Kugel (1992), 6–12. See also Baarda (1992), 36–40.

31. Indeed, the text implicates all Shechemites in the rape itself; *T.Levi*, 7:3.

32. *TLevi*, 6:8-11.

33. *TLevi*, 6:6-7.

34. *TLevi*, 6:8-11. Kugel (1992), 18, goes too far in claiming that foreignness as such is quite irrelevant to the tale.

brought into play, without pursuing the matter, an element of central importance: the issue of Israelite identity.[35]

The familiarity of the story can be illustrated by passing references in Second Temple texts that employ it for their own purposes, without endeavoring to recapitulate the narrative.[36] In the *Book of Judith*, for example, the heroine calls upon it without even having to mention Dinah's name. Judith appeals to God in a prayer before undertaking to save her city from the powerful Assyrian (really Babylonian) foe.[37] In doing so, she recalls the Lord's assistance to her ancestor Simeon in bringing vengeance upon the "foreigners," who stripped the virgin, defiled her womb and disgraced her.[38] She does not name Dinah nor the violator, nor even the site of the violation. The story was evidently too well known to require it. But she does delineate the criminals in the plural. The biblical version, of course, has Shechem as the sole ravisher. Judith's shift is hardly accidental. The author of *Judith* knew the Genesis tale, as did the audience. There were no multiple rapes. But the plural implicates the whole community in the crime and thus justifies the wholesale slaughter, plunder, and enslavement that followed.[39]

The assault on Dinah, of course, triggered the whole sequence of events. But Judith plainly paints with a broader brush. The plural "foreigners" already signified a collective offense that demanded retaliation. And more than vengeance for the dastardly deed is at stake here. The characterization of the enemies as foreigners hints at the ethnic contest stressed in *Jubilees* and alluded to in the *Testament of Levi*. And this appears forthrightly in the expression that the rape of Dinah constituted a "pollution of the blood."[40] More dramatically still, the role of God, a significant ingredient in the versions of Theodotus and *Jubilees*, becomes all-powerful in Judith's prayer. It was God who placed the sword of vengeance in Simeon's hand and who was responsible for the slaying of multitudes, from rulers to commons, in the sinning community. Simeon was a mere instrument in the divine plan. The author of *Judith* echoes the fateful line in Genesis that declares,

---

35. This aspect is downplayed in the discussion by Baarda (1992), 51.

36. Philo, of course, knew the tale and alludes to it very briefly in two different treatises, evidently to knowledgeable readers. But he has no interest in a recapitulation. He mentions Dinah, Shechem, Hamor, Simeon, and Levi only to discourse on the meaning of their names and draw out the allegorical significance of the characters; *Migr*. 253-255; *Mut*. 193-200. Pseudo-Philo, *LAB* 8:7, mentions the legend, but passes over it in a few words. On those texts, see Feldman (2004), 255–261.

37. On this segment of the *Book of Judith*, see the valuable commentaries of Gera (2014), 294–311, and Wills (2019), 279–285, with references to the literature.

38. *Judith*, 9:2.

39. *Judith*, 9:2-4. The notion that this represents Hasmonean resistance to Seleucid imperialism, as Wills (2019), 284 suggests, is wholly speculative.

40. *Judith*, 9:4: μίασμα αἵματος. Cf. Thiessen (2018), 165–188; Gera (2014), 310–311; Wills (2019), 282–285.

with regard to the rape, that "this ought not to be done." Whereas in Genesis, the identity of the deliverer of that line is unclear, in *Judith,* it is unequivocally the Lord.[41] The appeal to the Dinah story would naturally take such a course in a prayer to God by a woman for aid against a foreign enemy. But brief though this passage is, it touches on the themes that the story elicited in its Second Temple retellings: the horror at rape of an Israelite by an alien, the anxiety at the mingling of nations that might dilute Israelite character, and the reassertion of God's protection of the people of Israel.

Josephus did not dwell upon these events. Their troubling character may have deterred him. His summary is brief, with some telling omissions. He has the family of Jacob arrive in Shechem at festival time, with the innocent Dinah hoping only to enjoy the elegance of the women's apparel. Josephus records the rape, Shechem's falling in love with Dinah, and his father's request of Jacob for the hand of his daughter in marriage to his son. He conspicuously leaves out any reference to the brothers' crafty scheme, the Shechemites' generous submission to circumcision, and the treachery of Simeon and Levi. Instead, Josephus invents (or reproduces) a quite different scenario. He has Jacob respond diplomatically to Hamor's offer, being unwilling to brush off the request of a high-ranking official, and ask only for time in which to consult a council of his advisors, i.e. his sons.[42] Jacob thus emerges as a reasonable and fair-minded man who politely furthered the negotiations. The council, however, was divided. Most of the members declined to offer an opinion, but Simeon and Levi took matters into their own hands. They did not resort to a ruse, but attacked the Shechemites under cover of night in the midst of revelry, slew all the males, including the ruler and his son, and brought their sister back home. Josephus makes sure to assert that all this was done without Jacob's consent, and once Jacob learned of his sons' appalling acts, he expressed fury at their actions and indignation toward the perpetrators. God enters the picture here for the first time. He had had no hand in the events, and even now he simply asks Jacob to fulfill his vow of conducting sacrifices.[43] That is the end of the tale for Josephus.

The episode was perhaps too well known for Josephus to omit it altogether.[44] But he appears eager to pass it by as quickly as possible. He refrains from employing God as a means of lightening the load of guilt upon the brothers or Jacob, as Theodotus and the *Testament of Levi* did. He does, however, divorce Jacob from the offending sons and has him denounce the excesses to which they resorted, as

---

41. *Judith*, 9:2: εἶπας γάρ οὐκ οὕτως ἔσται. Cf. *Gen.* 34:7; Gera (2014), 307–308.

42. Jos. *AJ*, 1:337-338.

43. Jos. *AJ*, 1:339-341.

44. The tale is alluded to in passing in other texts without elaboration; e.g., Demetrius, in Euseb. *PE*, 9:21:9; Philo, *Migr.* 223-224; *Mut.* 193-195; *Jos. As.* 23:13; *4 Macc.* 2:18-21; *LAB*, 8:7. It was unnecessary to elaborate. Knowledge of the episode could be taken for granted. A useful summary of the later revisions of the story can be found in Standhartinger (1995), 155–169.

Genesis had indicated. Jacob is thus off the hook, and the enormity of the sons' action is recorded but swiftly passed over with a minimum of words. Josephus' truncated version of the Genesis text may well have stemmed from an awkward chagrin about the shameful actions of the house of Jacob. He could not suppress the disagreeable narrative altogether but he could eliminate the most disturbing elements like the deliberate tricking of compliant Shechemites, underscore the reasonableness and humanity of Jacob, and even ignore the idea of ethnic struggle for the soul of Israel.[45]

Dinah's misfortune and its consequences, as depicted in Genesis, plainly had resonance for numerous writers inspired to retell the tale. The grim narrative cast an unwelcome light upon the house of Jacob, thus motivating a variety of reinterpretations. The tale may have been too familiar to dispose of or to ignore. But the range of diverse versions revealed both strain and ingenuity. Some renditions brought God into the picture (he had not appeared in the Genesis original), thus to give sanction to the mass homicide, either to remove responsibility from the shoulders of Jacob's sons or to reinforce the justice of their actions. Others departed from Genesis to deny the compliance of Shechemites by stressing, exaggerating, and embellishing upon the wickedness of the clan. A different approach shifted focus from the rape of Dinah to the issue of mixed marriages, miscegenation, and Jewish identity. Some minimized or denied the deceitful trickery of the brothers or omitted the whole episode of the circumcision, while others embraced it and insisted upon the righteousness of the murderous deeds either through the depravity of the Shechemites or the judgment of God. The miscellany of approaches attests both to the power of the tale and the creativity of its re-tellers.

---

45. For Feldman (2004), 262–271, Josephus' omissions and changes formed an apologia, motivated by concerns about gentiles' hostile impressions of Jews. That is a repeated theme in Feldman's works, more an imposition upon than an inference from the text.

Chapter 7

THE CONFLICTING CHARACTER OF JOSEPH

The story of Joseph in the Book of Genesis echoes through the ages, retold, enhanced, or distorted, down to the great novels of Thomas Mann and even the musical theater of Andrew Lloyd Webber. (Abraham never got that much play.)

The Genesis narrative of Joseph portrays a complex and manifold personality, no mere one-dimensional man of virtue. The young Joseph, ambushed by his brothers, was hardly an innocent waif. His boastful recounting of dreams that forecast his own ascendancy not only angered his brothers but even troubled his father.[1] When he went in search of his brothers on what seems little more than a spying mission, he flaunted the multi-colored coat—thus leading directly to his humiliation, being dumped in a pit and then sold to the Ishmaelites.[2] Joseph, of course, was then taken to Egypt, where he nobly resisted the blandishments of Potiphar's wife, preserving his virtue and principles at the cost of imprisonment. When his reputation as interpreter of dreams brought him to Pharaoh's attention, his administrative talents put him in a position to run the country, and he took without hesitation the symbols of authority that elevated him to a rank second only to that of the king himself.[3] The rediscovery of and reconciliation with his brothers forms a moving story. But one should not omit to note that Joseph calculatingly put them through some severe anxieties and emotional trials before revealing himself to them. Joseph's magnanimity obviously had its limits. Further, his stern and exacting management of grain allocation during the famine years brought all Egyptian land under the king's control and transformed the entire Egyptian peasantry into vassals of the crown.[4] In short, Genesis supplies an intricate tale, a multifaceted personality, and rich material to be exploited by Second Temple Jews. And exploit it they did.

Space allows only a few illustrations of the variety of ways in which Joseph's image was molded by subsequent Jewish writers in antiquity.[5] The author of

1. Gen. 37:5-11.
2. Gen. 37:3, 37:12-24.
3. Gen. 39-41.
4. Gen. 47:13-26.
5. A brief summary of some selected portrayals of Joseph by later writers may be found in Hollander (1998), 237–263. The discussion here draws on Gruen (1998), 73–109.

Jubilees, for example, supplies a sanitized version. Not a hint of character flaws invades the portrait of the hero. According to *Jubilees*, Joseph's brothers turn upon him and sell him to the Ishmaelites for no apparent reason except their own innate wickedness. The narrator omits any mention of dreams, boasts, favoritism by Jacob, embroidered coat, or even fraternal jealousy. Joseph's adventures in Egypt show him in the most glowing light. He rejected the advances of Potiphar's wife by proclaiming adherence to ancestral precepts taught him by Jacob and stemming from Abraham, a solemn prohibition on adultery.[6] *Jubilees* embellishes liberally on Genesis by depicting Joseph's administration of Egypt as one of undeviating righteousness and integrity, devoid of all arrogance or pomposity, earning him the love of all those with whom he came into contact.[7] The discomfort that he put his brothers through upon seeing them again in Egypt, which receives no clear explanation in Genesis, is generously rationalized by the author of *Jubilees*: Joseph simply wished to see whether there was internal harmony among the brothers.[8] Nor does the text breathe a hint of dissention among the Egyptian populace in the wake of Joseph's sweeping economic changes. Whereas in Genesis the farmers welcomed the arrangement as rescue from famine, but described their situation as bondage to the king, a state of subjugation, *Jubilees* presents the new system as a sheer act of generosity on Joseph's part—no reference to indentured servitude. Joseph emerges without a flaw.

Philo of Alexandria wrote a separate treatise on Joseph, as he did on Abraham and Moses. The work alternates between a close rendering of the Joseph narrative in Genesis and a commentary by Philo, who plainly took as his mission in this work the idealization of Joseph, thus to present him as the epitome of statesmanlike qualities. The dubious or questionable features that appear in Genesis are smoothed over or rationalized. The hostility of the brothers, for example, stems from sheer jealousy, not any hubris or presumptuousness on Joseph's part. The young man's nobility and breeding earned him the complete confidence of Potiphar and a free hand in management of the entire household—a preview of his skills in administering the kingdom itself.[9] Philo does not dwell on the attempted seduction by Potiphar's wife, a tale rather marginal for his political theme. Unlike some of the other treatments of that episode, however, he has Joseph reject her advances not because of religious prohibitions, but because of social and moral obligations to his benefactor Potiphar. Philo further offers a most generous interpretation of Joseph's behavior toward his brothers after their arrival in Egypt. As in *Jubilees*, it was merely a test to discover whether there was dissension among the children of Jacob's two wives. When they displayed authentic family solidarity, all could be revealed—and forgiven. Joseph proceeded to administer the economy of Egypt with brilliance and effectiveness, while turning down every opportunity for

---

6. *Jub.* 39:5-8.
7. *Jub.* 40:6-7.
8. *Jub.* 42:25, 43:14.
9. Philo, *Jos.* 4–5, 37–39.

self-aggrandizement and self-enrichment.[10] And Philo ends the treatise with a flourish, assigning to Joseph a host of virtues, including intelligence, eloquence, a balanced disposition, great political and administrative skills—and, of course, good looks.[11]

The virtuous Joseph, scrubbed of all (or most) of his blemishes, appears also in Josephus' lengthy reproduction of the biblical narrative.[12] The brothers envied and hated him because of Jacob's favoritism, not because of any acts of Joseph.[13] Josephus pointedly omits Jacob's annoyance with Joseph for his excessive boasting, indeed even has him take pleasure in the recounting of his dream.[14] The historian embellishes liberally upon the Genesis text, a showpiece for his rhetorical training, as in the full-blown speech accorded to Reuben, based on just a few lines in the Bible.[15] He freely expands upon the encounter with Potiphar's wife, not only stressing Joseph's chastity and restraint on the basis of his obligation to his patron, but supplying him with a noble speech that reminded her of her marriage vows and even offered her sage advice about how she could better command her household as a chaste mistress than as a compromised woman.[16] The historian presents the exchange between Joseph and Potiphar's wife as a series of scenes with far more color and drama, including passionate avowals, tears, and ferocious anger, than the relatively brief and bland Genesis account. Joseph's steadfastness and composure stand out all the more.[17]

The Genesis version of Joseph's deception of and double-dealing with his brothers, by contrast, is a full one and does not reflect well on the hero. When they came to Egypt to purchase grain in order to relieve the famine in Canaan, as the famous tale has it, Joseph, now as chief minister of the Pharaoh, toyed with them to their deep discomfort and to his evident, even malicious, pleasure. He recognized them immediately, but they knew him not. He took advantage of the situation to accuse them of being spies and insist that, if they wished to purchase grain, they would have to return to Canaan and bring to Egypt their beloved youngest brother, Benjamin, the favorite of their father Jacob. The poignant scene has Jacob yield to

---

10. Philo, *Jos.* 257–260.

11. Philo, *Jos.* 268–270. Joseph's handsomeness is already noted in *Gen.* 39:6.

12. For a detailed comparison between passages in the biblical narrative of Joseph and those in Josephus' adaptation, see Feldman (1998b), 335–373, though he emphasizes too much the historian's impulse to make changes in accord with the presumed attitudes of his Roman readers.

13. Jos. *AJ*, 2:9-10.

14. Jos. *AJ*, 2:14.

15. Jos. *AJ*, 2:20-28; cf. Gen. 37:21-22.

16. Jos. *AJ*, 2:50-52. On Josephus' presentation of Joseph as an exemplar of rationality, see Feldman (1998b), 346–351.

17. Jos. *AJ*, 2:41-59. Feldman (1998b), 369–372, rightly stresses the heightened coloration added by Josephus to the episodes involving Joseph and Potiphar's wife, although it need not follow that the historian was adapting the tale of Phaedra in Euripides' *Hippolytus*.

their importuning and turn over Benjamin with much misgiving and dire forebodings.[18] Their arrival in Egypt, with Benjamin in tow, gave Joseph occasion to torment them further. He pursued the pretense of a stranger to his brothers, provided them with provisions, but had his personal silver goblet secretly slipped into Benjamin's travel bag. When it was discovered, Joseph compounded the ruse by threatening to enslave young Benjamin, thus calling forth desperate pleas from the other brothers, who proclaimed that they could not return without Benjamin for that would be a death sentence to their father.[19] Only then did Joseph relent, reveal the truth and declare reconciliation with his brothers, followed by tearful embraces all around and a happy ending.[20] But he had put them all through hell before disclosing the devious deceit. The author of the text supplies no explicit reason for this elaborate and hurtful game. It may indeed be implied that Joseph was finally exacting vengeance for his brothers' dastardly deed of so long ago. If so, however, it means that Joseph nursed this bitter grievance for many years, finally enjoying revenge when his brothers were most vulnerable. But this hardly commends the character of the perpetrator.

Josephus cleans up the picture. He supplies a motive for Joseph's dissembling: he simply wished to test his brothers' true feelings and qualities, an explanation similar to that offered by *Jubilees* and Philo.[21] When Joseph extended the plot by surreptitiously placing the goblet in Benjamin's luggage, the historian gives as reason Joseph's wish to see whether the brothers would protect Benjamin in his travail or would abandon him.[22] There is no suggestion or implication that Joseph wished to make them squirm because they had once betrayed him.

The biblical account of Joseph's restructuring of Egyptian economy and society delivers a mixed message, and a somewhat troubling one. The famine had left most Egyptian farmers desperate to find means for survival. Joseph controlled the grain supply and distributed it to the needy in return first for cash, then for livestock. When both ran out and starvation became even more imminent, the farmers offered to cede their lands to Pharaoh and become his slaves in order to survive. Joseph embraced the idea, the peasantry became serfs, and the lands became crown property. He went further still and resettled people from place to place, thus

18. Gen. 42:1–43:14.
19. Gen. 43:15–44:34.
20. Gen. 45:1-15.
21. Jos. *AJ*, 2:97. This coincidence may suggest that all three authors drew on an independent tradition, no longer extant, that sought to supply a defensible motive for Joseph's subjecting his brothers to such tortuous anxiety. The need to account, in some fashion, for this most troubling aspect of the patriarch's personality evidently affected several of the re-tellers of the narrative; cf. Kugel (1998), 461–463. Josephus further seeks to soften the negative implication of Joseph's temporary imprisonment of his brothers by suggesting that he simply wished to have more time to interrogate them; *AJ*, 2:105; cf. Gen. 42:17.

22. Jos. *AJ*, 2:125. Similarly, Philo, *Jos.* 232. That this was some form of test for his brothers is alluded to in Gen. 42:14-16, but as a means to prove that they are not spies.

separating them from their hereditary holdings, while still requiring them to pay a fifth of their produce annually to the king.[23] The author of this narrative makes no comment on the justification of this policy, but the effect is clearly a negative one. Josephus follows the outline of the account but was evidently uncomfortable with it and made some subtle and important changes. He acknowledges that all land was surrendered and became the property of Pharaoh, that people were moved from place to place, and even that the process enslaved both bodies and minds.[24] But the historian moved swiftly to repair the damage. Once the Nile resumed its normal flow and the famine abated, he has Joseph restore the lands to their proprietors to cultivate in perpetuity, with payment of a fifth as a token tithe, much to the delight of the peasantry and a marked boost for the reputation of the royal minister.[25] Nothing of this in Genesis, and all remarks about servitude were notably eradicated by Josephus. The biblical hero's repute is salvaged, and the whitewash predominates.[26]

The glowing portrait of Joseph, however, did not prevail among all Hellenistic Jewish writers. The dubious characteristics that can also be found in Genesis of the manipulator, the artful schemer, and the man enamored of worldly goods and power were not altogether repressed. For Hellenistic Jews, Joseph was more persona than personage, an acknowledged literary artifice available and versatile.

That fact emerges most conspicuously in the writings of Philo. The philosopher, as we have seen, devoted a treatise to Joseph, in which he stressed, and even stretched, the sterling qualities of his subject, an exemplar of political wisdom and moral principles. In another treatise, however, Philo draws out the more questionable features of Joseph's character that are also alluded to in Genesis. In that work, the *De Somniis* ("On Dreams"), Joseph is altogether transformed. Philo characterizes the ambitious dreams of the young man as boastful arrogance and over-reaching, thus justifying his brothers' hostile reaction and his father's sharp rebuke.[27] The dignities and honors bestowed upon him as Pharaoh's right-hand man become emblems not of rightful elevation but of hubristic ambition aimed at eradicating equality.[28] Joseph, a paragon of virtue in Philo's *De Josepho*, turns out to symbolize craftiness, deceit, and insincerity in the *De Somniis*. He was a man of empty vanity.[29] Much tortuous scholarship has attempted to reconcile or somehow account for Philo's blatant inconsistencies on this score.[30] However they may be explained, they reflect the

---

23. Gen. 47:13-26.

24. Jos. *AJ*, 2:189-191.

25. Jos. *AJ*, 2:189-193.

26. Feldman (1998b), 359–361, also correctly notes that Josephus plays down any divine influence in Joseph's admirable deeds. The hero's inner qualities are responsible.

27. Philo, *Somn*. 2:93-113.

28. Philo, *Somn*. 2:15-16.

29. Philo, *Somn*. 1:219-220, 2:42-47. 2:63; cf. *Mut*. 89-90, *Migr*. 203-204.

30. See the summary of scholarship in Hamerton-Kelly (1972), 3–26. Among later efforts, see Barraclough (1984), 491–506; Hilgert (1985), 7–13; Cazeaux (1995), 41–81. Niehoff (1992), 54–83, surprisingly, discusses only the *De Josepho*.

ambiguities of Joseph's character and achievements already apparent in the Bible, thus lending themselves readily malleable to serve a variety of purposes. Philo's conflicting and incongruous portraits of Joseph, employed to deliver his moral judgments, demonstrate that divergent representations can appear unblinkingly even in the works of a single author. The Bible left itself open to a range of twists and turns that accorded with the agendas of re-tellers.

The negative depiction of Joseph emerges more consistently and forcefully in the hands of a certain Artapanos, a Hellenized Jew in Egypt who composed a work on the Jews that seems to have combined a refashioning of biblical stories, historical reconstruction, and inventive fiction. We have it only in fragments quoted by later writers.[31] The extract on Joseph that we possess is all too brief—but enough to show that Artapanos freely adapted and refashioned the Genesis story to his own taste. He has Joseph's brothers conspire against him because he surpassed them in knowledge and intelligence. But, instead of falling into their trap, Joseph foresaw the plot and persuaded some neighboring Arabs to convey him to Egypt.[32] Joseph, in other words, landed in Egypt through his own shrewdness, escaping the machinations of his brothers, not victimized by them. For Artapanos, Joseph engineered the whole sequence of events, an account sharply at odds with the Genesis tale. Upon arrival in Egypt, Joseph became acquainted with the king and was installed as his chief economic minister, in charge of the entire land.[33] Not a word about Joseph as dream interpreter—let alone about a stint in prison as target of Mrs. Potiphar's spleen. The new minister proceeded to restructure Egyptian agriculture, put an end to the exploitation of the weak by the powerful, and bring neglected land back into cultivation.[34] This account, truncated and terse though it be, is a far cry from the biblical narrative. Genesis describes Joseph's agricultural changes as extending royal authority and ownership and making the peasantry of Egypt dependent upon the crown.[35] But Artapanos evidently felt free to ignore the testimony of the Scriptures. In the preserved text of that author, whether his own conception or following an unknown tradition, divine aid plays no part, moral lessons are absent, and the hero's inner character is irrelevant. Joseph appears rather as a clever calculator who impressed the Pharaoh, a farsighted economic reformer, and even a pragmatic inventor, the discoverer of measurements. Artapanos' Joseph merits neither praise for self-control nor blame for ambition and material desires. Joseph gained authority through his wits and employed it to reorder the institutional structure of Egypt. Artapanos simply made the point that the Egyptian nation owes its success to the brains of an Israelite.

One last text concerning Joseph gives a most dramatic instance of how far writers felt perfect comfort in departing at great distance from the supposedly

---

31. See the fragments assembled with commentary by Holladay (1983), 205–209, 226–230. Cf. the remarks of Gruen (2015), 31–44. Most recently, Adams (2020), 182–188.
32. Euseb. *PE*, 9:23:1.
33. Euseb. *PE*, 9:23:2.
34. Euseb. *PE*, 9:23:2.
35. Gen. 47:13-26.

sacred Scriptures. I refer to the romantic story entitled *Joseph and Aseneth*. This text moves in a realm quite different from the others involving Joseph, one closer to the *Testament of Abraham*, i.e. the realm of novelistic fantasy. Genesis provides barely a pretext for the invention. The Scriptures report only that Pharaoh gave to Joseph as his wife Aseneth, daughter of an Egyptian priest, and that she subsequently bore him two children.[36] That is all that the Bible tells us. All the rest is embellishment. And *Joseph and Aseneth* embellishes in style.

A brief summary of the yarn, at least its highlights, would be important. Joseph, gathering grain in the course of his duties as Pharaoh's agricultural minister, encountered the eminent Pentephres, an Egyptian priest, a royal official of the highest station, advisor to Pharaoh, and a man close to the throne. Pentephres happened to have a beautiful eighteen-year old daughter, Aseneth, reputed to be in a class with the most celebrated women of the patriarchal age, Sarah, Rebecca, and Rachel. Aseneth, however, scorned all men and rudely rejected suitors from noble houses in Egypt and royal families elsewhere. Pharaoh's son himself pressed hard for her hand but was overruled by his father, who preferred a match with another ruling house. The report of Aseneth's renowned beauty depended upon rumor rather than witnesses, for she had shut herself up in a lofty tower, not to be seen—let alone touched—by any man. Pentephres, upon learning of Joseph's imminent arrival, immediately proposed that Aseneth be betrothed to this righteous, pious, and powerful man. But Aseneth recoiled in anger: she would have nothing to do with one who was a stranger in the land, a shepherd's son from Canaan, sold as a slave and imprisoned as an adulterer. The arrogant Aseneth would accept marriage only with the son of Pharaoh.[37]

Once the young maiden spied Joseph from her bedroom window, however, everything turned topsy-turvy. Aseneth was smitten, immediately abandoned her haughty aloofness, and was overcome with self-reproach that the man she had despised as a shepherd's son turned out to be a dazzling divinity.[38] Joseph himself had his doubts when he caught a glimpse of Aseneth. He feared that she was yet another predatory female determined to bed him, like Potiphar's wife and a host of others who could not keep their hands off him. But Pentephres reassured his noble guest: Aseneth, he said, was a man-hating committed virgin, and no threat to Joseph's chastity. Pentephres now suggested that they exchange a friendly kiss, like a brother and sister, only to have Joseph this time recoil from the suddenly eager Aseneth. As a purist devotee of a sole god, Joseph would have no congress of any kind with an idolatress. He suggested instead that she acknowledge the true god, for only such a conversion could justify a relationship.[39] Aseneth grasped at the hope and turned her religious life around at a stroke. Much weeping and wailing ensued as she repented of former heresies, removed all false idols from her home, and fell to fasting and mourning, self-flagellation and humiliation, uttering

---

36. Gen. 41:45; cf. 41:50, 46:20.
37. *Jos As.* 1–4.
38. *Jos. As.* 5–6.
39. *Jos. As.* 7–8.

desperate prayers to her newly found god, seeking forgiveness for past sins and rescue from the fury of spurned divinities.[40] The maiden's prayers were answered. An angel of the Lord materialized, braced the woman's courage, offered her absolution for prior offenses, proclaimed her acceptance by God, and bade her put off sackcloth and ashes and dress herself in bridal attire to prepare for a wedding with Joseph. Aseneth's new dress restored her to the fullness of her beauty. And when Joseph returned for a second visit, she declared her renunciation of false idols and embrace of the true god. Joseph now infused his betrothed with the spirit of life, wisdom, and truth. Pharaoh himself presided over the wedding festivities, placed crowns on the heads of the couple, and sponsored a spectacular banquet that lasted for seven days. The marriage was consummated, and Aseneth subsequently produced two sons as Joseph's legacy.[41]

This was, in fact, only half the tale. The second half was an adventure story, involving efforts by Pharaoh's frustrated son to snatch Aseneth away, and a major battle that pitted some of Joseph's brothers against others who sided with the son of Pharaoh, culminating in the death of both Pharaoh and his son, with the throne now bestowed upon Joseph himself, who went on to rule Egypt for forty-eight years.[42]

So ends the narrative, an edifying and uplifting one. Its strikingly unusual character has called forth an extensive scholarly literature. Controversy swirls around the language, date, provenance, genre, message, and audience of the text.[43] This is not the place to get into any of that. We focus on the figure of Joseph. His treatment in a work of imaginative fancy, a form quite different from the other literary contexts in which he appears, adds a valuable dimension to the manipulation of his image in the Hellenistic era.

Joseph as the embodiment of piety and purity comes through loud and clear. But that aspect of character is by no means an unmixed blessing. Joseph's fussiness bespeaks a cramped disposition and his public display of abstinence at the outset of the work borders on the offensive. Upon entrance into Pentephres' house, he immediately planted himself upon his host's official seat as royal representative.[44] He took his meal in private, for he would not eat with Egyptians, an abomination in his view. Having caught a glimpse of Aseneth at her window, Joseph leaped to the conclusion that she was yet another in the long line of females who lusted after

---

40. *Jos. As.* 9–13.

41. *Jos. As.* 14–21.

42. *Jos.As.* 22–29.

43. See the fundamental studies of Burchard (1965) and Philonenko (1968). For other major works, see, especially, Chesnutt (1995); Standhartinger (1995); Bohak (1996); Kraemer (1998); earlier bibliography in Gruen (1998), 94–96; for more recent studies and bibliography, see Burchard (2003); Reinmuth (2009), 261–267; Standhartinger (2014), 350–406; Hicks-Keeton (2018), 16–40; Ahearne-Kroll (2020). On the relationship between *Joseph and Aseneth* and the Greek novel, cf. the remarks of West (1974), 70–81; Bloch (2013), 1–28; Whitmarsh (2018), 105–121, and Adams (2020), 168–181.

44. *Jos. As.* 7:13.

his body. And he did not hesitate to recount to Pentephres his stoical resistance to the flocks of beauties, the wives and daughters of Egyptian aristocrats and royal appointees, and indeed women of all classes, who were desperate to sleep with so handsome a creature. Joseph, of course, so he announced, was impervious to their charms and scorned the costly gifts with which they sought to win his affection.[45] This was not an attitude designed to endear him to his hosts—who, however, were too dazzled by his position to care. Joseph consented to receive Aseneth only when told that she was a virgin who hated all men, for this suggested that he was safe from molestation. But when Aseneth eagerly approached him, ready to offer a kiss, Joseph shoved her away disdainfully: no true worshipper of God could touch the lips of an alien woman polluted by contact with dead and dumb idols.[46] He does not hesitate to humiliate Aseneth in front of her father, thus driving her to self-abuse and mental torture before he would acknowledge her rejection of idolatry. The hero of this saga evidently did not prize graciousness or even civility.

Instead, Joseph exudes power and authority. He enters the gates of his host's estate in a royal chariot, resplendent in purple robes and a gold crown with precious stones. Pentephres and his entire family hastened to prostrate themselves before him. Aseneth declares him to be the sun from heaven, arriving in a chariot and shining its beams upon the earth.[47] Aseneth's prayer to the Lord describes Joseph as beautiful, wise,—and powerful. That last adjective carries major import.[48] Joseph underscored his stature by dismissing Pentephres' offer to provide a wedding banquet. He would have none other than Pharaoh perform that task.[49] Joseph disappears in the second half of the narrative, the adventure story. But he turns up again at its conclusion, to have the dying Pharaoh present him with the diadem, symbolic of royal authority. And the text has Joseph enjoy a long reign, before relinquishing the throne voluntarily to Pharaoh's youngest son.[50] This goes well beyond the biblical tale. Joseph remains mighty and unbending from start to finish.

The text of *Joseph and Aseneth* supplies revealing testimony on the manipulation of the Joseph image in Hellenistic times. It bears little relation to or concern for the biblical narrative. Yet the personality of Joseph that appears in Genesis interestingly reappears in this fictitious fantasy, modulated but unmistakable. Joseph emerges again as the favorite of God, trusting in divine beneficence, the loyal upholder of the faith, the fierce proponent of piety and rectitude, and the wielder of extensive authority in Egypt. But the author of this novella also heightens and intensifies those characteristics, subtly (or perhaps not so subtly) transforming them into haughtiness, prudery, self-righteousness, authoritarianism, and contemptuousness. In other words, while some Hellenistic texts sought to clean up Joseph's act, airbrushing some of the flaws that appear in the Genesis account, and others

---

45. *Jos. As.* 7:1-5.
46. *Jos. As.* 8:4-5.
47. *Jos. As.* 6:2.
48. *Jos. As.* 13:11.
49. *Jos. As.* 20:6–21:5.
50. *Jos. As.* 29:10-11.

portrayed him as a shrewd and rational schemer, *Joseph and Aseneth* exaggerated other characteristics to be found in Genesis, stressing his pomposity and arrogance.

The figure of Joseph thus lent itself to a variety of shapes. Jewish writers in general (there are many examples other than these) found him to be readily malleable.[51] Genesis itself had supplied a disjointed combination: a person of high moral principles, mingled with pride and prudery, resourceful but calculating and manipulative, a political and economic reformer who also advanced the centralization of royal authority, a wielder of power but one largely impervious to the sufferings of its victims. Hellenistic writers exploited the biblical material at will, taking and rewriting what they liked, omitting or freely adapting what they found unpalatable. Even when Joseph is portrayed as conducting himself with offensive sanctimoniousness, however, such traits need not compel a fundamentally negative impression or moral lesson. Joseph retains the character of a hero, however flawed, to the end, a devout champion of Hebrew ethical and religious superiority, elevated to royal rank with absolute sovereignty over inferior Egyptians. Self-esteem, even when expressed through swagger and condescension, can speak to, indeed intensify, the pride of Jews in the circumstances of the Hellenistic and Roman worlds.

---

51. For other examples, see Gruen (1998), 73–109.

Chapter 8

TAMAR AND JUDAH

The story of Judah and Tamar is one of the most engaging in the book of Genesis. It has been read as a comic satire, a feminist tract, an anomalous excursus, or a trickster's tale, among other things. Its entertainment value, in any case, cannot be doubted. The narrative seems awkwardly inserted in the midst of the life and deeds of Joseph. That anomaly may be more apparent than real. Although its position in the text is somewhat surprising, subtle links between it and what came before and after do exist.[1] Be that as it may, the story itself had a life of its own.

Judah was a figure of some importance, the fourth son of Jacob, and the man from whom the nation took its name. According to Genesis, Judah wed the daughter of a Canaanite who then bore him three sons, apparently in rather quick succession. He betrothed the first, Er, to Tamar, evidently also a Canaanite. The difference in ethnicity did not bother the author.[2] The expectation of an heir, however, came to naught. For reasons unexplained in the text, God struck down Er, who had displeased him. Judah then turned to his second son, Onan, to replace his brother as Tamar's husband and to do his duty in a levirate marriage, i.e. to produce the offspring that Er had failed to produce (or had been prevented from doing so).[3] Onan, however, did not go along with the plan. Irritated that any progeny of his would simply be proxy for his dead brother's line, he practiced coitus interruptus and "spilled his seed on the ground."[4] How often he performed this act we are not told. Tamar's frustration doubtless mounted, though the text is silent on that matter. The Lord, however, quickly lost patience. He terminated Onan's wasteful life as he had Er's. Judah was now done to one son, and had understandable doubts

---

1. Alter (1981), 3–12.
2. Gen. 38:1-5. On Tamar's ethnicity, see Gruen (2002), 291 – 292, with the literature cited there, especially Emerton (1979), 410–412; Menn (1997), 54–55. More bibliography in Amit (2013), 300, n. 20. According to Philo, *Virt.* 221–222, she came from Syria and was raised in an idolatrous family, but transformed herself into a paragon of piety.
3. On levirate marriage, see Deut. 25:5-10. By contrast, marriage to a brother-in-law is expressly forbidden in Lev. 18:16, 20:21. The legal issues are controversial, and cannot be pursued here. Cf. Menn (1997), 55–64; Weisberg (2004), 403–429.
4. Gen. 38:6-9.

about his fate. The track record was not good. Whether he blamed Tamar for this, as many believe, is unclear. But he was reluctant to take chances. He did promise Tamar his third son, young Shelah. But there would be no quick union. Tamar would have to wait until Shelah grew up—an unspecified period of time. Judah had no intention of speeding up the process. Tamar in the meanwhile would go back and live under her father's roof.[5]

Time passed, Shelah came to maturity, but Judah still dragged his feet. Tamar was not prepared to wait indefinitely. She consequently concocted a scheme to find a surrogate in the line of Jacob. Judah himself was now fortuitously available, having lost his Canaanite wife, completed his period of mourning, and ripe for a new relationship. A union of father-in-law and daughter-in-law was prohibited, but Tamar found a way around it. She was less interested in wedlock than in offspring. She appeared in disguise (her face covered by a veil) at the city gate, where she could be taken for a prostitute. Judah, as she knew, would be in the vicinity to have his sheep sheared. He fell neatly into her trap. The patriarch duly presumed that she was selling sexual favors and showed himself a willing customer. Haggling over a price resulted in Judah's promise to have a goat kid sent to her. As a token to guarantee the barter, Tamar demanded that he leave his seal, cord, and staff, items that would represent secure identification of the bearer. The bargain was sealed, Judah had his night of pleasure, and Tamar immediately conceived.[6]

Tamar now prepared the denouement. A friend of Judah, having produced a kid, returned to the scene of the tryst, with kid in tow, to fulfill the pledge and to reclaim the identity tokens. But there was no prostitute in sight and neighbors claimed no knowledge of one. Judah's friend returned empty-handed. Judah himself gave up the idea. Better to abandon the identity tokens than to conduct a wild-goose chase for a harlot, which would only make him a laughing-stock.[7]

Word soon spread that Tamar, hitherto presumed a chaste widow, was pregnant. Judah, as father-in-law still responsible for her character and well-being, flew into a rage at such a scandal. Without hesitation or interrogation, he ordered her taken from her family home and burned to death, the proper penalty for a whore. Tamar, of course, had anticipated this event. She produced the identity tokens that Judah had left with her and declared that their owner was the man responsible for her pregnancy. Judah, chagrined and humbled, had to acknowledge his paternity. Indeed he went further with a public assertion that Tamar was more righteous than he—a clear reference to the fact that he had withheld Shelah from his promised union with Tamar. Judah refrained from any further intercourse with Tamar.[8] The outcome of the tale proved momentous. Tamar proceeded to give birth to twins, thus perpetuating the line of Judah, and Perez, who emerged

---

5. Gen. 38:9-11.
6. Gen. 38:12-18. The tokens and the exchange are allegorized by Philo, *Fug.* 149–153; *Mut.* 134–136; *Somn.* 2.44.
7. Gen. 38:19-23.
8. Gen. 38:24-26.

first from the womb, elbowing out his brother, would become forefather of the house of David.[9]

This intriguing tale has clear entertainment value.[10] It also bears on the larger tableau of patriarchal history and the lineage of Judah, namesake for the nation of the Jews. The upshot of the narrative, however, sets Judah in a rather dubious light. Unsure of God's attitude toward his line, he failed to live up to his promise to Tamar, withholding his youngest son, thus triggering her ingenious plot. Tamar cleverly duped him and had her way, leaving Judah embarrassed, shamefaced, and compelled to admit his own character flaws.[11] Tamar plainly outstripped Judah in wisdom, determination, and effectiveness. The most remarkable feature of this memorable yarn is the fact that the Canaanite woman proved to be more committed to perpetuating the Israelite stock of the patriarch than Judah himself was.[12]

Fiddling with this text was no easy matter. The story evidently gained much popularity and the central narrative would be impervious to drastic revision.[13] Yet the flaws and transgressions of Judah were quite problematic. And his manipulation by a cunning woman—and a Canaanite at that—constituted a grave embarrassment for a patriarch, especially one who was forefather of the line of David. Josephus avoided this sticky issue simply by omitting the whole Tamar-Judah episode. Other re-tellers found different means to assuage the sensitivities of those who held the patriarchs in awe.

The *Book of Jubilees* took on the task of rehabilitating Judah to the extent possible with small, subtle, but significant changes in the biblical account. The issue of ethnicity is muted in Genesis, but takes on prominence in *Jubilees*, as it does elsewhere in that work. The Bible reports that Judah married a Canaanite, but makes nothing of it.[14] Tamar's ethnicity is unspecified in Genesis but sufficient clues exist pointing to Canaanite origins. This too plays no role in the narrative. For the author of *Jubilees*, by contrast, the matter is of high importance. He makes clear at the outset of the story that Tamar was no Canaanite. She was an Aramean. The Mesopotamian origin lent more respectability.[15] Judah's bride, however, was a

---

9. Gen. 38:27-30. On the link to David, see Ruth, 4:12-22; 1 Chron. 2:4-15. Cf. the discussion of Menn (1997), 82–86.

10. On the comedic elements, see Whedbee (1998), 108–111; Spencer (2003), 13–15. On the story as a "trickster tale," see Shields (2003), 31–51; Jackson (2012), 55–66.

11. Among his transgressions, Judah's fling with Tamar, even though unwitting, violated the biblical prohibition on intercourse with one's daughter-in-law; Lev. 18:16, 20:21.

12. Tarlin (2000), 176–177, offers an alternative interpretation, namely that Tamar, far from shoring up the Israelite patriarchy, actually demonstrates its fragility since a non-Israelite woman can so easily manipulate it. But readers who knew the genealogy that ran from Tamar to David would not likely draw that conclusion. That Tamar committed herself to the perpetuation of the Israelite nation was understood also by Pseudo-Philo, *LAB*, 9:5.

13. The very brief and quite incidental allusion to the story in Pseudo-Philo, *LAB*, 9:5, indicates that it would be quite familiar to his readers. Cf. Wassén (1994), 362–364.

14. Gen. 38:2.

15. *Jub*. 41:1; cf. 34:20-21.

Canaanite, a fact mentioned but passed over by Genesis. In *Jubilees* it takes on significance. When Judah designated Tamar as wife for his first-born Er, the son refused, indeed hated her, on the grounds that she was *not* a Canaanite, and he wished a bride from his mother's people. Judah, however, would not allow it. Er's death, at the hands of the Lord, followed thereafter. Neither Genesis nor *Jubilees* gives a reason for it other than Er's wickedness. But the latter suggests that Er's willfulness in seeking a Canaanite marriage against his father's wishes provides the context. Judah held firm on the ethnic issue, a position plainly approved by the author of *Jubilees*.[16] Judah was on the right side.

The withholding of Shelah, the third son, from Tamar's embraces, constituted Judah's principal transgression in the biblical narrative. *Jubilees* notably departs from that judgment. It was Judah's Canaanite wife who stepped in to obstruct any union between Shelah and Tamar.[17] The patriarch was off the hook.

A minor change may have some meaningful significance. In the bargaining over Tamar's fee as would-be prostitute, Genesis has her propose the identity tokens which Judah duly hands over to her. That is the lynchpin of Tamar's clever deception. In *Jubilees*, Judah proposes the tokens himself, having nothing more to offer, to which Tamar agrees, as a pledge for the sexual union.[18] The shift is small, but probably not inadvertent. The author of *Jubilees* gives the initiative to Judah, who is thus no mere instrument in Tamar's machination.[19]

The climactic scene in which the scales fall from Judah's eyes and he acknowledges that it was he who impregnated Tamar reads quite differently in *Jubilees* from its biblical precursor. Genesis has Judah declare that Tamar is more righteous than he, for he had promised Shelah as a husband to Tamar but had failed to carry through on the pledge. The self-condemnation and a decision not to sleep again with Tamar closed the proceedings. Judah is the culprit and duly chastised. The author of *Jubilees* was clearly dissatisfied with that scenario and provided a version rather more generous to the patriarch. The decision to prevent Shelah from bedding Tamar came *after* Judah had realized that he was responsible for her pregnancy.[20] In short, the enforced separation of Shelah and Tamar was the *result*, not the cause of this affair. Insofar as Shelah had previously been kept from the expected marriage, the villain was once more the Canaanite mother. *Jubilees* blames her for resisting a marriage for Shelah, as she had for Er, with a non-Canaanite woman.[21] Judah's remorse stemmed from a different offense:

16. *Jub.* 41:2-3. Endres (1987), 186, suggests that Judah's eagerness for his son's marriage to Tamar reflected a desire to rectify his own marriage to a Canaanite. An interesting possibility, but there is no hint of this in the text. The analysis of Wassén (1994), 359–362, overlooks the ethnic dimension altogether.

17. *Jub.* 41:7.

18. Gen. 38:16-18; *Jub.* 41:11-12.

19. It is not at all clear why VanderKam (2018), 1043, sees this as showing Tamar to be the stronger and more self-assured person.

20. *Jub.* 41:19-20. Cf. Gen. 38:26.

21. *Jub.* 41:7; cf. 41:2.

sleeping with Tamar inadvertently violated the biblical prohibition of sexual relations between father-in-law and daughter-in-law.[22] The *Book of Jubilees* softened considerably the burden of guilt.

The author indeed added a concluding section to this account not found in the Bible. He could not exonerate Judah altogether. But he gave poignancy and depth to his repentance. The patriarch underscored his own sin and iniquity in having engaged in sex with the wife of his son. He gave way to lamentation and supplication of the Lord. As a consequence, he was vouchsafed a dream, with heavenly voices assuring him that he was forgiven because of his genuine contrition and vow not to repeat the offense.[23] The text makes clear that the act itself was indeed sinful, and any future perpetrator would legitimately suffer the penalty of burning, but Judah gained forgiveness because his sin stemmed from ignorance rather than evil intention.[24] The author strove to mitigate the guilt of Judah, while reasserting the authority of Mosaic law against the transgression, and, perhaps most importantly, justifying the lineage that ran from Judah to David. He makes the point quite emphatically by stating that neither of Judah's sons had actually had intercourse with Tamar—not an obvious or likely inference from the Genesis account. But it underpinned the author's assurance that Judah's seed would generate the line that succeeded him.[25] The changes and additions in *Jubilees* were evidently thoughtful and weighty. They reclaimed the character of Judah, while reaffirming the authority of the law, and legitimizing the bond that traced Israelite genealogy from the patriarchal age to the kings of Judah.

A somewhat comparable effort to rewrite the tale and rehabilitate the reputation of Judah occurs in the *Testament of Judah*. This treatise forms part of the collection, *Testaments of the Twelve Patriarchs*. The *Testament of Judah* has the dying patriarch make reference to the embarrassing Tamar episode and endeavor to set it in context.[26]

The author picks up the ethnic theme that prevails in *Jubilees*, an indication that this motif may reflect a now lost tradition for which it was fundamental.[27] Tamar's origins are specified as Mesopotamian, a daughter of Aram. And the failure of Er to consummate his marriage with Tamar is also ascribed to his Canaanite mother, who insisted upon no offspring but Canaanites. The Lord, through his angel, expressed his fury by slaying Er. It was a matter of keeping the clan pure, an

---

22. *Jub.* 41:23. On the legal issues, see Segal (2007), 59–72, and the valuable notes by VanderKam (2018), 1049–1055.

23. *Jub.* 41:23-24.

24. *Jub.* 41:25-28. There is no need to assign some of these verses to an "interpolator," as does Kugel (2013), 429–430. See also Segal (2007), 65–71. See the criticisms of VanderKam (2018), 1050–1053.

25. *Jub.* 41:27; cf. 41:2.

26. For an extensive literary study of the Judah/Tamar story in the *Testament of Judah*, see Menn (1997), 107–213, especially 135–165.

27. That theme is the one element in the story noted by Ps-Philo, *LAB*, 9:5: Tamar preferred intercourse with her father-in-law, however sinful, to sexual relations with gentiles.

explanation lacking in Genesis, but shared by *Jubilees* and the *TJud*.[28] Their conjunction on the matter may reflect a wider tradition, drawn on by both, that injected the whole issue of ethnicity into the biblical narrative which had ignored it. Onan's abstention from full intercourse, according to *TJud*, also stemmed from the orders of his mother, and he suffered the same fate as his brother.[29] Judah plays a purely passive role. The question of the third son, Shelah, however, raises the more serious problem with regard to Judah's intent and action. Genesis holds Judah responsible for promising Shelah to Tamar but failing to act upon the commitment, thus triggering Tamar's scheme. For the *Testament of Judah* it was a different story. The culprit once more was the Canaanite mother. Judah wanted Shelah to be betrothed to Tamar but his wife would not allow it.[30] This absolves the patriarch of responsibility, but raises a more basic question. How is it that Judah's wife makes the decisions and dictates events? Is not Judah's weakness here, his inability to thwart his wife's demands, at least as damaging as the Genesis tale that has him duped by Tamar? And what induced him to marry a Canaanite in the first place?

The author of *TJud*, who places a deathbed speech into Judah's mouth, seeks to modify the patriarch's deficiencies. Judah affirms his hostility to the Canaanite race, but explains his wedding to a wife of that clan as a youthful indiscretion, his passion aroused by too much wine and the result of a drunken stupor.[31] He further expands on the wickedness of his wife by claiming that she not only blocked his efforts to have Shelah marry Tamar, but even found another wife for him, a Canaanite of course. This goes well beyond the Genesis original, for which Judah's wife is only a shadowy presence. *TJud* plainly gives centrality to her wickedness. But, although this might absolve Judah of evil designs, it only underscores the point that events were out of his control. He can do no more than curse his wife, and then benefit from her timely death.[32] Judah may not be evil, but he hardly emerges as an impressive figure.[33]

The scene of Judah's assignation with Tamar follows in the patriarch's speech. Yet the reproduction gives it a notably different implication. Genesis presents Tamar's appearance at the gate of Enaim as inauguration of her concocted scheme to entice Judah to her bed. *TJud*, on the other hand, skirts the idea of a canny ploy. In that account Tamar simply followed an Amorite custom that required widows to sit at the gate for seven days in a prostitute's garb. Judah was not tricked into a tryst

---

28. *TJud*. 10:1-3.

29. *TJud*. 10:4-5.

30. *TJud*, 10:6.

31. *TJud*. 11:1-2. Cf. 13:4-7, 14:6, 17:1. It is noteworthy that Judah depicts the Canaanites as an evil people, not as an ethnically deficient one.

32. *TJud*. 11:3-5.

33. By contrast, Menn (1997), 108, 152, sees the portrayal of Judah by *TJud* as consistently negative, a moralistic judgment by the author on Judah's drinking, lust, and greed. That misplaces the emphasis on the changes made by the author. Wassén (1994), 355–359, oddly sees the *TJud* representation as a primarily androcentric approach.

through Tamar's wiles, but simply (once again) gave way to lust brought on by excessive drinking.[34] Judah, in short, was not done in by Tamar's crafty cleverness but only by strong drink and sexual urge. The issue of pay for Tamar's services then follows. But the initiative to provide pledges in the form of identity tokens came from Judah, not Tamar.[35] The difference is subtle but meaningful. The text recognizes Judah's susceptibility, but avoids making him the plaything of a woman's guile.

TJud proceeds with an insertion quite distinct from the biblical narrative and gives a rather different flavor to the story. After Tamar's pregnancy was discovered and Judah proposed to have her killed, she then sent the pledged items but did so *secretly*.[36] This can only mean that she did not wish to expose Judah in public.[37] Judah seems quite baffled. He does indeed suspect trickery, but wonders whether she received the pledges from another woman. And since the townspeople knew of no whore at the gate, he surmised that she had come and gone, and no one would be the wiser. It was only when Judah summoned Tamar to a hearing and she revealed certain words that he had uttered during their lovemaking that he realized that she had indeed been the woman of the night. The truth was out, Judah canceled the orders to have her killed, and he refrained from any further sexual relations with her.[38] What the author has left out is quite telling: the assertion by Judah that "she is more righteous than I." And he has no scene of repentance like that in *Jubilees* which earns him divine pardon. The Judah of the *Testament* dropped the death penalty once he realized that he was the father of her unborn child (or children) and that she had not consummated a marriage with any of his sons. But there had been no entrapment by Tamar and no public remorse by Judah. The import of this retelling is significant. Judah had not covered himself with glory. But the author of *TJud* brought a separate angle to bear and created a picture markedly different from the scriptural portrait. Ethnic issues stand to the fore, putting in the shade any character flaws of Judah. The patriarch's plans for the marriage of his sons were foiled by a Canaanite wife who stood in the way of any union with a non-Canaanite. Judah escapes blame for the prevention of Shelah's marriage. Shelah's mother had been responsible. Too much drink rather than sinister intention account for both Judah's wedding and his dalliance. No legal issues arise to cloud Judah's actions. Any chicanery by Tamar is subdued or even excluded. Judah did not fall victim to a more clever and shrewd woman. The patriarch's reputation is slightly tattered, but remains intact.

34. *TJud*. 12:1-3.
35. *TJud*. 12:4.
36. *TJud*. 12:5: ἐν κρύπτῳ.
37. Although the text states that this act humiliated Judah, the humiliation must be an internal one, rather than open exposure. Cf. Kugel (2013), 1739, who wishes to emend the text to read that he was *not* humiliated. But if this is a private humiliation, the change is unnecessary.
38. *TJud*. 12:6-11. This whole section of the text is somewhat confusing. Kugel (2013), 1758–1760, accordingly reshuffles the lines to provide a more logical sequence. In any case, the basic sense seems clear enough.

This assemblage of assorted reinterpretations of the tale reveals a remarkably disparate range of attitudes among subsequent revisers. Some sought to shed a softer light on Judah's indiscretions, others focused on ethnic consequences of questionable intermingling, accounts differed over responsibility by the perpetrators for troubling deeds, and problematic reflections surfaced regarding the character and purpose of Judah. No consistent story line emerged, and no author felt bound by one. The story itself, however, even in variant versions and retold for multiple motives, retained a hold on later Jewish audiences as an engaging narrative and a window on the patriarchal age.

Chapter 9

MOSES AND GOD

The figure of Moses, of course, loomed large in the consciousness of Second Temple writers. A plethora of works owed inspiration to the Book of Exodus. Only a small sample will serve for our purposes. Exodus itself cannot and need not be summarized here. One particular Second Temple composition, however, warrants special notice. We possess a substantial portion of a remarkable Jewish tragic drama, the *Exagoge* or *Exodus*, composed in Greek by a certain Ezekiel some time between the late 3rd and early 1st century BCE. Of the author we know little more than his name. We do, however, know that the *Exagoge* was only one of several tragedies that Ezekiel wrote, although the others have sadly disappeared. That information is enough to show that tragic drama in Greek mode had a following of some significance among Hellenistic Jews.[1]

Ezekiel's play hewed closely to the narrative line contained in Exodus. But his drama was more than just an adaptation for the stage of the familiar Moses story. Among other things, Ezekiel added a stunning scene that has no biblical analogue. He has Moses report a dream in which he received the vision of a great throne high upon a summit extending to the cleft of heaven. Upon it sat a noble figure wearing a diadem and wielding a scepter. That imposing figure then handed the diadem and scepter to Moses, descended from the throne, and departed. Moses now had a panoramic view of earth and sky, with the stars falling on their knees before him. The dream then received an interpretation by Moses' father-in-law, who reassured him that it came as a sign from God that Moses will lift up a great throne, will issue judgments, and will serve as a guide to mortals.[2] This striking image corresponds to nothing in the Book of Exodus. Indeed no other tale anywhere in literature ascribes a dream vision to Moses. And certainly nowhere else does God relinquish his seat in the heavens to anyone. Ezekiel obviously wanted to capture his readers'

---

1. Text, French translation, and commentary by Lanfranchi (2006). See the excellent study of the *Exagoge* by Jacobson (1983). On the date and possible (though speculative) context, see Gambetti (2017), 188–217. On the play and its relation to Greek tragedy, see Stewart (2018), 223–252, and now Adams (2020), 45–54, with bibliography.

2. Euseb. *PE*, 9:29.4-6. Jacobson (1983), 89–97, provides valuable parallels for the several parts of the scene, but leaves little room for Ezekiel's originality.

attention here. The playwright had an arresting and powerful scene in mind: the forecast of Moses' future through a dramatic dream that gave him access to divinity. Moses will be executor of God's will on earth, with absolute authority on the model of Hellenistic kings.[3]

Ezekiel has thus applied the standard conventions of Greek drama to a Jewish theme presented in an altogether unique scenario. He draped Moses in the emblems of royal power that would resonate with those who lived in the era of the great Hellenistic monarchies. The Israelite hero therefore becomes a beacon for humankind, a representative of the divinity on earth, described in phraseology that struck responsive chords among Ezekiel's Hellenic or Hellenized compatriots. The tragic poet held scriptural authority in awe. But that did not prevent him from improving upon it.

A very different image of Moses emerges in the intriguing work of the author known as Pseudo-Philo. The portions on Moses offer an arresting picture. The famous story of the Golden Calf can supply an illustration. In the Book of Exodus, Moses came down from the mountain after receiving the sacred tablets of the Covenant from God, only to find that the Israelites, in despair of seeing him again and distrusting the deity, had fashioned out of molten gold the image of a calf as representative of the gods to whom they would now turn for worship. The Lord fumed with anger at this betrayal and vowed destruction of the nation. Moses then smashed the tablets, burned the golden calf, and scattered its ashes. At that point he implored God to spare the Israelites despite their grave offenses and even offered himself up as victim, thus prompting the Lord to pardon the innocent.[4] The author of the *LAB* is plainly familiar with the Exodus version but has his own take on it. His Moses does more than just make an abject appeal to God. He reasons with him and offers an argument for forgiveness. Employing the metaphor of a vine whose cultivator uproots it, he points out that if God should destroy the Israelites, his own cultivation of them will have been in vain, he will have no one left to glorify him, and no one will trust him. Indeed Moses asks whether anyone will be left to act in accordance with the divine will.[5] The argument, interestingly enough, is a purely pragmatic one, not a claim on clemency. It amounts to saying that if God knows what is good for him, he will spare the Israelites.

Perhaps even more striking is the episode in which the children of Israel faced destruction at the Red Sea (or "Sea of Reeds"). They cried out in fury to the Lord and to Moses his agent, denouncing them for freeing the Hebrews from Egypt only to have them die in the wilderness at the hands of the Egyptians. As the Book of Exodus has it, Moses reassures his people, guaranteeing that God will not abandon them. And sure enough the author has Moses stretch his staff over the sea and split the waters so that the Israelites can cross on dry land while the pursuing Egyptians

---

3. The recent remarks of Whitmarsh (2013), 215–227, on the play do not address this issue.
4. Exod. 32.
5. *LAB*, 12:9. See Jacobson (1996), I, 499–504. Cf. Murphy (1993), 68–73.

are swallowed up by the waves.⁶ Everyone knows the story. So did Pseudo-Philo. But he put his own twist on it. Rather than have Moses reassure the Israelites, confident of divine favor, he has him rebuke the Lord. Moses shouts out to him with a reproach for having led his people to the edge of the sea, their enemies now upon them. And he offers some stern advice: "think about your reputation!"⁷ That puts it rather boldly.

In fact, Moses is still at it on his deathbed. His final words sum up his lengthy mission as agent of the Lord, and he addresses him directly, pointing to the laws and institutions that he has bestowed upon his chosen people to which they have not always adhered. But then who is free of transgressions? Moses adjures God to show patience and mercy. Unless he does so, says Moses, how will his own legacy endure?⁸ His final request to God is to punish the transgressors, yes, but only for a time, and not in anger.⁹ The Israelite leader indulges here neither in plea nor in prayer. He serves as a counselor to God offering advice on what would serve the Lord's interest: live up to your promises or your credit will suffer.

The portrayal of Moses by Ps-Philo, in other words, is not of a merely dutiful and compliant servant of an infallible deity. Rather, his Moses can remonstrate with God, remind him of his promises, and caution him to think about his reputation and his legacy. This liberal refashioning of biblical episodes underscores Moses as one who reasons and argues with God—and usually wins the argument.

These two examples of portraying Moses' interconnection with God strike intriguingly different notes. The first invents a scene unauthorized by the Bible and bestows an ascendant quality upon its hero beyond scriptural imaginings. The second draws on its forerunners but gives Moses a more direct and more commanding association with the deity. We get no composite picture, rather a splintering of ideas and images that reflect the challenge presented by working out the relationship between the heroic and the divine. The two efforts noted here offer a glimpse of that problematic challenge.

---

6. Exod. 14.
7. *LAB*, 10:3-4: *et tu Domine, memor esto nominis tui.* Cf. Jacobson (1996), I, 439–440.
8. *LAB*, 19:9: *et nisi permaneat longanimitas tua, quomodo constabilietur hereditas tua si non misertus fuiris eis?*
9. *LAB*, 19:9: *emendabis autem eos in tempore, et non on ira.* There is nothing comparable in the Deuteronomy account of Moses' final days; Deut. 31–34.

Chapter 10

MOSES IN ETHIOPIA

Moses, of course, plays a very large role in the narrative of Josephus, as he does in much Hellenistic Jewish literature. This is not the place to engage in a wholesale examination of this central figure in the Josephan text. But one tale stands out in remarkable relief, for it possesses no biblical precedent at all: Moses' military conquests in Ethiopia. A single possible prompt in the Scriptures exists: a remark in Numbers that Moses married an Ethiopian woman, a fact deplored by both of his siblings, Aaron and Miriam.[1] It is unlikely in the extreme that this sole passing reference gave rise to a rather elaborate tale that had Moses as a successful general in Ethiopia whose triumphs induced an Ethiopian princess to fall in love with him and become his bride. Josephus drew on material well beyond the Bible and, to at least some degree, on his own imagination.

The narrative in summary proceeds as follows. Ethiopian forces invaded Egypt and plundered Egyptian possessions. Egyptians retaliated with an invasion of their own but were badly beaten, fled back to Egypt, and thus provoked a much more devastating assault in which the Ethiopians overran all the land, with little resistance, all the way to Memphis and the sea. The peoples of Egypt, in dire straits, resorted to oracles and divine prophecies, and received advice from God that they should have a Hebrew lead them into battle. Pharaoh consequently called upon his daughter to offer up Moses as general of the forces, which she consented to do, after rebuking the priests who had sought to have him killed as an enemy.[2] Moses gladly took on the job, to the delight of both Hebrews and Egyptians, the one because they saw him as future leader of his people out of Egypt, the other because they expected that after driving out the Ethiopians Moses would fall victim to Egyptian assassins.[3] Moses' expedition, however, proved unequivocally successful. He chose a land route through treacherous territory and managed to dispose of the menace of flying snakes by shrewdly bringing along baskets of ibises who consumed them. There followed smashing victories over the Ethiopians, to the point that they faced enslavement or extirpation.[4] The daughter of the king who

1. Num. 12:1.
2. Jos. *AJ*, 2:238-242.
3. Jos. *AJ*, 2:243.
4. Jos. *AJ*, 2:244-248.

witnessed Moses' impressive ingenuity and his warrior exploits became hopelessly enamored of him and made him an offer of marriage. Moses readily agreed, but only on condition of surrender of the Ethiopian capital, which he promised not to damage. The pact was made, and Moses led the Egyptians back to their homeland.[5]

Josephus evidently did not blanch at inserting an adventure tale and romance that had no basis whatever in the Bible. Moses emerges as a military hero, a shrewd and commanding figure who routs the hitherto invincible Ethiopians and captures the heart of an Ethiopian princess to boot.

How much of this story is Josephus' creation and how much is adapted from elsewhere we cannot know. What we do know is that Josephus was not the first to convey a yarn about Moses and an Ethiopian expedition. A comparable but fundamentally different version appeared already in the quirky treatise of the Hellenistic Jewish writer Artapanos.[6] In his inventive rendition, Moses brought numerous salutary changes to Egyptian culture, religion, society, and administration. His innovations, however, and the fame which he had attained stirred the jealousy of the Pharaoh who conceived the scheme of appointing Moses as commander of the army against the Ethiopian invaders but provided him only a ragtag group of forces, which should lead to failure and death. But Moses confounded the plan by winning every battle, founding a new city, and eventually even winning the affection of the Ethiopians.[7]

Much scholarly debate has been devoted to sorting out the relationship between these two fanciful tales. A variety of opinions has suggested either that Josephus employed Artapanos as a source or relied on an intermediary or that both authors drew upon a no longer extant text.[8] A definitive answer will always elude us. It is hardly likely that Josephus made up the story himself. Artapanos' version shows that diverse renderings of an expedition by Moses against Ethiopians had been floating about for some time. The significant differences between the accounts of Artapanos and Josephus renders any effort to see the one as dependent on the other or both dependent on a third source largely pointless.[9] One can dispute whether they were conveyed by written compositions or by oral transmission, whether they were based on folkloric traditions and popular memory or influenced by Jewish-Hellenistic historical literature or by writings that go back to the Persian period.[10] Nor does it help much to postulate apologetic motives that aimed to

---

5. Jos. *AJ*, 2:252-253.

6. The fragments of Artapanos are conveniently collected with text, translation, and commentary by Holladay (1983), 189–243. See also the French translation, with valuable notes, by Bloch et al. (2010), 25–39.

7. Euseb. *PE*, 9:27:4-10.

8. The bibliography is large. Useful compilations can be found in Feldman (2000), 200–202; Römer (2007), 169–193.

9. Sterling (1992), 269–279, usefully juxtaposes the two texts and underscores the discrepancies.

elevate Jewish virtues against the slanders of pagan critics and make the Jews more palatable to Roman readers. Few pagan critics would be disabused by reading a fanciful tale of Moses' exploits.

It would be preferable to eschew the speculation. What matters is that Josephus chose to transmit or reconceive an engaging narrative that combined an adventure story of military cunning and heroism with a romantic tale and a plot arising out of court intrigue—none of which had the slightest connection with Scripture. The Israelite lawgiver emerges with added dimensions, those of vaunted warrior and novelistic hero. The entertainment value of this addition stands out. Artapanos and Josephus evidently felt perfectly comfortable in enlivening their narratives by inserting this altogether unbiblical scenario into their reproduction of Israelite history.

10. Rajak (1978), 118–122, for example, sees a background of both Greek historical-ethnographic literature and oral traditions with folkloric elements. Runnalls (1983), 149–150, calls attention to the possibility that the story may have circulated among Jewish mercenaries in the service of the Persians or the Ptolemies. For Römer (2007), 188–190, both Artapanos and Josephus echoed legends of the Egyptian hero and ruler Sesostris. Feldman (2000), 200–202, sagely refrains from adopting any of the hypotheses.

Chapter 11

MOSES AS UNIVERSAL FIGURE

Artapanos' take on Moses and Ethiopia was merely a part of his quite remarkably inventive web of fables associated with the great Hebrew lawgiver. His most unusual Moses would be quite unrecognizable to those familiar with the Hebrew or Greek Bibles.

In the hands of Artapanos, Moses emerges as much more than the central personage of Israelite history. He is a polymath and multi-layered figure whose associations and influence left their mark on the worlds of both Egypt and Hellas as well. Moses single-handedly transformed Egyptian society, creating the administrative districts called nomes, assigning the gods to be worshipped in each, including the various animal deities to which Egyptians became attached, distributing land to the priests, and schooling them in sacred writings.[1] Connection with the Greeks was no less intimate. According to Artapanos, Greeks bestowed upon him the name of Mousaios (the similarity of names prompted it), and thus identified him with the teacher of Orpheus, the very emblem of music and poetry.[2] The Jewish writer indulged here in a special flight of fancy. Greek myth had Orpheus as teacher of Mousaios. Artapanos switched them around to have Mousaios (Moses) as the mentor rather than the pupil. The Egyptians gave him yet another honorific title, that of "Hermes," i.e. the Egyptian equivalent of Thoth, in acknowledgment of his mastery of sacred writings (hieroglyphics).[3] Moses' skills and achievements, however, transcended national and ethnic boundaries, bringing a host of benefactions to humankind in general, including the invention of ships, mechanisms for stone construction, weaponry, hydraulic engines, implements of warfare, and, not least, philosophy.[4] In Artapanos' vision, Moses taught circumcision to the Ethiopians, showed Egyptians the proper breed of oxen to plow their fields, and introduced the practice of animal worship.[5] His Moses is a culture hero and a world-historical figure.

1. Euseb. *PE*, 9:27:4.
2. Euseb. *PE*, 9:27:3.
3. Euseb. *PE*, 9:27:3.
4. Euseb. *PE*, 9:27:3-4.
5. Euseb. *PE*, 9:27:4-6.

The Bible, of course, has none of this. And Artapanos encases his account in a dramatic narrative that exhibits Moses' ingenuity, cleverness, and prowess. We have seen already the tale of Moses' smashing victories over Ethiopians and the wedding of an Ethiopian princess. Artapanos has still more. In his manipulation of the Exodus narrative, he has Moses wed the daughter of a Midianite priest who urges an invasion of Egypt upon him, in vain, but settles for a plundering of the land.[6] Even the burning bush turns into an instrument prompting Moses to wage war on Egypt.[7] And the adventurous escapades that follow have not the slightest relationship to the Scriptures. Moses' accomplishments, although welcomed by the populace and the priests, roused the jealousy of the Pharaoh Chenephres, who plotted against him and commissioned an assassin to kill him, only to have the villain overpowered by the formidable Moses. The next Pharaoh proved similarly incapable of containing Moses. He had him imprisoned, but prison doors miraculously opened, guards proved helpless, and Moses sauntered out with ease. His simple whisper of the divine name in Pharaoh's ear caused the king to collapse in a heap, and Moses emerged triumphant.[8]

Artapanos does not abandon the Exodus account of the plagues altogether. But he plays with it willfully. He includes some plagues and drops others, he reshuffles and reorders them—and he adds earthquakes. Moses' rod does not turn the Nile into blood, but he does have it flood its banks, the origin of its regular overflow, the very lifeline of the nation, for which the culture hero is responsible. Artapanos paints the arresting picture of Egyptians darting about to escape the plague of hail only to be felled by the earthquake, and vice-versa.[9] And one glaring omission stands out: no mention of the fatal tenth plague, the death of every Egyptian firstborn. Artapanos preferred not to associate God with that level of horror.

The concluding portions of the story revert to Exodus, but Artapanos continues to inject his own idiosyncrasies. On the miraculous crossing of the Red Sea, he offers two explanations, each ascribed to a different Egyptian source, thus casting a cloud on each.[10] That may be yet another declaration of independence from the received text, and even a means of expressing some doubts about it. And he has the pursuing Egyptians halted not only by the sea but by a burst of flame.[11] The waters were not enough for Artapanos. Fire and flood both consumed them.

The reasons for Artapanos' seemingly arbitrary and whimsical divergences have occupied many scholars. Some indeed have denied even that he was a Jew.

---

6. Euseb. *PE,* 9:27:19.

7. Euseb. *PE,* 9:27:21-2; cf. Exodus, 31:1-10.

8. Euseb. *PE,* 9:27:23-26.

9. Euseb. *PE,* 9:27:28-33.

10. Artapanus attributes one of the explanations to Memphites, the other to Heliopolitans. The first ascribed the deed to Moses' wait for low tide, thus to lead his flock through the dry portions of the water, the second to Moses' use of his rod to divide the waters and create a dry channel for his followers to cross safely; Euseb. *PE,* 9:27:35; cf. Exodus, 14:21-22.

11. Euseb. *PE,* 9:27:37.

What Jew would credit Moses with inaugurating animal worship?[12] But Artapanos' work depends upon extensive acquaintance with the scriptural version, so as to render meaningful the departures and deviations that would capture the attention of his readership.[13] Few gentiles would catch those allusions. Other explanations have sought to discern Artapanos' theological position as somewhere between a committed Judaism and a moderate paganism.[14] That approach leads down a fruitless path. Artapanos did not propound a theological or ideological program in his transformation of Moses. Nor should one saddle him with an apologetic agenda (the most common view), an effort to rebut gentile criticisms of Jews by presenting the life of Moses as one of heroism, of glorious cultural achievement, and of benefaction to all peoples.[15] Few hostile pagans (if indeed any of them ever read Artapanos) would be moved to revise their opinions on the basis of his fanciful tales.

Entertainment takes precedence over theology or didacticism in Artapanos' work.[16] Nor does he exhibit polemic or program. As we have seen, again and again, the upsetting of expectations is a frequent feature of later Jewish adaptations of biblical narratives. Artapanos stands very much in that literary culture. And he adds elements of whimsy and caprice that amuse rather than instruct. His wit and surprises give him special distinction. But his willingness to depart freely from received tradition is characteristic of a larger Jewish convention.

Artapanos was not alone in giving Moses a place as fount of cultural and intellectual accomplishment in a wider world. The Hellenistic Jewish writer Eupolemos (probably 2nd century BCE) accords him comparable stature. He describes Moses as the first sage (σοφός) and credits him with creating the alphabet for the Jews, who transmitted it to the Phoenicians, whence it came to the Greeks. And he adds, what the singularly eccentric Artapanos left out: the notice that Moses was the first to provide laws for the Jews.[17] The idea of Moses as a universal figure, whose benefactions extended well beyond his own people, evidently made the rounds. It was yet another exhibit of the multiple tales transmitted or concocted by Hellenistic Jews to refashion scriptural material in order to appeal to audiences who preferred amusement to theology.

---

12. See, especially, Jacobson (2006), 210–221.

13. Cf. Zellentin (2008), 31–32.

14. So, e.g., Schürer (1986), 523; Koskenniemi (2002), 26–29. Other works cited in Gruen (2015), 37.

15. For this view of "competitive historiography," see, e.g., Collins (2000), 39–40; Sterling (1992), 182–183; Droge (1989), 30–32; Johnson (2004), 102–105. Further bibliography in Gruen (2002), 232.

16. A fuller discussion on this point by Gruen (2015), 31–44. This element goes largely unappreciated in recent works; Zellentin (2008), 27–73; Ahearne-Kroll (2011), 434–456.

17. Clem. Alex. *Strom.* 1:23:153:4; Euseb. *PE*, 9:26:1. See the discussion of Gruen (1998), 153–154.

Chapter 12

BALAAM AND WAYWARD PROPHECY

A striking story surfaced as part of the biblical narrative of Israelite struggles and battles through the wilderness on the way to the promised land.[1] According to the book of Numbers, the Israelites had gained substantial victories over the Amorites, had pushed into Transjordan, and moved onto the borders of Moab. The Moabite king Balak was terrified by the vast numbers of the Israelites, whom he loathed. But he did not have the manpower to contend with them. He therefore turned to other means. Balak called upon the renowned seer Balaam, from Syria or Mesopotamia, whose powers were evidently widely known, to deliver a curse upon the Israelites.[2] Prophetic doom might be more effective than arms.

The ministers of the king went to Balaam, displaying their own skills as diviners, to persuade him to exercise his magic on behalf of Moab. The seer delayed and sought the counsel of God. Yahweh responded in no uncertain terms. He directed Balaam to reject the very idea of placing a hex on Israel whom the Lord himself had blessed. The diviner unhesitatingly obeyed the command. But Balak, when

---

1. On this "Balaam Pericope," see the excellent commentary of Levine (2000), 137–275. The briefer commentary by Vermes (1973), 127–169, still retains value. See, more recently, the remarks on the text by Robker (2019), 69–127. The topic has attracted much scholarly attention. Useful summaries of earlier literature can be found in Moore (1990), 1–11; Robker (2019), 10–68. Moore (1990), 20–109, also sets Balaam in the traditions of Near Eastern diviners, seers, and mantics generally, but does not discuss the post-biblical traditions. On Balaam's "profession," see further Robker (2019), 319–346. For a discussion of allusions to Balaam at Qumran and in Samaritan literature, see Greene (1992), 83–135. Too much of the modern literature on the appearance of Balaam in subsequent traditions, however, has focused on the issue of whether he is treated positively or negatively; e.g. Vermes (1973), 173–177; Kugel (1997), 482–495, van Ruiten (2008), 101–130. This dichotomy does not get us far.

2. Num. 22:1-7. The Balaam episode seems ill-fitting in the surrounding context and may be an insertion in the narrative. Some external validation for the tale may be found in an inscription unearthed in this region which records a certain soothsayer named Balaam; Milgrom (1990), 473–476; Levine (2000), 241–243, 261–275; Puech (2008), 25–47; Robker (2019), 271–305.

word reached him, was not to be put off. He sent another delegation, larger and with greater distinction, to make a more tempting offer: rich rewards for Balaam and a promise to do anything that the seer proposes. Balaam responded with defiance: no amount of treasure would deflect him from carrying out the will of the Lord. But he found it prudent to check once more with God and ask again for instructions. This time Yahweh changed his position somewhat. Balaam could go to the court of Moab but do nothing unless authorized by God.[3]

The trip to Balak produced the most celebrated scene of the story: the fable of the talking donkey.[4] Balaam accompanied the Moabite dignitaries to their king. But God shifted ground once more and became angry at the soothsayer's decision. He set an angel in the road, invisible to Balaam but fully perceptible to the donkey. When the animal saw this fearsome emissary of the Lord with drawn sword, she had no choice but to swerve from the road and seek refuge in the fields. The unknowing Balaam twice struck the ass to get her back on the path, and then a third time when she saw no room to move and lay down on the ground. God then opened the mouth of the animal, who lamented that she had done nothing wrong and wondered why her master had resorted to this undeserved punishment. Balaam exploded with fury, asserting that the donkey had made him a laughing stock and regretting that he did not have a sword at hand to kill her. The unfortunate animal observed that she had been a loyal helpmate throughout Balaam's life and had never let him down, a fact that Balaam had to acknowledge. At this point the Lord opened Balaam's eyes to reveal the angel with unsheathed sword, causing the seer to prostrate himself in humiliating fashion and receive severe rebuke from the angel before being told to proceed on to Balak, and to do or say nothing but what is ordered by God.[5]

The encounter between Balaam and Balak brought home the divine message. The soothsayer directed the construction of seven altars and the sacrifices set up in them to elicit the will of God. The divine directive then came through an oracle set in Balaam's mouth exclaiming that the people of Israel cannot be cursed for God has not willed it, indeed has made them a nation apart and as numerous as the dust. Balak, taken aback but not quite ready to give up, complained that he had enlisted the seer to apply a hex but got only a blessing. He makes another try by setting up seven more altars in hopes of getting a different result. But the Lord's response via a second oracle mouthed by Balaam simply reinforced the first, only more forcibly. The exasperated king let out his frustration by demanding that Balaam neither bless nor curse. But he recovered himself swiftly enough to have still another go at getting the desired pronouncement. Another seven altars were readied, and the spirit of the Lord once more expressed itself through the words of Balaam with clear favor to Israel and indeed an emphasis upon its might and

---

3. Num. 22:8-20. The sudden and unexplained reversal by God is often accounted for by the intervention of another source.
4. On the talking donkey tale, see Levine (2000), 154–159.
5. Num. 22:21-33.

power. This third pronouncement sent Balak into a rage. He scornfully dismissed Balaam, who dutifully left with a parting shot that reiterated God's commitment to the Israelites in yet a fourth oracular pronouncement. The issue was now closed. Balak had been put in his place. And no curse would be leveled at the children of Israel.[6]

This engaging fable, whether an independent insertion or part of a larger narrative, has its own appeal. And it also raises some intriguing questions. How is one meant to assess the seer? He possesses mantic powers, but fails to exercise them, indeed hardly makes a move without consulting the Lord. Why use a non-Israelite prophet to issue the Lord's instructions anyway?[7] And how does one understand the deity? He employs Balaam as a medium to deliver declarations with force and authority. But he also dupes him with an invisible angel and a talking donkey. He changes his mind more than once, without explanation. Further, the multiplication of oracles, altars, and sacrifices not only seems repetitious but hardly advances the narrative. Balak fumes in vain, gets nowhere, but keeps trying until he meekly withdraws. Is there any method in this seeming madness? The Israelites are in the same position at the end of this entertaining episode as they were in the beginning. Rewriters of the tale had something of a challenge.

Philo rehearses the story in some detail in his *Life of Moses*. But he was evidently bothered by the ambivalent and equivocal character of Balaam. Hence he determined to reshape him into someone more readily graspable. He simply transforms him into a villain. Philo expounds upon his mantic skills, filling out Numbers' brief notation with details of his augural talents and affording him speeches in his encounters with Balak.[8] But he undermines him right away. In Philo's representation, Balaam did not apply first to God for instructions, but engaged in deceit when presenting himself as a trustworthy prophet and claiming fraudulently that the deity had advised him not to go to the king. And when he consented to go, he again applied the false pretext, according to Philo, that God had authorized the trip.[9] Philo mentions the talking ass episode, but brushes past it quickly. His concern is to impeach the character of Balaam, not to present him as victimized by God. But he uses the episode to advance his case for loathing Balaam. He accounts for the angel's revelation as bringing Balaam to realize his own worthlessness and emptiness—for the angel pierced through his dissimulation.[10] Philo also omits the four oracles that Balaam delivered as the word of God, evidently devaluing the idea that the Lord would deliver potent pronouncements through the mouth of a despised individual. Balaam's words as

---

6. Num. 22:36–24:19.

7. On the difficult question of why a non-Israelite prophet should be consulting Yahweh, see Levine (2000), 217–225, who argues that Balaam's sources of authority constitute a consortium of divine powers, including but not limited to Yahweh.

8. Philo, *Mos.* 1:264–265.

9. Philo, *Mos.* 1:266.

10. Philo, *Mos.* 1:272-274.

dictated by the deity are briefer and less impressive in Philo's version, restricted mainly to singing the praises of Israel's singularity and divine protection.[11] And Philo adds that, although the words of God were implanted in the seer, he delivered them in bad faith because he longed to curse the Israelites but was prevented from doing so.[12]

Philo proceeds to add a wholly new dimension to Balaam's wickedness. The Book of Numbers concludes the story of Balaam with a whimper. Balaam returns to his place and Balak goes on his way.[13] The text continues with a brief recounting of Israelite men cohabiting with loose Moabite women who induce them to sacrifice to alien gods, thereby rousing the ire of the Lord. The event stimulated a bloody retaliation by the Israelite priest Phinehas, who slew two of the transgressors, accompanied by a pestilence that felled massive numbers of Midianites.[14] There is no hint here that Balaam had anything to do with this sequel or that the one episode grew out of the other. Philo, however, knits them together quite tightly. And he makes Balaam the villain of the piece. The soothsayer, having been restrained by God from imposing imprecations upon Israel, conceived another scheme. He advised Balak to choose the comeliest of Midianite maidens and have them prostitute themselves for the youthful Israelites. He even provides suggestions for the means of seduction: the young women should pretend shyness, coax and cajole the men to rouse their passions, and then declare the conditions under which they will give their favors: the abandonment of Israelite worship and the embrace of idols and images of Midianite deities. That, Balaam assured the king, would bring down Yahweh's wrath upon his own people. The plan worked, until Phinehas' spear pierced two of the offenders and triggered a wholesale slaughter of those who had succumbed to adultery and idolatry, as well as all members of their families, thus to purge the nation of pollution. Both Balaam and Balak then disappear from the story, as the nation of Israel under Moses proceeds to war on Midian.[15]

This alternative version was evidently known to the author of Numbers, who alluded to it much later in his text, though only in passing.[16] But Philo, or whatever source he may have used, transformed it into a major event, the capstone of Balaam's wickedness. He effectively revamps the weak and manipulable figure of the Bible into an evil and calculating deceiver. He levels a stream of invective against Balaam in brief volleys, usually as illustration of vices or failings, such as folly, vanity, subterfuge, hatred of virtue, and madness in a number of scattered

---

11. Philo, *Mos.* 1:281-284, 289–291.
12. Philo, *Mos.* 1:286: ἄμα δὲ καὶ τῇ διανοίᾳ καταρᾶσθαι γλιχόμενος, εἰ καὶ τῇ φωνῇ διεκωλύετο.
13. Num. 24:25.
14. Num. 25:1-9. The text seems to use the description "Midianites" and "Moabites" interchangeably.
15. Philo, *Mos.* 1:294-304.
16. Num. 31:16; cf. 31:8.

texts and contexts.[17] Just why the philosopher fastened his vitriol upon the seer remains a matter of speculation.[18] But he has certainly turned the ambiguous and largely vacuous figure of the Bible into a much more convincing purveyor of evil. Enhancement of the story, whether invented or adapted by Philo, may have been a principal motive for the retelling.

Josephus plainly found the story evocative and revised it with relish. His rewrite, in fact, occupies well over twice the length of the Hebrew version. And it possesses a rather different character.[19] Josephus takes a number of deliberate liberties. Like Philo, he streamlines some of the original, omitting the three oracular pronouncements by Balaam and reducing the talking ass fable, so as to bring more flow to the narrative. He applies a sharper character study to Balaam, and he attempts to straighten out some puzzling activities of God. And, also like Philo, he makes the seduction story and its baleful consequences dovetail with the Balaam episode and thus give a heightened flavor missing in the Bible. For Josephus, Balak is king of the Moabites but collaborates with the Midianites in seeking to check the advance of the myriads of Israelites.[20] The Midianites recommended the diviner Balaam, the best of his profession, and they took the lead in persuading the seer to place a hex on the invaders.[21] And the dramatic tale of deception and reaffirmation at the conclusion markedly expands and enhances the narrative.

The biblical Balaam is a rather disengaged and acquiescent character. He courteously delivers the wishes of the Moabite king to God but duly abides by the

---

17. Philo, *Cher.* 31–35; *Quod Deter.* 71; *Quod Deus Imm.* 180–183; *Conf. Ling.* 159–160; *Migr.* 113–114; *Mut.* 202–203. For an analysis of Philo's portrait of Balaam, with different purposes and approach, see Lester (2018), 75–89.

18. For van Kooten (2008), 135–142, Philo sees Balaam as emblematic of the sophist and the sophistical traits that the philosopher despises. So also, Lester (2018), 74–75. This is a strained hypothesis. Philo may indeed have been scornful of sophists. But, although he levels criticism at Balaam in several different treatises, only a single passage in his corpus actually labels him a sophist; *Quod Deter.* 71. And here the comparison is between Philo's conception of sophists as possessing an empty mass of contradictory and warring ideas and Balaam's attempts to curse Israel which God turned into a blessing. This is simply an analogy, and not a very good one. Other references to his "mantic sophistry" or "magic sophistry" (*Migr.* 113; *Mut. Nom.* 203), are mere slurs. They are certainly not tantamount to making Balaam the epitome of sophism.

19. Feldman (1993), 48–83, offers a useful comparison of Josephus' version with that of the Bible. See also his valuable notes on the text (2000), 364–384. But his view that most of Josephus' changes addressed themselves, in apologetic fashion, to supposed Greek or Roman criticisms of Jews strains plausibility.

20. They are mentioned once in the biblical text (Num. 22:7) as accompanying the Moabite leaders to Balaam, but disappear thereafter in the story. The suggestion of Feldman (2000), 376, that Josephus substituted Midianites for Moabites because Ruth, the ancestress of David, was a Moabite seems quite a stretch.

21. Jos. *AJ*, 4:102-104.

Lord's negative response. He shows a bit of vigor in affirming that he could not be bribed to act against the divine will, but proceeds to make a second and a third attempt to reverse God's judgment on the prodding of Balak. He exhibits anger against the talking ass but offers abject submission when the angel revealed himself. All in all, a well-meaning but ineffective and unimpressive figure.

Philo's Balaam is a more striking character, but largely one-dimensional, exuding evil, a schemer and a dissimulator. For Josephus, he takes on a more complex persona. He asks the Lord for his view on the matter of the curse, receiving only the answer that he opposed the idea. But Balaam's report to the Midianites goes beyond a mere parroting of the divine message. He claims that he would have been happy to comply with their requests and deliver imprecations upon the Israelites, but Yahweh blocked him, the very deity who had been responsible for Balaam's own high esteem as a truthful prophet.[22] The notice that God had bestowed divining powers upon the alien seer adds an intriguing aspect to the tale, implying that there is more here than a simple clash between Israel and Moab (or Midian). Not only does the non-Israelite soothsayer have a direct line to God, but his own skills and success are owed to the Israelite deity. And this despite the fact that Balaam had expressed zeal for the cause of the Midianites against Israel. He offers counsel to the Midianites to back off and drop their animosity toward the Israelites, an act unattested in the Bible. It suggests that the differences between the people were not irreconcilable. Balaam acquiesces in the Lord's decision, but evidently against his own inclinations.[23] The account brings to light internal tensions between Balaam's subservience to God and his desire to gratify the Midianites. Despite divine injunctions, which required obedience, he accedes to Balak's requests for a second and third attempt to change God's mind, even in the wake of the talking ass episode. Balaam is in two minds throughout.[24]

The role of God himself is equally problematic. His actions in the scriptural narrative seem quite inscrutable. He first directs Balaam not to accompany the king's envoys to the court, and then, after the second offer, reverses himself, for no obvious reason, and authorizes Balaam's visit, only then to flare into anger when the prophet actually does so.[25] The puzzling double reversal goes unexplained in the Bible. Josephus does at least endeavor to account for it. But in so doing he casts yet a further cloud upon God's behavior. He views the divine intention as setting up a trial, indeed a deliberate deception, of Balaam. The deluded seer duly saddles up his donkey and undertakes the trip wherein he is denied a vision of the angel and suffers the reproaches of the talking animal, redoubled by the angel's own reproaches after he revealed himself. In Josephus' presentation, Balaam is stunned, never imagining that God would deceive him. Completely panicked by the events, he endeavors to return, only to have the Lord enjoin him to continue the journey, while adding that he must say nothing except what the divinity puts into

22. Jos. *AJ*, 4:105.
23. Jos. *AJ*, 4:106.
24. Jos. *AJ*, 4:107, 4:113, 4:123, 4:127.
25. Num. 22:7-22.

his mind.[26] Josephus' effort to clarify God's purpose here only muddies it the more. God both sanctions Balaam's trip to Balak and disapproves it. And worse, he devises a devious scheme to entrap the very seer whose powers he had himself instilled for expounding the divine wishes. The seemingly arbitrary actions leave a dubious impression of the Lord.

The interactions between deity and prophet present a challenge to the reader. In the biblical account, God seems somewhat puzzled as to what is going on and the seer has to explain to him the requests made by Balak. When the Lord requires Balaam not to cooperate with the Moabite, the mantic unequivocally obeys. His response to a second and more generous offer by Balak is still more unequivocal. He asserts in ringing tones that he would not disobey Yahweh for all the gold and silver in the king's household. In Josephus' presentation, however, these affirmations become considerably more ambiguous. The prophet's connection to the Midianites takes on greater significance. When Balak reacted in fury because of the seer's betrayal of his mission to curse Israel, Balaam's speech presents himself in an arresting fashion. He expresses sentiments that amount, in effect, to an apology to the king. Balaam indicates that he would have been happy to carry out the Midianite wishes and deliver a curse upon the Israelites, but the power of God held him in its grip and required him to carry out the divine will.[27] This reaffirms Josephus' earlier depiction of Balaam as one who sympathized with the Midianites.[28] Indeed Balaam himself, not Balak as the Bible has it, suggested a second attempt to persuade God to endorse a hex upon the Israelites.[29]

That Balaam spouts the words of God's will receives strong emphasis in Josephus' version. Balaam's speeches, as composed by the historian, invoke God's providence bestowed upon Israel, and are characterized as infusion of the divine spirit which dictated the message.[30] Yet Balaam is a conflicted soul. He had not yet abandoned the idea of advancing the interests of the Midianites. After a third failure, the frustrated and furious Balak dismissed the prophet without remuneration. But, in still another reversal, the prophet, already on his way, turned back to offer Balak yet a new suggestion that might reap some success, even if it violates the wishes of the Lord.[31] The seer still endeavors to reconcile the irreconcilable motivations. Josephus evidently sought to provide a more vivid tale than the Scriptures present. His Balaam grapples with two clashing pressures, allegiance to the Midianites and demands of the deity. The inner struggle dominates. Balaam is manipulated by God but persists to the end in attempts to implement his allegiance to the Midianites.

26. Jos. *AJ*, 4:107-111. On the deception and Balaam's bafflement, see 4:107: ὁ δ' οὐχ ὑπολαβὼν ἀπάτῃ ταῦτα τὸν θεὸν κακελευκένι συναπῄει τοῖς πρέσβεσι.

27. Jos. *AJ*, 4:120-121: ἥν τέ μοι δι' εὐχῆς μηδὲν ἀδικήσαιί σου τὴν ἐπιθυμίαν. κρείττων δὲ ὁ θεὸς ὢν ἐγὼ χαρίζεσθαι διεγνώκειν. Cf. 4:118.

28. Jos. *AJ*, 4:103, 4:105, 4:107.

29. Jos. *AJ*, 4:123. Cf. Num. 23:13-14.

30. Jos. *AJ*, 4:114-122. Cf. Num. 22:9.

31. Jos. *AJ*, 4:126-127: παρὰ βούλησιν τοῦ θεοῦ χαρίσασθαι ὑμῖν.

The final turnabout puts the seer in the spotlight. After three fruitless attempts to sway God through smoking altars, Balaam proposes a very different approach. Josephus here introduces the episode of the young Midianite women prostituting themselves to deflect Israelite youths from the worship of Yahweh to reverence of alien idols. It receives mention in just a single line in the Bible but is given a lengthy narrative by the historian, longer indeed than Philo's account. The historian here abandons the Bible altogether to deliver the alternative version.[32]

In Josephus' narrative, the seer acknowledges that the Hebrews cannot suffer defeat by war or calamity because of the protection of God, but his scheme for seduction and conversion would do the trick. God's ire would be directed against the lapsed Hebrews.[33] Josephus proceeds to unfold the dramatic tale. The Midianite women do indeed successfully seduce the Israelite men, reduce them to despair by preparing to depart, and then with impressive rhetorical skills gain their agreement to abandon the laws of their fathers and embrace the full-blown polytheism of the gentiles. The episode reaches a climax in the dramatic confrontation between the renegade Israelite Zambrias and Moses, and then culminates in the death of Zambrias at the hands of the zealous patriot Phinehas, whose deed inspired his fellow Hebrews to massacre all the Hebrew transgressors, with the sanction of the Lord.[34]

Josephus has thus appended the episode of seductive women, impressionable youths, apostasy, and divine vengeance, with due rhetorical flourishes, to the blander tale in Numbers and in much fuller fashion than Philo. He had no qualms about inserting a lively story that improved on the original.[35] And he rounded out his recital, most interestingly, by bringing Balaam back in at the end. In his final paragraph, Josephus shows a noteworthy respect for the seer. He observes that Moses himself incorporated Balaam's prophecies in his work (the Pentateuch) without rewriting or claiming them as his own. Balaam, despite a divided personality, remained a figure of substance. Josephus thus wrapped up his tale by reminding readers, who may have been entranced by the seduction fable and Phineas' dramatic act, that Balaam had set it all in motion by his scheme to annihilate the Israelites, even after failing to deliver a curse upon them. He thereby gave coherence to the narrative as a whole.[36] And he ends with a cautious caveat: let readers judge these matters as seems best.[37]

Josephus has not smoothed out all of the bumps. But the historian's version gives more life to Balaam, puts the intents of the divine in question, endeavors to

---

32. Num. 25:1; Jos. *AJ*, 4:126-158.

33. Jos. *AJ*, 4:126-130.

34. Jos. *AJ*, 4:131-155. On this narrative, see van Unnik (1974), 241–261.

35. The biblical version alludes only to whoring with the daughters of Moab. And it does provide the story of Phinehas, but without any connection to the Balaam periscope; Num. 25:1-18.

36. Jos. *AJ*, 4:157. Cf. Feldman (2000), 385. See the interpretation of Balaam in Josephus, with very different emphasis, in Lester (2018), 89–99.

37. Jos. *AJ*, 4:158: καὶ ταῦτα μὲν ὡς ἂν αὐτοῖς τισι δοκῇ οὕτω σκοπείτωσαν. This is a caveat which Josephus often employs in his writings; see Feldman (2000), 39, n. 271.

resolve certain problems, expands freely with non-biblical material, and provides a generally more successful recasting of the original.

The mixed messages of the Balaam pericope in Numbers reappear in Ps-Philo's *Liber Antiquitatum Biblicarum*. The author eschews the one-sided denigration of the seer by Philo. But he does not endeavor to clear up some of the riddles that Josephus tackles. In his compact recapitulation, he leaves the complexities of character intact, refrains from exercising judgment, and, while offering some nuances, presents as entangled a tableau as the biblical account.[38]

Ps-Philo's introduction of Balaam departs almost immediately from the Bible and provides a novel perspective upon the soothsayer. After Balak asks him to curse the Israelites, the prophet does more than merely consult God. He already knows the ways of the Lord without inquiring. His speech in *LAB*, which owes nothing to the Bible, declares that Balak is ignorant of the world's governance: God's plan is not that of men; the divine will govern all; the spirit of the Lord is bestowed only for a time.[39] This is remarkable self-awareness on Balaam's part. Even before he consults God, he knows that whatever mantic powers he may possess stem directly from divine inspiration—and only for a limited period. This immediately gives Balaam more substance than the baffled and confused mantic of Numbers of whom Josephus tried to make sense or the one-dimensional villain of Philo. *LAB* offers insight also into the peculiar question posed to the seer by God, "who are the men who have come to you?" How could the omniscient deity not know? Ps-Philo has Balaam see through it right away. He even rebukes the Lord for posing a test to humans when he knew everything that would happen in the world before he founded it.[40] Balaam again emerges as a figure of some substance.

The Lord also receives a dimension denied him in Numbers. Instead of merely issuing an order to Balaam that he refrain from any curse upon a people whom God has blessed, he reminds him of the promises made to Abraham and Jacob and even cites the tale of Jacob's wrestling with the angel.[41] Yahweh thus offers explanation rather than abrupt directive. And he interestingly elaborates upon his own rationale. He adds the acute question: "if you curse those whom I have chosen, who will be left to bless you?"[42] Ps-Philo has produced a brief but pointed dialogue,

---

38. The dense and detailed commentary of Jacobson (1996), 575–611, remains indispensable on all textual matters. Van Ruiten's article (2008), 101–130, supplies a valuable comparative table that juxtaposes the scriptural narrative to *LAB*, thus giving a handy view of omissions and additions. But his analysis focuses too heavily on which passages present Balaam positively or negatively. That oversimplifies the objectives of the writer.

39. *LAB*, 18:3: *nescit quoniam non ita est consilium Dei sicut consilium hominis. Ipse autem non novit, quoniam spiritus qui nobis datus est in tempore datus est, vie autem nostre non sunt directe nisi velit Deus.*

40. *LAB*, 18:4. *Ut quid Domine temptas genus hominum ? Hi ergo non possunt sustinere, quoniam tu plus scis que habentur in seculo antequam fundares illud.*

41. *LAB*, 18:5-6.

42. *LAB*, 18:6: *Quod si maledixeris eos, quis erit qui benedicet te?*

unmoored in the Bible, that shows both deity and seer to advantage, a marked improvement over the original.

The next scene gains further meaning in the author's hands. Balak urges the soothsayer to try again and Balaam generously consents, but in entirely clear-eyed fashion. The Scriptures have him proclaim assertively that he will take no bribe from the king, even if he should offer all the gold and silver in his household, yet he goes on a second try anyway. This makes little sense. But Ps-Philo endeavors to give it some meaning. Balaam's response to the ministers of the king minces no words. He asserts that Balak is like a fool who is unaware that he is actually dwelling among the dead.[43] Just exactly what this means is somewhat obscure, but, at the very least, Balaam makes clear that such a mission, requested by one who is out of touch with reality, would be fruitless. He nonetheless asks the envoys to spend the night while he seeks confirmation from Yahweh.[44] Ps-Philo thus portrays a prophet who courteously respects Balak's wishes, but is perceptive and fully knowledgeable about the anticipated outcome.

The perspective of God is not quite so intelligible. He endorses Balaam's second voyage to the king of Moab, but warns that the trip will be a stumbling-block and will presage the ruin of Balak.[45] The ways of the Lord remain mysterious. Just why he now puts Balaam to the test of the talking donkey is unexplained. Ps-Philo mentions the episode (he could hardly avoid it), but brushes past it in three quick sentences, omitting almost all of its details.[46] It did not fit with his narrative.

The Lord now abandons all subterfuge and trickery. He infuses Balaam with the divine spirit that issues potent pronouncements through his mouth. God's protection for Israel is unshakeable, and his omnipotence will shatter the kingdom of Balak, whose ignorance and presumption only hastened his own destruction.[47] Balaam's hopeful effort to balance his deference to Balak with his obedience to God has now collapsed. The seer himself has come to a sharper self-awareness, indeed blames himself for having complied with Balak's wishes at all, thus shortening his own life because the spirit of God within him is now waning.[48] The prophet can freely forecast doom for Moab but berates himself for having been led astray and violated what had been communicated to him.[49] All this represents Ps-

---

43. *LAB*, 18:8: *Ecce insipiens est filius Sephor, et nescit quoniam inhabitat in gyro mortuorum*. On the problems with the text, see Jacobson (1996), 590–591, although he implausibly opts for the reading *inscipiens*, instead of *insipiens*.

44. *LAB*, 18:8.

45. *LAB*, 18:8: *erit via tua in scandalum, et ipse Balac erit in perditionem*.

46. *LAB*, 18:9.

47. *LAB*, 18:10. The text reads *non permansit in eo spiritus Dei*. But that surely cannot stand. Balaam's declarations to the king plainly express the thoughts of Yahweh, as is clear from 18:11; cf. Numb. 24:2. See also Jacobson (1996), 594–595.

48. *LAB*, 18:11: *quia modicum mihi superset sancti spiritus qui manet in me, quoniam cognovi et per quod suasus sum a Balac, perdidi tempus vitae meae*.

49. *LAB*, 18:11-12.

Philo's expansion of the biblical narrative, which provided little more than Balaam's oracular declarations from God and nothing of his self-reflections.

Ps-Philo has created a sympathetic portrait of Balaam, a more rounded figure than in Numbers, certainly not the pure villain presented by Philo, nor the conflicted soul of Josephus' presentation who would have preferred to curse than bless. The Balaam of *LAB* sought to appease Balak, a fatal error, but never swerved from allegiance to the Lord. He was himself thwarted by the divine will and had to confess his own liability—even though the text had not hitherto suggested it. God's own actions, enigmatic and less than praiseworthy in the Bible, remain no less so in *LAB*. The manipulation of Balaam, though not quite as blatant as in the other texts, leaves God's motives similarly opaque.

Ps-Philo concludes the pericope, somewhat surprisingly, with Balaam's regrettably wicked advice to Balak to send beautiful Moabite and Midianite daughters to lure Israelites into idolatry thus to insure their defeat.[50] This seems out of character for the persona whom *LAB* has created. One can only suggest that this finale, unauthorized by the biblical narrative but regularly fostered in other retellings, had become a fixture in the tradition and could not be ignored by Ps-Philo. It can hardly be taken as the pivot for *LAB*'s whole understanding of the seer.[51] The author has taken an independent line from the earlier versions, and, even in a shorter compass, has offered a fuller and more engrossing portrait of Balaam.

A few other references to Balaam occur in the Hebrew Bible. But each is quite brief, not part of a narrative. They speak to his subsequent reputation in various ways. In three texts he is simply a soothsayer hired to curse the chosen people and turned by the Lord into providing a blessing.[52] Elsewhere his death is recorded, evidently as a deserved end.[53] A single passage gives him some agency: Balaam responds to Balak that the Lord will reveal his bounties.[54] None of these constitutes anything like a retelling of the tale. But they do indicate the resonance that the tale continued to have as an exemplar of gentile resistance to the Hebrew resettlement and of the power of Yahweh to protect his people.[55]

---

50. *LAB*, 18.13-14.

51. Jacobson's claim (1996), 611, that *LAB*'s representation of Balaam is fundamentally a negative one and renders him a villain is quite unwarranted. Vermes (1973), 173–177, rightly sees it as a more favorable judgment, but his interpretation of *LAB*'s Balaam as a tragic hero goes too far. See Feldman (1971), cf. Murphy (1993), 84.

52. Deut. 23:4-6. Josh. 23:9-10; Neh. 13:2.

53. Num. 31:8; Josh. 13:22.

54. Micah, 6:5. One other text makes reference to Balak, but without mention of Balaam; Judges, 11:25.

55. Noort (2008), 3–23, does his best to find threads that run through these brief references in passing and discerns a gradual darkening of the picture of Balaam as villain. A fuller exposition but with similar interpretation occurs in Robker (2019), 207–253. But the few scraps do not readily lend themselves to a diachronic interpretation. A single allusion to Balaam appears in Revelation, 2:14, but it refers to the seer's advice to Balak to induce the

The figure of Balaam was a fascinating but frustrating one for those writers who took up the narrative. The Scriptures had left a tale full of puzzles. The motivations both of the prophet and the Lord begged for answers that the authors of Numbers failed to provide. Philo sought to narrow Balaam to a single dimension, a purveyor of evil, and links the story to another episode that underscores his villainy, thus rendering him still less worthy but more intelligible. Josephus provides a more involved analysis of both prophet and deity and delivers a lengthy, more thoughtful, and more provocative rendition. Ps-Philo has yet a different, generally agreeable, depiction of Balaam, though a less successful effort to pierce the puzzles of God. The stimulus provided by the biblical rendition is clear, and the results correspondingly provocative.

Israelites into illicit sex and idolatry, which is attached to the account in Philo and Josephus, but is not part of the narrative in Numbers. Cf. on this van Henten (2008), 247–263; Lester (2018), 41–48. Two other brief mentions in the New Testament turn up in 2 Peter, 2. 15–16 and Jude, 11, noting Balaam's greed for gain, with 2 Peter adding that he was thwarted by the talking donkey and his own irrationality. The absence of any further context in these passages indicates that the story was widely known and required no elaboration.

Chapter 13

YAEL AND THE DEATH OF SISERA

A grisly and gruesome scene occurs in a central narrative of the Book of Judges. The overall setting is the struggle of Israelites to establish themselves in the land of Canaan against determined foes designated as Canaanites or Amorites. The rulership of the embattled Israelites passed from hand to hand in this era of the "judges," a succession of military commanders, tribal chiefs, prophets, priests, political leaders, and heroic warriors. At some point power came into the hands of a woman, the redoubtable Deborah, a prophetess who was enlisted as judge to head the nation. She called to her side the military man Barak to head the forces and conduct warfare against the Canaanite enemy and their commander Sisera. The response was a rather surprising one. Barak was willing to take up the cause, but only if Deborah would share the martial responsibilities with him. Deborah seemed somewhat taken aback but agreed to the joint command, though not without a warning. The prophetess predicted that God would indeed deliver Sisera into the hands of the Israelites, but any credit would not redound to Barak, rather to a woman.[1]

The biblical account proceeds to the climactic episode. Deborah and Barak jointly led Israelite forces, ten thousand of them, with Deborah issuing the orders. Sisera could muster nine hundred chariots and a large army, but the Israelite advance threw him into a panic. The Canaanite general abandoned his chariot and fled on foot. Barak's men pursued the chariots and soldiers of the enemy, eventually slaying every last one of them. Sisera himself sought refuge in the tent of a certain Yael, a Kenite of a clan sympathetic to the Israelites. Yael graciously (so it seemed) welcomed Sisera into her tent, reassuring him that he need not fear and covering him with a blanket. At his request for a drink of water, she supplied instead some milk and covered him again. Sisera, obviously still in a most anxious state, asked Yael to stand at the entrance to the tent and to deny to inquirers that anyone was within. When Sisera had fallen asleep from exhaustion, Yael took a sharpened tent peg, crept up to him stealthily, and hammered the peg through his temple with such force that it reached to the ground, thus killing him instantly. Barak arrived at that time in pursuit of Sisera, only to be greeted by the triumphant Yael who

---

1. Judges, 4:1-9.

showed him the man he sought—lying on the ground with a tent peg through his skull.²

This repugnant tale appears twice in the Book of Judges, first in the prose version summarized above, then followed directly by a poetic rendition as part of the celebratory hymn, the "Song of Deborah." The second is briefer, but adds a noteworthy coda. It includes a rather poignant scene which has Sisera's mother, peering out her window, awaiting his arrival, and wondering what delayed him. Her friends sought to reassure her by suggesting that he and his troops must be dividing the spoils of their victory. That closing verse of Deborah's song thus delivers a final irony.³

The Israelites had therefore gained a grand victory, celebrated in prose and poetry. Yet for some readers it may well have left a bitter taste. The Israelite captain Barak does not come off particularly well. His courage and confidence leave something to be desired. He declines the job of leading his troops unless he can share the command with a woman. That would not likely inspire admiration in his cultural world. Although the Israelite troops, under joint leadership, wipe out the enemy, leaving not a soul alive, Barak's hunt for his Canaanite counterpart Sisera ends in some ignominy since another woman, Yael, had anticipated him in finishing off the Canaanite. Yael's ironic retort to Barak, "I will show you the man you are looking for," can only have increased his discomfiture.

Yael herself, despite the claim in Deborah's song that she is "most blessed of women," seems well short of that laudable distinction. Sisera evidently had reason to expect a friendly reception when seeking asylum in her tent. And she led him on with guile and deceit, offering promise of safety and comfort, only to lull him to sleep and then execute him in ghastly fashion.⁴ Those actions cast a shadow on Yael's character.

The troublesome aspects of the story were evidently recognized by Ps-Philo, the author of *Liber Antiquitatum Biblicarum*. His version elaborated on the original, shifted its emphasis, and produced a more agreeable portrait of its characters. The narrative opens with Deborah's summoning of Barak to do battle with Sisera, as if it were individual combat. But, notably, Ps-Philo omits Barak's plea that Deborah join him on the battlefield, or else he would not enter the fray. The general betrays no reluctance.⁵ Deborah then proceeds to set the coming contest in terms of a

---

2. Judges, 4:10-22.
3. Judges, 5:24-30.
4. The author's attitude toward Yael is, at best, ambivalent. For different views on the presentation of her character, see Bellis (1994), 119–123, with references. Others have found sexual implications in the texts, notably in the Song of Deborah's reference to Sisera's falling between Yael's legs; Judges, 5:27. On possible sexual allusions, see Niditch (1999), 305–315; Jackson (2012), 105–111.
5. *LAB*, 31.1. There may be a hint of the biblical version in Deborah's encouragement of Barak to "gird your loins like a man," but the text pointedly leaves out Barak's insistence that he would not go to battle without Deborah.

heavenly clash and to prophesy the outcome as orchestrated and predetermined by God. Whereas the Lord makes no actual appearance in the biblical account, the *LAB* presents him as the mover of all events, the actions by the principals dictated by his will. Deborah announces that the stars themselves are on the side of the Israelites, moving in their course to thwart the chariots of Sisera and foil his wicked plans. God, of course, directs their path. And when fighting commenced, the Lord ordered the stars to intervene, with the consequence that Sisera's whole army was burned up in the conflagration—almost nine million of them![6] In recasting the reference to Yael in the Song of Deborah, Ps-Philo gives full credit to Yahweh. It was he who commanded the stars to leave their posts in the sky and burn to death the enemies of Israel. Yael finished off Sisera, a source of great pride. But she had simply carried out the will of the Lord.[7]

The Book of Judges' depiction of Sisera is a surprisingly neutral one. He heads the armies of the enemy, to be sure. Yet he is far from a formidable figure, nor even an especially evil one. When his troops faced the Israelite multitudes, he panicked, fled by foot, and headed straight for Yael's tent where he was greeted warmly, easily duped, and treacherously slain. Ps-Philo, by contrast, ascribes dastardly schemes to Sisera. The Canaanite leader had in mind a division of spoils in which he would take captive for himself the most beautiful of the women to serve as his concubines. This naturally adds a further sting to the narrative, for the author adds that Sisera will be felled by the hands of a woman and the spoils from his camp would be confiscated by the very girls whom he had expected to carry off.[8]

The encounter between Yael and Sisera also takes on more vivid coloration in the hands of Ps-Philo. Yael does not simply welcome Sisera with duplicitous hospitality. She takes pains to make herself as alluring and seductive as possible (much as in the tale of Judith and Holofernes), she sprinkles rose petals on the bed, she has Sisera sleep while she goes out to her herd and personally milks a cow to bring fresh drink to her guest, and, in the course of it, explains to God in detail her plan for inducing sleep upon Sisera and then killing him. But she needs some reassurance. Evidently her conviction that she is carrying out God's will is less than ironclad, and she asks for a divine signal to authenticate the propriety of her deed—which she gets.[9] She can now make sure of a second and deeper sleep by Sisera through mixing some wine with the milk (another parallel with the Judith story).[10] Ps-Philo also drags out the death scene, with Yael communicating once more with God, asking him for adequate strength, and requesting yet another sign before she goes ahead with the fatal blow. Sisera, like an operatic character in death throes, still has a final exchange with his slayer. The fallen commander fittingly exclaims that he is dying like a woman, and Yael rubs it in by suggesting that he

---

6. *LAB*, 31:1-2.
7. *LAB*, 32:11-12.
8. *LAB*, 31:1. Cf. Jacobson (1996), II, 844–845.
9. *LAB*, 31:3-5.
10. *LAB*, 31:6. Cf. Gen. 24, with Jacobson (1996), I, 852–853.

report to his father in the underworld that he had fallen victim to a woman.[11] *LAB* includes also the biblical coda, the scene with Sisera's mother, who awaits her son's triumphant return, but makes the irony a bit more pointed by having her anticipate the arrival of Sisera with daughters of the Hebrews who would become his concubines. And the author adds a final touch by having Barak, who had just praised Yael's deed as the work of the Lord, cut off Sisera's head and send it to his mother—spoils of war, but not the ones she had expected.[12]

Ps-Philo thus keeps faithfully to the gist of the biblical narrative. But the alterations, however slight, supply some significant nuances, and the embellishments provide a more engrossing and more vibrant tableau. The author makes Sisera both more villainous and more pathetic than in the biblical version, thereby implying greater justification for his fate. Barak, who seems rather weak and confesses his own dependency upon Deborah in the Book of Judges, is somewhat relieved of that disturbing deficiency by Ps-Philo, who leaves out his self-deprecating remarks. And he concludes his tale by having Barak sever the head of Sisera and deliver it to his mother with a fitting flourish. Yael still entraps Sisera, but the author fills out her designs with details of craftiness and manipulation that supply a more vivid and even theatrical picture. And, most significantly, the emphasis on the divine management of the characters and the events diminishes the culpability of the Israelite figures for distasteful actions. The Lord had planned it all for the sake of his chosen people.

Josephus offers an abbreviated account of this episode, with only minor changes. He evades most of the problematic aspects embedded in the scriptural version. But his narrative does offer a slightly different angle. God is there from the beginning. When Deborah summons Barak to take up arms against the foe, she exclaims that God had willed it and had promised victory. Barak's reply that he would not take up the cause unless Deborah shared the command, however, drew a rebuke from the prophetess. The Bible has Deborah warn Barak that, with a joint command, the glory for the fall of Sisera would go to a woman. Josephus sharpens the point by having Deborah express irritation at Barak for resigning sole generalship to share it with a woman, even while she accepts the proposition.[13] The expression may reflect Josephus' own indignation at Barak's timidity, unworthy of an Israelite captain of the host. Unlike Ps-Philo, Josephus is not interested in salvaging Barak's reputation. On the contrary. Whereas the scriptural account has Barak sally forth to battle on Deborah's prompting, Josephus has him panicked by the size of the enemy's forces and prepared to retreat until Deborah orders him to engage in combat that very day on the promise of divine assistance.[14] The contest itself, won handily by Barak in the Bible, was decided largely from above in Josephus' version. Not stars, as in *LAB*, but great winds and rainstorms in the face of the Canaanites

---

11. *LAB*, 31:7.
12. *LAB*, 31:8-9. Cf. Murphy (1993), 143.
13. Jos. *AJ*, 5:202-203. Cf. Judges, 4:8-9.
14. Jos. *AJ*, 5:204.

were instrumental in delivering the victory. Barak gets no credit.[15] Josephus presents the demise of Sisera at Yael's hand swiftly and curtly, with no embroidery.[16] The story, with its somewhat disagreeable features, was not one that Josephus elected to dwell on. He was evidently disturbed by Barak's hesitancy and ostensible cowardice and thus heightened Deborah's exasperation with him.[17] He gave short shrift to the Yael episode, which he may have found distasteful. Josephus appears eager to get on with more satisfactory narratives.

The two variants on the biblical narrative by *LAB* and Josephus illustrate the divergent approaches that Jewish authors confidently took in rewriting scripture. The original tale had its disturbing aspects. Ps-Philo chose to present Barak in a somewhat more favorable light, to stress the unsavory character of Sisera, and to provide a fuller and more engrossing portrait of Yael. Josephus, evidently discontent with elements of the tale, amplified, rather than diminished, Barak's flaws, and passed over Yael's craft and deceptiveness in a hurry. And both authors gave principal credit to the designs of the Lord. The biblical story remained intact, but the recastings gave it their own seasonings.

---

15. Jos. *AJ*, 5:205-206.
16. Jos. *AJ*, 5:207-208.
17. Josephus does, however, record the death of the Canaanite king as an accomplishment of Barak; *AJ*, 5:209, although the Bible speaks only of an Israelite victory; Judges, 4:23-24.

Chapter 14

JEPHTHAH AND HIS DAUGHTER

The wrenching tale of Jephthah and his daughter leaves a poignant and painful impact. It occupies a single chapter in the book of Judges but its resonance was meaningful and memorable. In the biblical account Jephthah had gained significant renown as a warrior but carried some genealogical baggage. He was son of a prostitute and when his father's legitimate sons grew to adulthood they drove him out of the household and denied him any rights of inheritance. Jephthah consequently dwelled in an unsavory location and surrounded himself with desperados. But at a time of dire need for the Israelites in Gilead, the nation facing a war with the Ammonites, its leaders called upon Jephthah, with his martial reputation, to lead them into battle. The disgruntled warrior reminded the elders of Gilead that they had endorsed his banishment from his father's household, but expressed willingness to command the forces, provided that they name him not just captain of the host but head of the entire community of Gilead. The elders accepted the bargain, and Jephthah exchanged tense communications with the Ammonite king over which people had a legitimate claim on the land in dispute. Once they broke down, Jephthah readied for the contest. Before engaging, however, he uttered a vow to God, promising that if he should gain victory, he would sacrifice to him as a burnt offering whatever came first out of the door of his house after his victorious return. That vow proved to be fateful. Once Jephthah returned in triumph, the first to emerge from the door with timbrels and dances was his beloved virginal daughter and only child. The totally distraught Jephthah could do nothing more than tear his garments, berate himself for the foolish vow, and acknowledge that the pledge had to be honored. His daughter willingly submitted herself to the sacrifice as the vowed recompense to the Lord, asking only that she be allotted two months in the mountains in the company of her nubile companions to mourn the fact that she will die a virgin. Her father granted that last wish and, after two months, performed the fatal deed. The event would be commemorated annually through lamentations by the daughters of Israel.[1]

The biblical text provides almost no comment on this grim tale. Jephthah castigates himself for having made the vow once he sees his daughter emerge from the house, but does not question his obligation to fulfill the promise. And the

---

1. Judges, 11:1-40.

daughter (the text never gives her name) accepts her fate unquestioningly. She bemoans the fact that she will die as a maiden, and that lamentable outcome gains commemoration in an annual lament. But the issue of justice or righteousness does not arise. The ostensible scriptural parallel that springs to mind, the would-be sacrifice of Isaac by Abraham, is far from a perfect fit. The aqedah constituted an express test by God of Abraham's devotion and adherence to divine command. Isaac plays a purely passive and unknowing role. And Abraham's undeviating loyalty to the divine averts an unhappy fate.[2] Jephthah's sacrifice of his daughter was the straightforward carrying out of the warrior's oath and an active acquiescence by the maiden. However anguished readers may feel, the biblical author refrains from passing judgment.

Josephus' version of the story closely follows the biblical presentation. But not altogether. In Josephus' narrative, Jephthah does not censure himself for having uttered the fatal vow but blames his daughter for undue haste in coming to meet him![3] And the historian allows himself a brief but pointed reflection that contrasts sharply with the biblical writer's reticence. He branded the deed as unlawful and displeasing to God. And he adds that Jephthah failed to take into account the possible consequences of his vow or to ponder how it would be perceived by those who learned of it.[4] Josephus, evidently dissatisfied with the absence of a moral verdict on Jephthah in the biblical tale, did not withhold judgment. He took the liberty of adding an important dimension to the received text.

The gripping story of Jephthah and his daughter reappears in Ps-Philo's *Liber Antiquitatum Biblicarum*.[5] The author adopts the outline of the narrative conveyed by the Bible but expands upon it liberally and recasts it to his own purposes. He inserts vivid dialogues that enliven the tale, he elevates the role and centrality of the daughter, and he makes God a major character in the drama.[6]

The expulsion of Jephthah, and then his restoration to command his people against the forces of Ammon, recur in the *LAB*. The events are driven, however, by Jephthah's brothers. They banish him out of envy, not because of his bastard birth, and they, not the elders of the land, take the lead in persuading him to return in a pointed exchange. The brothers resorted to the ploy, familiar from the Book of Esther, that Jephthah had been spared precisely for the purpose of leading his people to victory. Jephthah's sharp rejoinder questions their sudden change of

---

2. Gen. 22. A closer parallel, of course, is Agamemnon's sacrifice of his daughter Iphigenia, a legend most vividly recorded by Euripides' *Iphigenia in Aulis*. Many have noted this. See, e.g., Römer (1998), 27–38; Gnuse (2021), 150–164. It does not follow that the biblical author found his inspiration in Euripides' tragedy.

3. Jos. *AJ*, 5:264.

4. Jos. *AJ*, 5:265.

5. See the brief but insightful analysis by Alexander (1988), 108–111, whose suggestion that Ps-Philo sought to create a national epic, however, goes too far.

6. The magisterial commentary by Jacobson (1996), 945–977, is an indispensable guide. See also the summary and analysis by Murphy (1993), 162–169. Alexander (1988), 108–111, provides a brief analysis of literary elaborations in *LAB*'s treatment of the Jephthah story.

heart, their shift from hatred to love, and the dialogue proceeds with contrasting arguments about the intentions of God. The brothers, in seeking to deflect Jephthah's wrath, remind him of God's own history of punishing Israelite sinners and then showing mercy, thus a model for Jephthah to emulate. But Jephthah supplies a clever retort: God has infinite opportunity to choose time and place for release of suffering and exercise of forgiveness, but mere mortals do not have that luxury.[7] Nothing like this occurs in the biblical version. Jephthah there simply bargains for his appointment as chief of the nation. Ps-Philo introduces theological argumentation, thus supplying a quite different character to the episode. Jephthah yields to the Israelites' entreaty after prayers to the Lord by the entire populace. His role thus transcends that of renowned military warrior. He becomes champion of God's law against idolatrous Ammonites.[8] The repartee between Jephthah and the Ammonite king before battle in the Book of Judges concerns itself solely with the issue of which people have legitimate claim on the land. In *LAB*, however, the exchange between the leaders includes a contrast between the God of Israel and the inferior deities of Ammon who are no gods at all. Here again Ps-Philo underscores a clash between rival theologies.

God himself is no mere distant deity but an active player in the drama. When Jephthah exclaimed that, if he were vouchsafed victory over the Ammonites, he would provide a burnt offering to the Lord of the first who comes to meet him, that did not sit well with God. He burst out with anger, denouncing the vow of Jephthah: "What if the first creature he encounters is a dog? Will he offer up a dog to me?" The divine wrath expressed itself unequivocally. God determined to have the vow fulfilled, but the victim would be fruit of Jephthah's loins, his first born and only child. And he added that he would indeed free the Israelites from their enemies, but only because of the prayers of his chosen people—and not because of Jephthah.[9] The biblical version is rather bland by comparison. Ps-Philo brought the Lord of Israel back on stage as orchestrator of the fatal finale.

The daughter of Jephthah also emerges as a full-blown figure. Ps-Philo even gives her a name, Seila, which the biblical author saw no need to do. Her encounter with her father after learning of his vow gains but a brief exchange in the Bible: Jephthah bewails his oath but cannot reverse it; she simply concurs. The *LAB* adds poignancy and intensity. Jephthah bemoans the very name of Seila which heralded an eventual sacrifice. His decision itself was not foredoomed, for he weighed his heart and his soul in the scales, the one being his joy in victory and the other his grief in the potential death of his only child. He chose the latter as inevitable, but the agonizing over alternatives underscores the passion that is absent in the biblical model.[10]

7. *LAB*, 39:1-5.
8. *LAB*, 39:6-7.
9. *LAB*, 39:11: *Ego autem liberans liberabo populum meum in isto tempore, non pro eo sed pro oratione quam oravit Israel.*
10. *LAB*, 40:1: *Et nunc quis dabit cor meum in statera et animam in pondere, et stabo et videbo quis preponderabit, utrum epulatio que facta est an tristicia que contingit mihi?*

Seila's speech too augments the emotion and expands on the meaning of the episode. She emerges not just as one who accepts her fate, but as a source of reassurance to her father of the deeper significance of the event. She declares that her death counts for far less than the liberty of her people which it has brought about. And she proudly recalls to mind the aqedah when Isaac willingly consented to be sacrificed in order to fulfill the will of God, a moving model for her own acquiescence in her fate.[11] Ps-Philo here massages the biblical account, for Isaac is there as an unwitting actor in the drama. Seila, by contrast, is a forceful figure in the *LAB*. She insists that Jephthah not deviate from his vow. She stresses that her sacrifice is a voluntary one, thus evincing no sadness, she recognizes that her father was trapped by his promise, and she offers yet another rationale for reassurance: if she had resisted her fate, it might have been unacceptable to God and her death would be in vain.[12]

Not that Seila is without regret. As in the Bible, she requests a postponement so that she can shed tears in the mountains together with her virginal friends. Indeed she anticipates accompanying laments from the beasts of the fields and even the trees.[13] Ps-Philo once again gives God a central role in the narrative, unanticipated by the Scriptures. He has Seila consult with the sages of the community, none of whom was capable of offering counsel, for the Lord had shut up their tongues. God proceeds to explain his own actions: he wanted no obstacle raised to the fulfillment of his plan. And he further pays tribute to Seila as wiser than her father, indeed wiser than all the sages, for the voluntary offering of her life will make her death forever precious in the eyes of the Lord.[14]

Seila's final speech constitutes the emotional climax. She freely pours out her lamentations to the hills and the rocks, reiterating that her death should not be in vain but should serve as a lesson to any father who might vow to sacrifice a daughter or any ruler who might promise to make an offering of his only child.[15] The Seila of *LAB* thus articulates the long-term implications of the deed more eloquently than any other participant in the drama, even God. She continues by underscoring, even as she reconfirms her decision, the root of her sorrow: the failure to enjoy the splendors of a wedding, the perfumes, oils, white gown, and bridal wreathe that would have marked her transition to full womanhood. She will mourn this loss together with her virgin companions, with the trees and beasts of the forest joining in her sorrow.[16] The episode closes, as in the Book of Judges, with Jephthah performing the fatal deed, the burial

---

11. *LAB*, 40:2.

12. *LAB*, 40:3.

13. *LAB*, 40:3. Jacobson, II (1996), 963, rightly notes the parallel in Vergil, *Ecl.* 10:50-69.

14. *LAB*, 40:4: *erit mors eius preciosa ante conspectum meum omni tempore*.

15. *LAB*, 40:5: *ut pater non epugnet filiam quam devovit sacrificare, ut princeps illius ungenitam audiat in sacrificio promissam*. On the difficulties in this passage and various efforts to resolve them, see Jacobson (1996), II, 970.

16. *LAB*, 40:6-7.

of Seila by the weeping virgins of the community, and the establishment of the annual commemoration.[17]

The author of the *LAB* has plainly woven a fuller tapestry than that provided by the biblical precursor. This constitutes no challenge to the original nor any distortion of its narrative, for Ps-Philo adopts it in outline. But he provides a much richer and deeper account, filling in the gaps with more vivid depictions of Seila and God, drawing out the theological overtones, and transforming the tale into a thoughtful and meaningful drama.

Both Josephus and Ps-Philo reproduced the story in their own way. Josephus added a moral judgment to a bare narrative, Ps-Philo expanded it boldly to produce a more extensive and more powerful tale. The heartbreaking story of Jephthah and his daughter moves to a different level of nuance and significance in the hands of the re-interpreters.

---

17. *LAB*, 40:8.

Chapter 15

SAMSON AS SUPERHERO

The familiar tale of the imposing but ill-fated Samson stands among the Bible's most memorable narratives. The character of Samson in the scriptural account, however, is a less than fully admirable one. This character presented an awkward dilemma for later retellings, wherein it took quite different shapes.

An annunciation scene heralded the birth of Samson, according to the Book of Judges. An angel or an emissary of God reported to a hitherto barren woman that she would conceive and produce a child, a scene reminiscent of comparable biblical episodes, as in the cases of Hagar, Sarah and Rebecca. In this case, the coming child is to be a holy man, a nazirite devoted to God from the womb. But, more than that, he is destined to take up the cause of the Israelites, who are currently under the oppression of the Philistines.[1] So a glorious future was in store for Samson, both as a man of God and as a warrior. But the biblical tale severely undercuts that prospect.

Samson's initial adventure involves neither his sacred mission as servant of the Lord nor his armed struggle with the Philistines. Instead, he became enamored of a Philistine woman, to the dismay of his parents. Over the objections of mother and father, who warned against consorting with Philistines, Samson insisted that he be given permission to wed the woman for no other reason than that "she is right for me." The strong-willed youth had his way, unaware that this was all part of God's plan to entangle the Israelites in a contest with their Philistine overlords.[2] The awesome strength of Samson, a superhero in the mold of a Hercules, showed itself immediately in the trip to claim his woman.[3] He tore apart a young lion with his bare hands. Events then speeded up. On a second trip, the wedding ensued, and thirty companions were assigned to Samson. The Israelite now posed a riddle to his Philistine associates, offering the rich reward of fine garments for each if they solve it, and, if not, he would be the recipient of similar gifts. Samson's posture, in

---

1. Judges, 13:3-7.
2. Judges, 14:1-4.
3. On parallels between the Samson story and Greek legends regarding Herakles, often noted, see, especially, Margalith (1987), 63–70; Gnuse (2021), 131–149. Efforts to construct influences from one direction or another, however, remain quite speculative.

other words, is not as brave warrior but as trickster hoping to show superiority over less clever Philistines. It is noteworthy, however, that the Israelite did not play fair. His riddle involved the slaying of the lion, an event they had not witnessed and could hardly imagine.[4] In fact, however, the Philistines outwit him by enlisting his new wife (through threats) to wheedle the answer of the riddle out of him, which she proceeds to do. Samson yielded to her importuning and revealed the solution, which she then transmitted to her countrymen, who triumphantly became victors in the riddling contest. The outcome not only stirred Samson's wrath but provoked use of his superpowers in the most damaging fashion. He immediately slew thirty Philistines in order to wreak vengeance.[5] Samson hardly emerges as an admirable figure.

The fury of the superhero only escalates from there. Samson failed to gain access to his wife and scorned the offer of a younger sister by her father. And he exercised his revenge upon the larger community of Philistines. Somehow he miraculously captured three hundred foxes, tied them up tail to tail with a torch between each and set them onto the Philistines' grain fields, olive groves, and vineyards to spread fire throughout. The tit-for-tat then had the Philistines in turn burn up Samson's erstwhile wife and father-in-law, thus justifying still further devastation by Samson, who struck his enemies "hip on thigh." The escalation continued. The Judahites preferred to avoid further conflict by binding Samson and turning him over to the Philistines. Samson deceptively went along with the plan but at the moment of falling into Philistine hands, he burst the bonds, conveniently found the jawbone of an ass, and clubbed no fewer than a thousand Philistines to death with it.[6] The Lord, to be sure, supplied the hero with his superpowers, but Samson consistently applied them with ruthlessness, vengefulness, and excess.[7]

The climax, as is well known, carries through with the same themes. Samson first consorted with a Philistine prostitute in Gaza, and when word reached the citizens of the town they sought to entrap and kill him, only to be thwarted when Samson simply pulled down the very gates of the city and transported them on his shoulders to the top of a mountain.[8] But the Herculean superhero succumbed once again to lust, this time with another Philistine, Delilah, who ultimately encompassed his demise. The story has her engage in wiles similar to those of his first Philistine bride. Under prodding (and the promise of substantial cash) from her fellow citizens, she endeavored to elicit from Samson the source of his immense physical power. Three times she thought that she got the right answer, but three times Samson deceived her with false responses, stirring her anger and intensifying her entreaties until he gave in and revealed the secret. The long tresses of the superman, a requirement for

4. Judges, 14:5-14.
5. Judges, 14:15-20.
6. Judges, 15:1-17.
7. The often insightful analysis of the Samson story by Leveen (2017), 85–106, puts perhaps too much weight on God's manipulation of events. The divine plan, to be sure, lurks behind the circumstances, but the Lord is not conspicuous in the narrative.
8. Judges, 16:1-3.

any nazirite, uncut since birth, contained the source of his potency. The game of deception vs. deception was finally over. The strongman who had so cleverly kept the root of his power under wraps was once more out-deceived.[9] Delilah snipped his locks when he slept, and Samson fell helpless into the hands of the Philistines, who gouged out his eyes and reduced him to a mere grinder of mill in a prison. They then imposed a further and devastating humiliation by having him put on some sort of performance in the temple of their god Dagon, an exhibit of the superiority of their deity to that of the Israelites. The symbolism of that culminating divine contest came to the fore when God answered Samson's prayer, breathed new life into him (some hair had grown back), and Samson pulled down the pillars of Dagon's proud temple, crushing to death more people than he had ever slain in his lifetime—including himself.[10] The biblical story concludes with a notable pronouncement not to be overlooked. Samson's poignant appeal to the Lord for the final infusion of strength did not come as a means to demonstrate the predominance of his deity over that of the Philistines. That may have been God's intent. But Samson expressed it only as a personal desire to settle scores for the loss of his sight.[11]

The will of the Lord was done. But his instrument was no saint. The exploits of the Herculean hero are rather less than gratifying. Samson is repeatedly motivated by lust rather than by principle. He engages in deception as well as brute force to gain his ends. But he is outfoxed by scheming women and by evil Philistines. And his slaughter of enemies attains colossal proportions. A certain obtuseness holds almost to the very end. The scriptural account has Samson, even after waking with hair shorn, unaware that his strength is gone and that God has abandoned him.[12] Samson is more brawn than brains. Not exactly a model to be emulated.

The questionable character of Samson presented a challenge for Josephus. The awesome champion of the Israelites against the oppressive Philistines was, in fact, a flawed figure. To Josephus' credit, the historian does not seek to blot out Samson's blemishes. What he does is something else altogether. He minimizes God's responsibility for them. God, of course, plays a key role in the scriptural story at its outset, with regard to the annunciation of Samson's birth and the expectation of his devotion to the deity as a faithful nazirite. Josephus follows this narrative, indeed elaborates upon it with emphasis on the beauty of Samson's mother and the jealousy of his father, thus to add some spice to the tale.[13] But the anticipation of a dutiful servant of the Lord pervades the opening segment. The Scriptures add that Samson received the divine blessing, and Josephus expresses this as heralding the life of a prophet.[14]

Samson, however, never suits the conventional prospect of the holy man. As the plot commences, he ignores his parents' warnings and wins the hand of a Philistine

---

9. Judges, 16:4-17.
10. Judges, 16:18-30.
11. Judges, 16:28.
12. Judges, 16:20.
13. Judges, 13; Jos. *AJ*, 5:276-285.
14. Judges, 13:24; Jos. *AJ*, 5:285.

maiden who has captured his fancy. The Bible notes that his parents were unaware of God's plan to entangle Samson with the girl, thus to set in motion the events that would ultimately lead to disaster for the Philistines, a point picked up by Josephus.[15] One might observe that Samson too was oblivious to the divine scheme, the first instance of his obtuseness. Erotic attraction alone motivated the hero, no aim to serve the interests of the Lord.

God, in fact, remains an occasional presence in the biblical account, but hardly surfaces in Josephus. Samson's Herculean feat of single-handedly tearing apart a young and aggressive lion was due to divine inspiration, according to the Bible. No such inspiration in Josephus: Samson did it on his own.[16] A similar contrast holds in the recounting of Samson's wreaking of vengeance after his riddle was solved through the betrayal of his new wife. The biblical version has him infused by the spirit of the Lord; Josephus leaves God out of it.[17] The historian seems to shrink from saddling God with responsibility for Samson's excesses.[18] When the superhero easily breaks the bonds placed on him by the Judahites, it is the Lord again who breathes spirit in him and the bonds simply fall apart if we follow the Book of Judges. Josephus, on the other hand, simply has him burst the bonds without outside help.[19]

The final episodes of the drama underscore the absence of God. When Samson awakes after the sleep in which Delilah has shaved off his hair, the biblical author pointedly notes that he fails to realize that God has abandoned him.[20] This not only offers another illustration of Samson's cluelessness, but also implicates God in his fate. Josephus omits this notice altogether.[21] For him, God is not a player here, whether in presence or absence. Samson's own foolishness brought about his end. When the blinded Samson gropes for the pillars that will bring the temple of Dagon down upon himself and thousands of Philistines, he calls upon the Lord to revive his strength just one more time so that he can have his revenge upon those who put out his eyes. So says the biblical narrative.[22] Nothing of this is in Josephus. For him, Samson is led into a Greek-style symposium to be mocked and jeered at by the guests, and he determines, without divine assistance, to avenge the mockery by removing the pillars and crushing his tormentors, himself with them.[23]

15. Judges, 14:4; Jos. *AJ*, 5:286.
16. Judges, 14:5-6; Jos. *AJ*, 5:287.
17. Judges, 14:19; Jos. *AJ*, 5:294.
18. Josephus does have Samson disingenuously claim that his slaughter with the jawbone came from his own valor rather than the fact of divine aid; Jos. *AJ*, 5:301. But the reference is to God's infusion of strength, not to his support of the deed.
19. Judges, 15:14; Jos. *AJ*, 5:300. Cf. Feldman (1998b), 471–472, 484.
20. Judges, 16:21.
21. In Josephus' version, when Samson gives away his secret to Delilah, he adds that he is under God's protection so long as his hair remains untouched. But the historian points out that, notwithstanding God, Samson's fate was already sealed; Jos. *AJ*, 5:312; cf. 5:306; Begg (2005), 78.
22. Judges, 16:28.
23. Jos. *AJ*, 5:314-316. Cf. Feldman (1998b), 485.

In one scene only does God take an active part, a rather odd and incongruous one. After Samson conducts his massacre of Philistines with the jawbone of an ass, he is afflicted with a mighty thirst. On that occasion, he acknowledges God's role in allowing him to slay multitudes of his foes, but he also issues a complaint: you gave me a great victory, but are now plaguing me with a deadly thirst that will deliver me into the hands of the uncircumcised Philistines. God responds by splitting a rock and providing a spring that refreshes the hero.[24] Just what this anomalous event has to do with the rest of the story is quite unclear. But Josephus duly repeats it and makes it the sole occasion on which Samson actually credits God with running the show. And that emerges only when Samson rebukes the Lord and elicits some action on his part. Until that point, Samson had brazenly boasted of his jawbone success without expressing any debt to the divine.[25] No other action of God appears in Josephus' text.

A telling fact deserves notice. After echoing the scriptural remark that the Lord set the entire course of events in motion, Josephus largely keeps him off stage. Samson's deeds, his successes, and his missteps are fundamentally his own doing. And, while his awesome physical power provides him with spectacular achievements, his susceptibility to women, his wildly disproportionate acts of cruelty, his resort to deception, and his repeated mental lapses deeply tarnish his character. This may help to explain why Josephus keeps God's interventions to a minimum, so as not to involve him too much with Samson's transgressions.

The transgressions, however, could not be gainsaid. Josephus maintained throughout his declared general policy of keeping to the text by recording all the key episodes that disclose Samson's questionable qualities.[26] But the historian strikingly seeks to rescue Samson's reputation at the conclusion of his narrative. His summary ascribes to the hero the features that compel admiration: bravery, strength, magnanimity at the end, and righteous wrath. This is hardly what one might have expected. Samson's flaws are here conveniently suppressed. Josephus has to admit Samson's vulnerability to feminine wiles, but he excuses it as a symptom of general human failing, quite minor when set next to his surpassing *arête*.[27]

24. Judges, 15:18.
25. Jos. *AJ*, 5:301-303.
26. That Josephus' narrative largely follows the biblical presentation is rightly noted by Roncace (2004), 185–207, as against Feldman (1998b), 461–489. But Roncace oddly fails to discuss the closing portion of Josephus' account, which is most glaringly at odds with the rest of his retelling.
27. Jos. *AJ*, 5:317: θαυμάζειν δὲ ἄξιον τῆς ἀρετῆς καὶ τῆς ἀρετῆς καὶ τῆς ἰσχύος καὶ τοῦ περὶ τὴν τελευτὴν μεγαλόφρονος τὸν ἄνδρα καὶ τῆς ὀργῆς τῆς μέχρι τοῦ τελευτᾶν πρὸς τοὺς πολεμίους καὶ τὸ μὲν ὑπὸ γυναικὸς ἁλῶναι δεῖ τῇ φύσει τῶν ἀνθρώπων προσάπτειν ἥττονι ἁμαρτημάτων οὔσῃ, μαρτυρεῖν δὲ ἐκείνῳ τὴν εἰς τὰ ἄλλα πάντα τῆς ἀρετῆς περιουσίαν. Begg (2005), 79, surprisingly, does not comment on Josephus' striking reversal here. Mason, in Feldman (2000), xxxii, ascribes it to a tendency in Josephus for balancing both good and bad qualities in characters who appear in his works.

The combination of omission and addition gives Josephus' narrative a decidedly different flavor from its precursor. By reducing the involvement of God, he relieves the deity of responsibility for Samson's vices and offenses. Whereas God determines the overall plot, Samson makes his own decisions, including the blunders, the ill-fated erotic entanglements, and the excessive butchery, none of which is imputed to God. Josephus' belated efforts to rescue the hero's reputation at the close soften the negative record, but do not erase that dominant narrative. In the end they stand as an unresolved anomaly.[28] But the arresting shift at the conclusion underscores the historian's willingness to compromise the impact of the sacred tale by leaving readers with an altogether different impression of the hero's character and quality. The admirable features of the superhero stand side by side with the unpleasant ones, leaving an awkward composite image. In this reconception Josephus complicates, even confounds, the Scriptures at the risk of leaving his readers at a loss.

Ps-Philo retells the story in his *Liber Antiquitatum Biblicarum*, but does not pretend to duplicate it.[29] The basics remain the same but there are both additions and contractions, some quite drastic, thus delivering a rather different variant from the original. Ps-Philo expands notably on the backstory, that of the problem of conception and the resolution through an angelic annunciation. He inserts an abrasive quarrel between husband and wife as to where blame lies for the failure to conceive, each accusing the other with repeated and unresolved indictments, until the woman appeals to God to provide an answer. The angel's arrival identifies her as the source of the difficulty but promises that God will open the womb and guarantee offspring. This triggers a flurry of activity, including an apology by the wife and a number of other divergences from the original. The author felt free to supply his own accretions to the text.[30]

The main line of the narrative, however, with regard to the accomplishments and the destructiveness of Samson, receives sharp reduction rather than embellishment and leaves a quite different impression from that of the Bible. This is not mere compression, but a conscious decision to be highly selective. The author states specifically that he will leave out certain episodes for they are well known from the Book of Judges, namely Samson's killing of the lion, the jawbone slaughter of Philistines, the fiery foxes, and the snapping of bonds from his arms.[31] He also omits the anecdote of the riddle, thus leaving the story bereft of much of its drama. These expunged events, of course, constitute perhaps the most notorious escapades in the biblical story. Ps-Philo here signals quite overtly that he will provide his own unique version.

---

28. Whether Josephus presents the Samson story as a Greek tragedy, as suggested by Feldman (1998b), 484, 489, is a more dubious proposition. There are few resemblances.

29. For *LAB* on the Samson story, see the text, translation, and valuable philological analysis by Jacobson (1996), I, 61–64, 162–165; II, 979–1002.

30. *LAB*, 42.

31. *LAB*, 43:4.

Unlike Josephus, whose work he may or may not have known, the author of *LAB* gives a more conspicuous role to God. When Samson was blockaded in the city of Gaza, he appealed to the Lord for strength to escape this confinement. The result was an exhibition of superpower even more formidable than the parallel scene in the scriptures. Samson simply shook the gate in the city wall and removed it, seized one of the doors to use as a shield, put another on his shoulders, killed 25,000 Philistines with this makeshift material, and set it all up on a mountain.[32] Ps-Philo then rests his principal focus on the Delilah portion of the story and the demise of the hero. Samson encountered her in a Philistine city, was seduced by her, and took her as his wife. God surfaces here as observer and commentator rather than as active participant. But his remarks are remarkable. He bemoans the fact that Samson has been "seduced through his eyes" and has failed to remember the deeds of courage that the Lord provided him with. God here takes credit for the awesome achievements of Samson but disclaims any responsibility for his consorting with the daughters of the Philistines.[33] Samson had thus made his own bad decisions, no mere agent of divine direction. But all this would now change. God compares Samson unfavorably with Joseph, who had fended off Potiphar's wife and would not allow the commingling of an Israelite with an alien. Since Samson had transgressed, his lust would be his undoing, says the Lord, whose intervention would now be decisive; he will deliver Samson to his enemies and will assure his blinding—although in the end he will allow him to exercise vengeance upon the Philistines. God, not Samson, is in charge.[34]

LAB abbreviates the scriptural account of Delilah and Samson's mutual deceptions as she endeavors to cajole him into revealing the secret source of his power, reducing those vivid and memorable scenes to just a couple of lines. The author adds only that she got him drunk and that he passed out before she sheared his locks. The blinding and imprisonment of Samson and the symposium scene in which he is mercilessly mocked by the Philistines also shrinks to two sentences.[35] Ps-Philo's version offers a much blander and less engrossing tableau than the original. It omits even the growing back of Samson's hair. Further, the symbolically critical contest for supremacy between God and the Philistine deity Dagon receives no allusion. Indeed the author makes no mention even of the fact that the structure pulled down by Samson was the temple of Dagon—or any temple at all. The two columns he took down were simply two columns.[36] But the author makes sure to include Samson's last-minute appeal to God to reinvest him with the strength needed to accomplish the task. This is the indispensable element. And it takes an even more pointed form. Samson's prayer not only pleads for God's help, it stresses

---

32. *LAB*, 43:2-3.
33. *LAB*, 43:5.
34. *LAB*, 43:5.
35. *LAB*, 43:6-7.
36. *LAB*, 43:7-8.

the fact that the sight which the Philistines had deprived him of had been accorded him by God himself.[37]

Ps-Philo plainly composed an idiosyncratic text. He reproduced the main outline of the biblical story. It was perhaps too famous for a drastic distortion. Yet he shifted its emphasis and provided a rather different picture for his readership to consider. The backstory of Samson's parents and the annunciation got fuller treatment. It had the Lord, his messenger, and his message on center stage. The rest of the narrative, with Samson's adventures, the intrigues with women, and the superhuman feats of the hero get short shrift. The author dismisses most of them simply by referring the reader to the Book of Judges. Ps-Philo has little interest either in the exploits of Samson or in his character flaws. What matters is the working of the Lord. He provides the means of conception, he sets Samson up for the struggle against the Philistines, he expresses great disappointment at Samson's dalliance with Delilah, he orchestrates the hero's fate at the hands of the harlot and his foes, and he has him crush the Philistines as a last gasp, while crushing himself in the process. Ps-Philo constructs a tighter narrative than the biblical one. It lacks most of the flair and excitement of the original. But it keeps the divinity at the forefront. Those who wish to get the more colorful version are referred to the Bible. Ps-Philo had different ends in view.

What is noteworthy here is that Josephus and Ps-Philo moved in exactly opposite directions in the emphasis placed (or diminished) on the role of Yahweh. Josephus soft-pedaled God's engagement, thus absolving him of responsibility for Samson's recklessness and foolishness. Ps-Philo attenuated Samson's flaws and gave freer rein to the Lord's responsibility for Israelite triumph over the Philistine foe. But both felt comfortable in rewriting the biblical tale for their own purposes and to their own taste.

---

37. *LAB*, 43:7.

Chapter 16

THE JUDEAN MONARCHY AND SAUL

The origins of monarchy in Judea are fraught with complexity and controversy. Did the Judaeans need a king to lead them into battle against their enemies? Did they indeed want one or did they have a ruler foisted upon them? Was the outcome a salutary one, a mixed blessing, or a harbinger of evils to come? The text of 1 Samuel contains the principal account of the Judeans' dilemma and their struggles over it. But that text itself is riddled with puzzling shifts and inconsistencies, most of them centered upon the problematic character of Saul. The fluctuations have prompted commentators to conceive of at least two separate strands woven together somewhat awkwardly to produce a composite version. That may well be true. But the composite text, or something like it, was the basis for subsequent rewritings and served as their jumping off point.

A brief summary of key passages in 1 Samuel on the installation of monarchy and the personage of Saul can supply the foundation.

The immediate background involves the narrative of Samuel's birth and his designation as seer and minister of the Lord, successor to the priestly house of Eli.[1] He took the position at a time when his nation faced a dire crisis, under assault from the powerful Philistines, who had even absconded with the Ark of the Lord. Divine intervention, upon appeal from Samuel, wrought vengeance upon the Philistines and allowed Samuel to administer his flock as "judge" to the end of his days.[2] But his final years brought another crisis. Samuel's sons proved to be unfit to step into his place. The elders of Israel now urged the seer to institute a new form of rule and to set a king over them, like other nations. Samuel sharply resisted the idea, pointing to the deleterious effects of such a change, especially the likelihood of an autocratic ruler with unlimited authority who would impress the young men not only into military service but into his personal service, as he would the young women, and expropriate the property, slaves, and livestock of the people to his own purposes, imposing a tithe that would reduce all to the status of slavery.[3] The narrative, however, possesses intrinsic difficulties not readily resolvable. Where does God stand on this? The ambiguity is surprising. He ostensibly shares Samuel's

---

1. 1 Sam., 1–3.
2. 1 Sam., 4–7.
3. 1 Sam., 8:1-6, 8:11-18.

deep discontent with the idea of a monarch, although he has his own personal motive. God ascribes the proposal to the Israelites' turning away from him and preferring a different ruler, another example of Israelite forsaking of the divinity who had made them the chosen people and looking to other gods.[4] But the Lord takes an unexpected stance. Instead of backing Samuel's efforts to discourage the establishment of monarchic governance, the Lord instructs him to heed the wishes of the people, though warning them of the evils of the institution.[5] Why this apparent double-stance? Did God deliberately encourage monarchy for his wayward flock in order that they should suffer its injustices and see the error of their ways? Not especially likely. They may have to endure an unsatisfactory king in the person of Saul, but the institution of kingship was unaffected and lasted well beyond his disquieting reign. God has simply placed Samuel in the tortured situation of condemning monarchy while adhering to the popular will and creating a monarch.[6] The tension in the text stands, thus creating a challenge to readers and re-tellers.

God does not disclaim responsibility for this major change in Judean governance and history. Nor for the appointee himself. The biblical text has him declare to Samuel that he will supply the man whom the seer should anoint as ruler over the nation.[7] And Samuel does indeed perform that function, while announcing that the anointment of Saul was the choice of Yahweh.[8] Yet the very institution evidently remained a delicate matter. When Saul was questioned about his encounter with Samuel, he pointedly omitted any reference to the kingship.[9] Samuel himself, however, despite initial misgivings, proclaimed the establishment of the monarchy and introduced the new monarch unequivocally as the choice of God, a decision duly hailed by the populace.[10]

The ambivalence nevertheless persists. Saul proved his mettle right away, leading forces to victory over the Ammonites. The people then did more than rejoice. They seized the occasion to reaffirm the correctness of the decision to make Saul a king, to denounce, indeed to execute, those who had resisted the idea. This was judgment not only on Saul's qualifications, but evidently on the institution of monarchy. Samuel's subsequent calling of an assembly to renew the kingship confirmed the decision.[11] The popular pressure to execute those who had opposed the appointment suggests that divisions about the virtue of installing monarchy still stirred passions. Samuel acknowledged that he adhered to the voice of the people who sought monarchy—but, now in his final days, he seemed well short of

---

4. 1 Sam., 8:7.
5. 1 Sam., 8:7-9. Cf. the comments of McCarter (1980), 159–162.
6. 1 Sam., 8:19-22.
7. 1 Sam., 9:15-17.
8. 1 Sam., 10:1, 10:24.
9. 1 Sam., 10:14-16. . Josephus, *AJ*, 6:63, ascribes Saul's hesitancy to self-control and moderation, ἐγκράτεια καὶ σωφροσύνη, rather than to any doubts about the institution.
10. 1 Sam., 10:23-25. Cf. 15:1, 15:17.
11. 1 Sam., 11:11-15.

embracing the concept. The speech put in Samuel's mouth is notably equivocal. The seer reminds the Israelites, with a touch of sarcasm, that it was they who had insisted upon a king even though the Lord God was already their king, and he had granted their wish. Samuel exhorts them to follow their ruler as the agent of God, but not without adding that their wish was itself an act of wickedness. The people's reaction underscores the tortuous equivocation. They plead with Samuel to intercede on their behalf with the Lord for they repent of their unconscionable desire to have a king set over them. The seer's response combines reassurance with rebuke. He urges them to follow the dictates of God (and his appointee) who will keep faith with them—while adding the sting in the tail, that their wish for a king was itself an evil act. If they stray once more, he points out, Yahweh will sweep them away, together with their king.[12] This whole segment of the text drips with irony and increases perplexity. The author's judgments of the players in this drama, Samuel, Saul, the populace, and indeed God, defy simple conclusions and leave matters, perhaps deliberately, in some confusion. Whereas neither God nor Samuel ever declares explicit endorsement of monarchy as such, the institution evidently gained unspoken acknowledgment without explanation. The author or authors refrained from commenting and left the matter in a curious limbo.[13]

The troubling ambiguity about monarchy is closely tied to a comparable ambiguity about the first monarch. The text introduces Saul in a most positive light. He is a good man, none better among the Israelites, and one of great stature, a head taller than all others.[14] God had marked him out as royalty from the start and designated him as leader of his people against the Philistines.[15] Samuel confirms that judgment publicly by asserting that there is none like him anywhere among the people.[16] Saul himself enters the scene in humble fashion, declaring his unfitness, for he is a member of Israel's smallest tribe.[17] After anointment by Samuel, he refrained even from mentioning anything about its significance for kingship.[18] When spurned and criticized by some members of the community, he did not respond in kind but stoically maintained restraint.[19] And when his more ardent followers called for the death of those who had opposed his elevation, Saul magnanimously declared that none should be harmed.[20] The initial sign of disfavor came only when Saul made sacrifice before a major battle without waiting for the seven days specified by Samuel, thus rousing the ire of the seer, who charged him

---

12. 1 Sam. 12:12-25.

13. When God lost confidence in Saul, he turned immediately to another choice for the kingship and orders for his anointing; 1 Sam. 15:35, 16:12-13. Continuation of the monarchy was assumed and unquestioned.

14. 1 Sam. 9:2.

15. 1 Sam. 9:16-17.

16. 1 Sam. 10:24.

17. 1 Sam. 9:21.

18. 1 Sam. 10:16.

19. 1 Sam. 10:27.

20. 1 Sam. 11:12-13.

with violating the Lord's commands. The episode, however, suggests no wickedness on Saul's part. The delay in beginning the war, the assemblage of the Philistines, and the absence of Samuel even after seven days induced the king to make sacrifice and engage in battle before it was too late.[21] Saul does not come off badly in this encounter. The text, in fact, implies that Samuel's failure to arrive in time and his impetuous rage bear more blame than any lapse on Saul's part.

The king's second major offense in the eyes of Samuel may also have a less offensive meaning from a different perspective. The seer had delivered the divine dictate that Saul destroy the Amalekites root and branch, sparing no man, woman, child, or beast. The king followed orders, but not quite altogether. He spared the life of Agag, the Amalekite ruler, as well as the best of the livestock. That decision brought the wrath of God, who pronounced through Samuel that Saul had forfeited the kingship as consequence of his disobedience.[22] The event seems to have been the pivotal point in the withdrawal of divine favor. Yet the offense itself does not appear drastically egregious. Saul may have wished to keep Agag alive as a display of victory with mercy. With regard to the animals Saul offers a perfectly reasonable explanation: the best of the livestock would be kept to serve as a suitable sacrifice to God.[23] And he immediately repents of any transgressions that may have offended the divine will, adding that he acted in the interests of the troops but is prepared to bow down to the Lord. It is Samuel who remains rigid and unmoved, declaring that the king has now forfeited his rule, and proceeds to perform the grisly execution of Agag himself.[24] God's rejection of Saul is now complete. But that outcome receives minimal justification and hardly reflects ill on Saul.

Divine favor had turned instead to the prospective future king, the young David, and Saul had good reason to feel anxious.[25] Yet his actions even now show worthy character. He embraced David, made him his armor-bearer and expressed love for him.[26] The portrayal of Saul to this point has him more as victim than as perpetrator of evil.

The portrayal becomes more tangled thereafter. Saul betrays terror at the challenge by the giant Philistine warrior Goliath. But he also seeks to dissuade David from entering into combat with him out of concern for the lad.[27] After David's slaying of the giant, however, jealousy began to grip the king. The women who celebrated David's accomplishments sang forth their famous lines: "Saul has struck down his thousands and David his tens of thousands," thus stirring the wrath of the king and initiating his doubts and suspicions of David, a herald of the tragedies to come.[28] Yet there was no linear progression to disaster. The twists and

21. 1 Sam. 13:7-14; cf. 10:8.
22. 1 Sam. 15:1-19.
23. 1 Sam. 15:15. 15:21.
24. 1 Sam. 15:24-35.
25. 1 Sam. 16:1, 16:13-15.
26. 1 Sam. 16:21-22.
27. 1 Sam. 17:11, 17:33.
28. 1 Sam. 18:7-9.

turns reveal a tortured personality rather than one bent on evil. Saul twice hurled a spear at David with intent to kill, but also paid him the signal honor of giving him a royal daughter as wife.[29] The narrator here takes a dark and cynical view of the development: Saul hoped that the bride would undermine David's efforts, and he further sent him as captain of the hosts against the Philistines in the expectation that he would perish on the battlefield.[30] Whether this was, in fact, Saul's intention stands as an open question.

The text's depiction of the king remains convoluted. Saul allegedly instructed his son Jonathan and all his servants to encompass David's death. But when Jonathan defended David, Saul immediately reversed himself and swore an oath to keep David safe.[31] That did not prevent him from making another futile attempt to skewer David with a spear and to send agents to murder him in his bed.[32] Saul's jealousy extended even to his son Jonathan because of his loyalty to David, and he once fired a spear at him as well (yet another miss).[33] The king's paranoia now haunted him, causing him to turn on all those whom he saw as siding with David, going so far as to order the slaying of priests.[34] Saul went further still, mobilizing troops to conduct hostilities against David's men, once more without success.[35] The about-faces, however, recurred still again. When Saul fell into David's hands, the younger man graciously let him live, indeed exclaimed that he could not and would not act against the anointed of the Lord. Saul in turn burst into tears, declaiming that David is a better man than he, forecasting his well-deserved ascension to the throne, and concluding with reconciliation.[36]

That, however, was not the end of it. Unsurprisingly, another reversal followed. Saul mobilized yet again against David, and fell into his hands once more. David refused the advice of a comrade and let the king live, lest he slay God's anointed.[37] The earlier scene received a full replay. Saul broke down as before, acknowledged his own errors and folly, and gave David his blessing.[38] The text reduced the once powerful king to a pitiable figure.

Saul's final days underscored his lamentable situation. He sought out a medium in order to consult about what future remained to him, having forgotten that he himself had expelled all mediums, wizards, magicians, and fortune-tellers from the land. He managed to find just one surviving necromancer, the "witch of Endor," who conjured up the ghost of Samuel. The seer, however, irritated at his summons from the deep, had nothing reassuring to offer and reduced the hapless Saul to

29. 1 Sam. 18:10-11, 18:17-21.
30. 1 Sam. 18:21, 18:25.
31. 1 Sam. 19:1-8.
32. 1 Sam. 19:9-10, 19:14-16.
33. 1 Sam. 20:30-33.
34. 1 Sam. 22:11-19.
35. 1 Sam. 23:7-14.
36. 1 Sam. 24:5-23.
37. 1 Sam. 26:1-11.
38. 1 Sam. 26:17-25.

despair.[39] A final battle against the Philistines resulted in a rout, the death of Jonathan, and a plea by the king to his armor-bearer to run him through. Even this desperate move was unsuccessful, as the armor-bearer refused, and Saul was compelled to fall upon his own sword. The ultimate humiliation came when victorious Philistines cut off his head and impaled his body on the wall at Beth-Shean.[40]

The fluctuating fortunes of Saul parallel the rapid reversals, the volte-faces, and the switches in behavior and personality that make him so intriguing and so frustrating a character. The biblical rendition defies any uniform appraisal. Saul, of course, serves as inferior precursor to and contrast with the exemplary and admirable (at least as a young man) David. But it is insufficient and misleading to view him simply as a foil whose every flaw sets David's virtues into sharp relief. Nor is the depiction of Saul that of a gradual disintegration from a promising young warrior to a despicable and pitiful figure. The shifts are too frequent and too sudden. Saul's story is no linear one. And it presented a daunting prospect for any rewriting that might reduce it to a pattern.

The closely integrated issues of the desirability of monarchic rule and the character of the first monarch are central for 1 Samuel. Both remain unresolved. And another unresolved matter deserves attention. Where is the hand of God in this drama?

Surprisingly, the divine entity takes a back seat through most of it. He is there in the entreaties of Samuel and of David. But he keeps Saul at a distance. And his role in the matter of monarchy is curious and minimal.

"The Lord's word was rare in those days," says the text, referring to the priesthood of Eli and the time of Samuel as novice.[41] He did emerge to summon Samuel to his post as successor to Eli and as prophet to the Lord, and spoke through him.[42] He could intervene in Israelite battles against the Philistines and to restore the Ark to its proper place. When the suggestion of instituting monarchic rule arose, however, Yahweh did not take the initiative. The elders of Israel conceived the idea and pressed it upon Samuel, who sought God's advice. The response that came was surprising and somewhat paradoxical. Yahweh instructed Samuel to follow the wishes of the people. Why? His reasoning, such as it is, lacks graspable logic. God reassures Samuel that the desire for a monarch is not a rejection of the seer but of God himself, an example among many of Israelite denial of the true God for false idols. Just how this accounts for the demand for a king is quite unclear. And it hardly explains Yahweh's instruction to Samuel to abide by the people's wishes while warning them of the despotic behavior that a king is likely to bring to his subjects.[43] Does he endorse monarchy as a means of punishing recalcitrant Israelites? Is this a begrudging acquiescence to popular outcry, a manipulation of

39. 1 Sam. 28.
40. 1 Sam. 31.
41. 1 Sam. 3:1
42. 1 Sam. 3:4-21.
43. 1 Sam. 8:7-22.

the reluctant Samuel, and a trap for the faithless flock? There is more perplexity than direction in this account. Yahweh's position is shrouded in mystery.

The muddle persists. Despite the dark forecasts of royal misrule, God has Samuel anoint Saul, whom he presents as the man of his own choice and one through whom he will deliver the Judaeans from the oppression by Philistines.[44] Is this miscalculation on God's part—or a deception of his nation? No clarification is forthcoming. The king, it appears, has sanction and inspiration from God.[45] Samuel's impassioned speech to the nation both reminds them that God has provided them with a king and rebukes them for having asked for one in the first place, claiming it to be an evil in the eyes of the Lord.[46] Just where does God stand? He has not previously and will not subsequently denounce monarchy itself as a wicked institution. Is Samuel representing divine sentiments or misconstruing them? Too many questions and too few answers.

Samuel, in berating Saul for his premature offering of sacrifice without waiting for him to arrive, adds that this was a commandment from God.[47] But nothing in the prior text suggests God's participation in this event. The text credits God for delivering victory in a battle against the Philistines, as Saul's son Jonathan had predicted and his troops confirmed.[48] Saul subsequently directs that an altar be built to the Lord.[49] But when he called upon God to assure him about the outcome of the war, he received no answer.[50] Allusions to God recur in the statements of Samuel, Saul, and David, but active engagement by the divinity is sparse. Yahweh himself expresses regret that he had ever bestowed the kingship on Saul, an interesting admission.[51] Did he err? That would be a surprising confession on God's part. Samuel in fact insists that God never repents, only humans do so.[52] On the face of it, that is a direct contradiction of God's own expression of remorse, recorded a few lines earlier and again a few lines later. Bewilderment about the nature of God's part in the tale only increases. He did at last determine upon the removal of Saul and the anointing of David.[53] But the reasons for this change of heart seem far less than obvious. A premature sacrifice by Saul (for which he had good reason and for which he apologized) would appear to be quite inadequate grounds and cast God in a rather dubious light.

The closing portions of 1 Samuel show Yahweh more as reactor than initiator. David, now chosen as the anointed one, had access to the Lord, to whom he could

---

44. 1 Sam. 9:15-17, 10:1-2, 10:9, 10:24; cf. 12:12-13, 15:1.
45. 1 Sam. 11:6, 11:13.
46. 1 Sam. 12:13-17.
47. 1 Sam. 13:13.
48. 1 Sam. 14:2, 14:23, 14:45.
49. 1 Sam. 14:35.
50. 1 Sam. 14:37, 14:41.
51. 1 Sam. 15:10-11, 15:35.
52. 1 Sam. 15:29. McCarter (1980), 268, maintains that this must be a late addition to the text. Be that as it may, the glaring inconsistency stood to confront subsequent readers.
53. 1 Sam. 16:1, 16:3, 16:12-14.

appeal and who responded to his requests as patron for his conflicts against both the Philistines and Saul.[54] He even called upon God to serve as arbiter between him and Saul.[55] But no arbitration took place. And the Lord disappears from the scene for the rest of the tale through the death of Saul, apart from a single reply to a request of David regarding pursuit of an Amalekite raiding party.[56]

The biblical text presented a challenge for readers and for any who wished to recast it. Was monarchy a blessing or a curse? The attitudes of both God and Samuel seem pliant and perplexing on both sides of the issue. Saul himself enters the picture as a humble and restrained new monarch. His subsequent acts that generated disfavor from the powers that be do not seem to be so serious as to justify the harsh reaction that they generated. Saul's darker side emerges in his jealousy of David and the efforts to thwart and even eliminate him. But those actions occur only after an initial welcome and embrace of David and despite later shifts of attitude and reconciliations that leave a quite fragmented image of Saul's character. And even the portrait of God is clouded and murky on the issue of kingship and his disposition toward the king. Did later writers seek to resolve the discrepancies?

Ps-Philo, author of the *Liber Antiquitatum Biblicarum*, seems to have made an attempt. When the people of Israel clamored for a monarch, citing Moses as a model, he has Samuel express misgivings not about the institution but about the timing. It is too soon, so the seer proclaims, and the Lord may reject the idea. He was wrong. God endorsed the idea.[57] The biblical text has God approve the appointment of Saul out of personal pique: since the people have chosen a king to rule them instead of the Lord, they can have him—and it will be to their cost.[58] *LAB* omits the peevish motivation and suggests that the whole episode was part of God's prior plan: he will send a king to destroy the Philistines but will eventually destroy that king himself.[59] This suppresses the sense of mere retaliation against Israelite failures and puts the episode into a larger context of divine orchestration. But it avoids any comment on the propriety of kingship itself.

Ps-Philo follows his precursor in having the people initiate the idea of royalty. But it is God who issues the directive unequivocally and Samuel who conveys it (despite his own wishes) immediately.[60] Samuel's principal motive seems to be to exculpate himself from this decision, without, of course, resisting it.[61] The Lord is in control.

It is noteworthy that the one justification for monarchy comes not from Samuel or from God, let alone from Saul who was reluctant, but from the people of Israel.

54. 1 Sam. 23:2-4, 23:10-13.
55. 1 Sam. 24:13-16.
56. 1 Sam. 30:6-8.
57. *LAB*, 56:1-3; cf. 58:4.
58. 1 Sam. 8:7-9.
59. *LAB*, 56:3.
60. *LAB*, 56:5-7.
61. *LAB*, 57:3.

In the Bible they are prompted simply by the inadequacies of Samuel's sons. In *LAB* a deeper reason surfaces. The people lament their own inadequacies. They are no longer worthy of governance by a prophet: they require a king to whip them into shape.[62] That striking statement, unanticipated in *LAB*, and altogether absent in the Bible, represents an apparent effort by Ps-Philo to offer some kind of rationale for the installation of monarchy.[63] It is, to be sure, far from a satisfactory solution, but, for the author, a possible answer for why this novel institution came into being. He does not pursue the matter. One can only presume that the subsequent entrenchment of the monarchy over many generations induced Ps-Philo to probe no further into its problematic origins.

The author of *LAB* also tried to give some coherence to the disjointed portrait of Saul. Like the biblical account, he has Saul first express reluctance and self-deprecation when summoned to the throne.[64] But admirable traits of character swiftly dissipate. Ps-Philo omits Saul's initial forbearance from mentioning his anointment as ruler, his restraint in responding to those who carped at and criticized him, and his opposition to execution of his harshest detractors. *LAB* moves directly to Saul's grievous sin in the eyes of the Lord: the sparing of Agag, king of the Amalekites, and leaving the livestock alive. Saul offers reasons in the biblical narrative, but Ps-Philo gives only a sinister motive: he let Agag live because he promised to show him his hidden treasures. And God immediately perceived the greed for gain, denouncing Saul for being corrupted by the lure of lucre.[65] Nor does Ps-Philo include the biblical passages in which Saul makes David his armor-bearer, declares love for him, and seeks to dissuade him from contending with Goliath out of concern for his safety. Instead he focuses on Saul's envy of and hatred for David, his effort to kill him, and his fear of being replaced by him, thus stressing David's innocence and blamelessness throughout.[66] The Saul of Ps-Philo is largely one-dimensional, jealous, greedy, and wicked, with no redeeming features. The author largely leaves out Saul's about-faces, reversals, repentances, and expressions of remorse.[67] The portrait is almost fully hostile. But it is at least consistent. By removing or smoothing out the shifts and switches, *LAB* avoided much of the difficulty of the prior text—but only by making it far less captivating.

This flattening out applies also to God. Unlike the ambiguities in 1 Samuel, *LAB* has God in charge from the start. When Philistines abscond with the Ark, the Lord

---

62. *LAB*, 57:4; cf. 1 Sam. 8:5-6.

63. It does not follow that this is a disparaging assessment of monarchy, as Murphy (1993), 205, proposes.

64. *LAB*, 56:6.

65. *LAB*, 58:2-3. On these lines, see Jacobson, (1996), II, 1162–1165.

66. 1 Sam. 62:1, 62:3-6, 63:2, 63:5.

67. The one exception comes at the very end. As his last wish, Saul asks the Amalekite who was about to finish him off to deliver a message to David: "do not remember my hatred nor my injustice" (*LAB*, 65:5). This should not be seen primarily as "a note of reconciliation," as by Murphy (1993), 219, and Jacobson (1996), II, 1215, but as a death-bed effort to salvage some reputation.

assures Samuel that he will bring it back and will inflict vile punishments upon the enemies of Israel.[68] As we have seen, Yahweh indicates to Samuel that he has already devised a long-term plan that involves the selection of a king who will destroy the Philistines and eventually suffer destruction himself.[69] Samuel proceeds to inform Saul that the Lord has dictated his appointment, determined his paths, and will direct his future.[70] God himself reasserts his command of events by instructing Samuel to effect the anointment and adds that he will not only bring about Saul's kingdom but will eventually destroy it.[71] The Lord thus controls both the present and the future. He also plays a more direct role in David's slaying of Goliath, having provided an angel to help the youth and the smooth stones that effected the kill.[72] Even the death of Saul, foreshadowed by Yahweh already before his appointment as ruler, was finally accomplished by the son of Agag the Amalekite, as God had forecast well before.[73]

Ps-Philo had thus faced the complexities of circumstances and characters in 1 Samuel and determined to smooth out the inconsistencies. He did so, however, by evading the problems, simplifying the protagonists, and repressing the ambiguities. The result was a more readily comprehensible story, but a rather less interesting one.

Josephus faced an equally formidable task in attempting to make sense of this convoluted story. Instead of flattening it, he chose to follow closely the outline of the biblical narrative but to expand upon it liberally, to give it more vividness, and to provide more range to its characters. The historian gives full play to his rhetorical skills by supplying lengthy speeches to the protagonists, and adds numerous details to the confrontations, thus making a richer tableau. The result is a notably longer text than the scriptural version itself. He even pauses at one point to inject his own assessment of Saul, a rather surprising—and not altogether convincing—evaluation, and, as we shall see, one that makes the overall narrative less rather than more coherent.

The historian did not come to grips with the issue of monarchy as a desirable or undesirable mode of governance. Writing, as he did, under the Roman Empire and as a beneficiary of the Flavian dynasty, he could hardly denounce the institution itself. He deviates little from the scriptural account in presenting the people's demands for a king, Samuel's reluctance to embrace the idea, God's authorization of the prophet's yielding on this score, and Samuel's warnings of the evils of one-man rule.[74] But Josephus adds a small item of no small significance. He observes that Samuel's hatred of kings stemmed from his deep commitment to aristocracy,

---

68. *LAB*, 55:2.
69. *LAB*, 56:3.
70. *LAB*, 56:5, 57:3. Cf. Murphy (1993), 203. On the wording here, see Jacobson (1996), II, 1153–1154.
71. *LAB*, 59:1.
72. *LAB*, 59:5, 61:3, 61:5-8.
73. *LAB*, 58:4, 65:4.
74. Jos. *AJ*, 6:35-44.

which he regarded as a divine and blessed form of government.[75] Josephus thus transforms, without making an issue of it, the theological and Deuteronomistic matter of the people's rejection of God into a constitutional matter. By ascribing the view to Samuel (the Bible has none of this), the historian alludes to the political significance without taking a stand on it. Samuel, as the Scriptures have it, called another assembly, railed once more against the grievous drawbacks of kingship, and delivered the Lord's message that by choosing monarchy the people have cast aside God's own rulership—but monarchy they will have.[76] Josephus provides a faithful paraphrase of that text and expresses no judgment.[77] The inner tension of the original is thus restated, and Josephus refrains from attempting to elucidate it. When Samuel anointed Saul for the second time to confirm his position, the biblical narrative has the prophet remind the populace that the installation of a king was their idea, and a wicked one at that in the eyes of the Lord.[78] Josephus here again inserts his addition that the πολιτεία of the Hebrews had been transformed into a monarchy.[79] While Samuel might deplore it, Josephus held back an explicit judgment. But a close reader could read between the lines. Josephus does observe that under Moses and Joshua, and subsequently under the Judges, the Israelites remained under aristocratic rule.[80] He did not say, but did not need to say, that this was the preferable regime. If any Roman reader should suspect an indirect questioning of monarchy, Josephus had deniability.

Once the fraught beginnings of monarchic rule were over, the issue disappears as if uncontroversial and unquestioned. Although Saul as first king is a most problematic character, there was no turning back on the institution. Josephus nurtured the notion (through Samuel) of a slide from admirable aristocracy to terrible tyranny, but the subject disappeared with stunning swiftness. When Saul confronted the likelihood of displacement by David, the expectation of succession was already established fact.[81] It was assumed and confirmed by Samuel from the grave, although his initial stance had been fiercely hostile to one-man rule.[82] Josephus' general assessment of Saul in his concluding digression includes the striking statement that the king determined not to flee from his fate lest he

---

75. Jos. *AJ*, 6:36: ἥττητο γὰρ δεινῶς τῆς ἀριστοκρατίας ὡς θείας καὶ μακαρίους ποιούσης τοὺς χρωμένους αὐτῆς τῇ πολιτείᾳ. Josephus' references to aristocracy are generally favorable; *AJ*, 4:223, 5:135, 6:84-85, 6:268. But he recognizes that it did not always hold. Cf. 11:111, 20:229; Attridge (1976), 139; Schwartz (1983-4), 30–52; Spilsbury (1998), 161–171; Mason, in Feldman (2000), xxvi–xxvii, 414. The issue of aristocracy in Josephus was reassessed recently by Feeley in his unpublished PhD dissertation "Josephus as a Political Philosopher: His Concept of Kingship" at U. of Pennsylvania (2017).

76. 1 Sam. 10:17.
77. Jos. *AJ*, 6:60-61, with the notes of Begg (2005), 114–115.
78. 1 Sam. 12:12-24. Cf. Jos. *AJ*, 6:88-91.
79. Jos. *AJ*, 6:83: καὶ οὕτως ἡ τῶν Ἑβραίων πολιτεία εἰς βασιλείαν μετέπεσεν.
80. Jos. *AJ*, 6:84-85.
81. Jos. *AJ*, 6:291.
82. Jos. *AJ*, 6:335-336.

disparage the dignity of kingship.[83] In the end, according to Josephus, Saul showed intense concern for his future reputation—something especially appropriate for kings.[84] The legitimacy of kingship was already beyond question.

The transition from contested and reluctant installation to established system occurred as if in an instant and without apparent resistance—or at least without notice either by the biblical writer or by the Jewish historian.

The inconsistencies and contradictions that characterize the behavior of Saul could not be so easily ignored. Ps-Philo endeavored to soften or dismiss them by focusing his lens upon the negative side of the personality, thus providing uniformity but repressing ambiguity. Josephus held more firmly to the biblical text and reproduced the discordance and incongruities that seemed to signalize Saul's makeup. Yet in the end he felt the need to step back and find some essence that would expose a core of character—or at least provide some closure to his narrative.

For the most part Josephus is content to replicate the course of Saul's career as found in his sources. He draws it out with lengthy speeches and fuller descriptions but sticks to the main line of events and actions.[85] He records Saul's initial reluctance and modesty in taking up leadership of his people, the brilliance of his military exploits, and his unwillingness to execute fellow-Israelites who had opposed his elevation.[86] He even contrasts Saul's compassion for the Amalekite king with God's ferocity and hatred of the Amalekite clan, while reproducing his repentance at having disobeyed the divine command.[87] But he criticizes Saul's recklessness in calling down a curse on any Israelite who takes food prior to the battle with Philistines that almost cost the life of his son.[88] Josephus narrates the on-again, off-again relations with David, some to the credit of Saul, others exhibiting his jealousy, resentment, and murderous inclinations.[89] The act of most horrendous sort, the murder of the High Priest of Nob simply for hosting David, followed by massacring his whole family, then all the inhabitants of the town, is duly registered by Josephus and condemned by him in no uncertain terms.[90] The deed did, however, prompt general reflections that were not drawn from the Scriptures. Josephus uses Saul as an exemplar of a deep character flaw fundamental to humanity itself. In Josephus' jaundiced view, all persons exhibit gentleness, moderation, and righteousness when they lack power. But once they are in a position of untrammeled authority and sovereignty, they strip off the mask, abandon their false benevolence, and give free reign to irrationality, malevolence,

---

83. Jos. *AJ*, 6:344: καθυβρίσαι δὲ τὸ τῆς βασιλείας ἀξίωμα.

84. Jos. *AJ*, 6:349; cf. 6:343.

85. On Josephus' portrait of Saul, see Feldman (1998b), 509–536, although his emphasis on the praiseworthy qualities of Saul is one-sided and exaggerated. For a more judicious literary analysis, see Avioz (2015), 23–56.

86. Jos. *AJ*, 6:51, 58-59, 80-82.

87. Jos. *AJ*, 6:137-138, 151.

88. Jos. *AJ*, 6:116-119.

89. E.g. Jos. *AJ*, 6:168-169, 181, 193-198, 205, 211-214, 237.

90. Jos. *AJ*. 6:255-262.

and cruelty, of which a prime instance is Saul's calamitous vengefulness at Nob.[91] Josephus concludes his devastating digression there and makes no more of it. He returns directly to his narrative with close adherence to the scriptural story. But the excursus leaves an ineradicable impression. The idea that absolute power brings out the darkest traits of human character would reverberate with those subject to the rulers of the Roman Empire. Josephus gave voice to but swiftly dropped that line of reasoning—a prudent move. But he had already left a suggestive hint that owed nothing to the Bible.

Saul's tergiversations continued to the end. The king pursued plots against David, but then reverted to repentance and praise of his young rival, whom he acknowledges as a future monarch.[92] That turnabout occurs a second time in an episode which is a near doublet, duly followed by Josephus.[93] Saul's final scene presents him in a pitiable state, after defeat by the Philistines. Unable to convince his armor-bearer to finish him off, he persuaded an Amalekite to help him thrust a self-inflicted wound as a final blow. This too reproduces the biblical account with a bit more detail and vividness.[94]

Josephus, however, deviated in one very important regard. He provided yet another digression, inserted just prior to the culminating scene of Saul's death, without any scriptural authority, in order to leave his own stamp on the meaning and significance of Saul's life and deeds.[95] It comes quite unexpectedly and seems to have a life of its own. After remaining largely true to the biblical account, Josephus stepped back to draw broader conclusions about his subject. Unlike the earlier excursion that deployed Saul as archetype of inner human wickedness, this one draws out worthy traits that would inspire those who emulated them to deeds of virtue and renown. The historian points to Saul's courage and perseverance at the end: he faced his fate unflinchingly, rejected the idea of clinging to life and besmirching the dignity of kingship; he would go down fighting and provide those left behind with a model of bravery that would earn him eternal renown. Josephus' lofty encomium makes Saul the very epitome of righteousness, courage, and wisdom.[96] He reiterates the point more than once in this section, holding up Saul's determination and valor at the end as the true means for all, but especially kings, to leave a lasting lesson for posterity.[97] This is a quite remarkable, even startling, parenthesis in the text. Coming shortly before the description of Saul's suicide, which Josephus commends (although he notoriously shunned that choice for himself), it is particularly striking. Is this indeed a model to be emulated? And how does one reconcile this powerful praise of Saul's virtues with the rest of the

---

91. Jos. *AJ*, 6:262-268.
92. Jos. *AJ*, 6:290-291.
93. Jos. *AJ*, 6:310-318.
94. Jos. *AJ*, 6:368-372.
95. Jos. *AJ*, 6:343-350.
96. Jos. *AJ*, 6:346: δίκαιος καὶ ἀνδρεῖος καὶ σώφρων.
97. Jos. *AJ*, 6:349-350. On Josephus' attitude toward self-killing more generally, see van Henten (2007), 203–207.

narrative that suggests nothing of the sort? Josephus seems almost embarrassed and sheepish about the excursus. In its concluding lines, he claims to have much more to say about Saul's fortitude but forbears to continue lest he appear excessive and tasteless in his panegyric.[98]

The tensions between this final laudation and the twists and turns of Saul's prior history remain unresolved.[99] Indeed the sharply different, even mutually contradictory, judgments delivered in Josephus' two digressions on Saul, the one epitomizing internal immorality and the other exemplary virtue, resist reconciliation.[100] Whereas Ps-Philo strained to present a consistently evil character, Josephus appears to have had an attack of bad conscience at the end and labored to provide a different side of Saul. It did not bring coherence to the convoluted portrait stemming from the Scriptures, indeed only added to the incoherence. The suicide of Saul plainly resonated with Josephus' own personal experience. He felt an urgency to confront it and its reverberations. But he left the discordance with his earlier remarks unaddressed and unresolved. Readers would have to put the pieces together themselves.

Where does God fit into this picture? The Bible made him a somewhat secondary character. The tale revolved around Samuel, Saul, and David, with God for the most part letting it play out on its own. Ps-Philo brings him onto center stage and has him orchestrate much of the plot. Josephus clings closer to the Scriptures, but adds some subtle supplements that suggest a somewhat different perspective on the deity.

Yahweh enters to assure Samuel's victory over the Philistines, even sending earthquakes, thunder, and lightning to debilitate the enemy and underscore the superiority of the chosen people.[101] Josephus essentially repeats without comment the tortured logic of God's authorization of monarchy out of pique because the people sought it, instead of being content with God's own dominion over them.[102] But he nuances the original by having Samuel explain the divine intention. Samuel infers that the Lord is putting his people through a trial. The harsh brutality of a king will drive them to implore God for succor, but he will not heed their prayers,

---

98. Jos. *AJ*, 6:350: ἔτι τούτων πλείω περὶ Σαούλου καὶ τῆς εὐψυχίας λέγειν ἠδυνάμην, ὕλην ἡμῖν χορηγησάσης τῆς ὑποθέσεως, ἀλλ' ἵνα μὴ φανῶμεν ἀπειροκάλως αὐτοῦ χρῆσθαι τοῖς ἐπαίνοις, ἐπάνειμι πάλιν ἀφ' ὧν εἰς τούτους ἐξέβην.

99. The analysis of Dormeyer (2005), 147–157, does not address this fundamental tension. His proposal that the praise of Saul represents a parallel to his attitude toward the Hasmonean dynasty is undefended and implausible.

100. Avioz (2015), 54, suggests that Josephus included the encomium simply because it was a literary convention or because he wished to soften the negative portrait of Saul and the institution of monarchy. That does not account for his willingness to let the blatant inconsistency stand.

101. Jos. *AJ*, 6:25-28.

102. Jos. *AJ*, 6:38-39.

thus to teach them a lesson for seeking a monarchy in the first place.[103] This spells out what was unexpressed in the original and endeavors to account for the divine motivation.[104] In a subsequent popular assembly summoned by Samuel, the prophet again voices Yahweh's will as punishing the Israelites for having preferred a ruler other than himself.[105] The Deuteronomistic character of the story stands forth: an affront to God followed by divine retaliation. God's will is expressed through his prophet and represented by his choice of king. But the agents of the Lord play the principal roles. Yahweh is appealed to, spoken for, even disobeyed, but more detached than engaged. His order for the extermination of the Amalekites, however, does draw Josephus' attention. Samuel conveyed it and Saul implemented it. And Saul's failure to include the Amalekite king among the slaughtered draws the implacable anger of God, a fury that seems excessive and unjustified in the biblical narrative. Josephus felt the need to give some accounting for this rage. He ascribes it to God's unrelenting hatred of all Amalekites, the people who ambushed the Hebrews during the Exodus.[106] Indeed Josephus adds to the biblical text an express contrast between the unremittingly irascible Yahweh on the one hand and Saul, who showed at least a modicum of compassion, on the other.[107] That contrast forecast Saul's demise. His sparing of the Amalekite ruler found God quite unforgiving and bent on retribution.[108] The Lord is not especially admirable in the biblical version. Josephus' additions make him even less so. The historian, in short, endeavors to account for the Lord's actions that the biblical author apparently reckoned as self-evident.

Unlike Ps-Philo, who sought to trim the troublesome aspects and leave a more coherent story, Josephus on the whole faithfully reproduced the tangled tale of Samuel and Saul in the web of an inscrutable God. But he did not disentangle it. Instead he exercised to some advantage the historian's craft. His insertion or elaboration of speeches in the tradition of classical historiography, his commitment to find some rationality in seemingly irrational behavior, and his pauses to reflect upon the effects of character upon events and as exempla for the future, provide historical perspective that far exceeded mere reproduction of a narrative. Josephus did not tie up the loose ends. But his new version, prompted by historical considerations and broader issues, added ingredients that could provoke serious rethinking and reflection beyond the basic story.

---

103. Jos. *AJ*, 6:40-42. ὁ δ' οὐ προσδέξεται τὰς δεήσεις, ἀλλὰ παραπέμψας ἐάσει δίκην ὑποσχεῖν ὑμᾶς τῆς αὐτῶν κακοβουλίας. See Begg (2005), 107–108.

104. Cf. 1 Sam. 8:4-22.

105. Jos. *AJ*, 6:60-61.

106. Jos. *AJ*, 6:138.

107. Jos. *AJ*, 6:137-138: οὐκέτι τοῦτο ποιῶν κατὰ βούλησιν τοῦ θεοῦ, πάθει δὲ νικώμενος ἰδίῳ καὶ χαριζόμενος ἀκαίρως περὶ ὧν οὐκ εἶχεν ἀκίνδυνον ἐξουσίαν οἴκτῳ; 142–151. On Saul and the Amalekites, see Avioz (2015), 37–39.

108. Jos. *AJ*, 6:142,150, 335-336, 378.

Chapter 17

SOLOMON AND THE BUILDING OF THE TEMPLE

The construction of a Temple to Yahweh in Jerusalem was an event of immense magnitude for the nation of Israel. The Lord had promised such a structure to David, but would not authorize it until the Israelites had subdued their foes and brought peace, thus leaving the actual task and the glory to David's son Solomon. The king duly carried out this charge, aided crucially by Hiram, the ruler of Tyre. The cedars of Lebanon would be the implements of construction. The cordial relations between the kings and collaboration between the nations of Israel and Phoenicia made it all possible, a matter of foreign policy as well as divine direction that implemented the deed. The first book of Kings conveys the story, and it is reproduced with slight variation by the first book of Chronicles.

Hiram took the initiative, sending servants to congratulate Solomon upon ascending to the throne and to renew the friendly relationship that he had had with David. The Israelite king then announced his plan to build a house of the Lord and proposed, as Yahweh had ordered, that the cedars of Lebanon would provide the most suitable material. The Sidonians themselves would be indispensable in the operation. Hiram eagerly embraced the proposition and promised to supply the best lumber and personnel for the job. His men would join Solomon's own impressed labor to accomplish it. Solomon would, in turn, provide ample wheat and oil for the Phoenician land, and the arrangement was sealed with a pact.[1] Twin tasks indeed were fulfilled, the building of the temple and a similarly elaborate structure, the palace of the king, a twenty-year project, achieved with the indispensable assistance of Hiram of Tyre, who advanced the efforts with expert carpenters, the finest cedar wood and cypress wood—and gold. In recompense, Solomon bestowed various towns upon Hiram, a somewhat poor exchange in Hiram's view, but the settlement evidently sufficed.[2] The collaboration of Israel and Phoenicia created the most majestic splendors of Jerusalem.

This negotiation and its effects caught the attention of a Jewish-Hellenistic historian, Eupolemos, probably of the 2nd century BCE. His work, *On the Kings in*

---

1. 1 Kings, 5:15-32. The account in 2 Chron. 2:1-17 has Solomon take the initiative, and embellishes somewhat on the tale.
2. 1 Kings, 9:10-15.

Judaea, known only from fragments preserved by Clement of Alexandria and Eusebius, drawn from Alexander Polyhistor, focused primarily on the era of the monarchy. He is usually identified with Eupolemos, son of John from the priestly family of Akkos, who served as envoy of Judah Maccabee to Rome in 161. The identification is widely accepted, but rests on a number of dubious presumptions.[3] In any event, a late Hellenistic date for the author is not implausible. And whether or not Eupolemos had a Hasmonean agenda, his rewriting of Solomon's foreign diplomacy with an eye to constructing the great temple sets the story in a wider Hellenistic context.

The Bible signaled an exchange between Solomon and Hiram of Tyre. The Chronicler gives a somewhat more elaborate version than the author of 1 Kings. But Eupolemos supplies an actual correspondence in the epistolary style of Hellenistic rulers.[4] The historian has Solomon take the initiative in writing to Hiram (who is Souron in Eupolemos' account) and adds that it is God himself who commanded that he write to ask the assistance of the Phoenician.[5] The Israelite king writes with special authority in the version of Eupolemos. In addition to divine authorization, Solomon declares to Hiram that he has also sent messages to various principalities—Galilee, Samaria, Ammon, Moab, and Gilead—to furnish grain and wine for the endeavor. None of these areas is specified in the scriptural narratives. Their appearance in the letter plainly serves to exhibit Solomon's extensive territorial control, a sign of superiority over his collaborative partner. He adds even that cattle for food will be coming from Arabia at his command.[6] The far reach of the Israelite monarch, however anachronistic, here receives strong emphasis.

Hiram's letter in reply, as given by Eupolemos, has a model in the biblical accounts. They accord him a most gracious and compliant response.[7] The letter conveyed by Eupolemos, drawn in part from the Chronicler, is fulsome and effusive in praise of Solomon. Hiram addresses him as "great king," a not too subtle hint

---

3. The fragments, with commentary, are conveniently collected by Holladay (1983), 93–156. The identification of the historian and the envoy, with various inferences about the Hasmonean flavor of his work, has long been the prevailing view in the scholarship. See, especially, Wacholder (1974), 4–9; Mendels (1987), 29–31; Sterling (1992), 207–209. Additional bibliography in Gruen (1998), 139, n. 8 and Keddie (2013), 203, n. 5. Doubts about the identification were raised by Gruen (1998), 138–141, endorsed more recently by Berthelot (2018), 436–438; White and Keddie (2018), 304–307; cf. Adams (2020), 203–213. On Eupolemos' treatment of Solomon and the temple generally, see the discussions of Wacholder (1974), 173–215; Mendels (1987), 29–46, 131–143.

4. On the Hellenistic epistolary style, see the documents and commentary in Welles (1934), especially, xxxvii-l. Cf. the treatment of Wacholder (1974), 155–160; Holladay (1983), 143; White and Keddie (2018), 303–315, and, especially, Keddie (2013), 208–225.

5. Eupolemos in Euseb. *PE*, 9.33.1. Hiram takes the initiative in 1 Kings, 5:15, but the Chronicler gives it to Solomon; 2 Chron. 2:3.

6. Eupolemos in Euseb. *PE*, 9:33:1.

7. 1 Kings, 5:21-24; 2 Chron. 2:10-15.

that they belong to two different levels of authority and power. He also hails the god of the Israelites "who created heaven and earth and also chose an auspicious man, son of an auspicious man" as ruler.[8] The two kings, ostensibly rulers of comparable realms, are here set on different planes. Eupolemos, in fact, had earlier noted that David had reduced Hiram, king of Tyre and Phoenicia, to a tribute-paying status.[9] Hiram is plainly more subordinate than equal.

Eupolemos' drive to enhance the international stature of Solomon through epistolary exchange becomes still more striking with another set of letters. The correspondence with Hiram did at least have a biblical basis, even if somewhat embellished. But the historian includes an additional pair of letters that have no foundation in the Scriptures. In this case, the Israelite king wrote to Vaphres, ruler of Egypt, an epistle nowhere else attested, announcing that God commissioned him through David to build a temple for Yahweh and to seek the assistance of Egyptians for the job. Vaphres responded positively, expressing joy at the contact and, in parallel with Hiram's words, lavished praise upon Solomon as a man who stemmed from an illustrious father and was sanctioned by so great a god. And Vaphres promised 80,000 men from various Egyptian nomes who will implement the project.[10] The letters are doubtless fictitious, but the concoction served Eupolemos' purpose of elevating the prestige of the Israelite monarch as a major player on the international stage. In Vaphres' epistle, as in that of Hiram, the salutations alone signal the discrepancy in power. Solomon greets each as "king" but he is hailed as "great king." Not that the Egyptian or Phoenician ruler is denigrated. That would diminish Solomon's own ascendancy. Each ruler, in fact, makes sure to assert that his men should have all their needs provided for and that their return, after the mission was accomplished, should be assured.[11] These are no minor princes, but they do not bear comparison with the king of Israel.[12]

Eupolemos plainly had no qualms about improving on the biblical text by embellishing Solomon's exchange with Hiram and inventing a comparable one with Vaphres. Solomon's reputation for wisdom and his crowning achievement of building the temple had already been well entrenched in the tradition. But the Hellenistic historian added a further dimension in giving him diplomatic relations not only with Phoenicia but also with Egypt and in portraying the Israelite king as superior to both.

---

8. Eupolemos in Euseb. *PE,* 9.34:1. Cf. 1 Kings, 5:21; 2 Chron. 2:10-11.
9. Eupolemos in Euseb. *PE,* 9.30:4.
10. Eupolemos in Euseb. *PE,* 9.31:1-32:1.
11. Eupolemos in Euseb. *PE,* 9.32:1; 9.34:3.
12. Cf. Mendels (1987), 29–46, 133–136, who sees this as polemic arising out of the political situation of the Hasmonean era. Keddie (2013), 209–215, 225–229, also recognizes Eupolemos' effort to elevate Solomon's position in relation to the other kings. Unlike Mendels, he is rightly skeptical about the identification of "Eupolemos" with the ambassador of Judah Maccabee. But his argument that Eupolemos was a propagandist for the Hasmoneans is thus largely speculative.

The final line in the preserved fragments of Eupolemos is the most arresting of all. After recording Solomon's return of the Egyptian and Phoenician workmen to their homelands and the substantial gifts that the king supplied to Egypt in recompense for their labors, he adds a startling item that was sent to Tyre. The historian declares that Solomon shipped to Souron (Hiram) a golden column that is now installed at the temple of Zeus in Tyre.[13] That gift has caused some consternation in scholarship. Why would the ever wise and devout Solomon, creator of the great Temple for Yahweh, send an expensive offering to the shrine of an alien god? Nothing of the sort, of course, stems from the biblical tradition. What significance did it have for Eupolemos, who either invented or transmitted it?[14] The historian, whose narrative (what we have of it) is consistently favorable to Solomon, would hardly have injected this item to disparage the king or compromise his reputation. The Bible itself attests the king's penchant for foreign gods and foreign women, at least in his later years, including the goddess Astarte of the Sidonians.[15] For the biblical author, that represented descent into impiety and wickedness. It is hardly accidental that Eupolemos omitted it. Whoring and idolatry had no part in his presentation. Yet he did not blanch at recording Solomon's dispatch of a golden pillar to Tyre for the temple of Zeus. Some have endeavored to explain it away as an embarrassment.[16] But the effort is unnecessary. Eupolemos simply included this present with the other generous gifts bestowed upon Hiram for his collaboration in building the house of the Lord. The linkage was a natural one and added to the prestige of the king. Solomon's authority had elicited the assistance of foreign nations for the erection of his magnificent homage to Yahweh, and he could now exhibit his patronage even to the worshippers of alien gods. The Hellenistic historian had taken the liberty of amplifying the Scriptures by widening the reach of the Israelite king and broadening the expanse of Israel.

---

13. Eupolemos in Euseb. *PE*, 9.34:18 τῷ δὲ Σούρωνι εἰς Τύρον πέμψαι τὸν Χρυσοῦν κίονα, τὸν ἐν Τύρῳ ἀνακείμενον ἐν τῷ ἱερῷ τοῦ Διός.

14. A certain Theophilus, otherwise unknown, bears witness to this tradition in a slightly different form. He has Solomon send to the Tyrian king the gold that was left over after construction of the temple that he then used for a statue of his daughter, to be covered by a golden column; Euseb. *PE*, 9:34:19. Josephus, *CAp.* 1:215-216, does mention a Theophilus among pagan writers who wrote about Jews. He may or may not be the same man. But an author who wrote about Solomon was far more likely to be a Jew. The pagan author Dios refers to a golden pillar installed by Hiram in the temple of Zeus, but gives no indication that it had been sent by Solomon; Jos. *CAp.* 1:118.

15. 1 Kings, 11:1-6.

16. Wacholder (1974), 217, offers as alternatives that Solomon simply sent the gold as a gift while Hiram refashioned it as a religious object or that some later author added this notice to the fragment. Eupolemos' account, to be sure, does not state explicitly that Solomon sent the gold with the express intent of having it converted into a sacred offering. But the implication seems clear, and Eupolemos feels no need to take Solomon off the hook.

Josephus offered no dramatic deviation from the biblical source. In supplying the communication between Solomon and Hiram, he follows the Scriptures in having Hiram make friendly contact upon the accession of Solomon to the throne, then a missive by Solomon requesting assistance from the Sidonian in the building of the temple. Unlike Eupolemos, he does not present a formal correspondence with salutations. Nor does he have Solomon claim that he speaks for a number of principalities under his dominion. There is no evidence indeed that Josephus was aware of Eupolemos' work.[17] Unlike the Hellenistic historian, Josephus does not endeavor to expand Solomon's territorial dominions or international reach. His concern lies elsewhere: an effort to burnish his own credentials as a thorough and reliable historian. In recording the inauguration of work on the temple, he is careful to set it in a specific chronological context, outlined in years from the era of the Flood, the coming of Abraham to Canaan, the Exodus, and even the creation of Adam, as well as its timing in relation to the foundation of Tyre.[18] He furnishes extended details on the nature of the building, its proportions, its dimensions, its materials, the accompanying porches and porticoes, every room, chamber, stairways, walls, floors, furnishings, and decorations in impressive specifics and statistics well beyond even the admiring biblical descriptions.[19]

This is more than mere embellishment. Josephus seeks to establish his worthiness as a serious and trustworthy researcher. In paraphrasing the letters between Solomon and Hiram alluded to in the Bible, he makes certain to insist that they can be found also in the archives of Tyre (which he had evidently visited). Josephus here, in a somewhat defensive manner, explicitly contrasts his assiduous work in extra-biblical sources from writers who prefer to captivate their readers for purposes of entertainment and deceit. Indeed he challenges readers to find anything in his work that is not backed by demonstrations and solid evidence.[20] The historian's craft constitutes a key element in Josephus' presentation.

Josephus reinforces this point by citing external sources. He calls upon the pagan author Menander of Ephesus who, according to Josephus, translated Tyrian archives from Phoenician to Greek, thus supplying independent testimony for the linkage between Solomon and Hiram.[21] Menander, of course, as a Greek writer, would have no axe to grind for Solomon, so Josephus could proudly parade him as unbiased confirmation of the biblical story. He makes the point with greater force in his later treatise, the *Contra Apionem*, where he showcases Menander as a

---

17. He shows no knowledge, for example, of the correspondence between Solomon and Vaphres, the ruler of Egypt, which appears in Eupolemos and is altogether extra-biblical.

18. Jos. *AJ,* 8:61-62.

19. Jos. *AJ,* 8:63-98; cf. 1 Kings, 6; 2 Chron. 3–4. On Josephus' presentation of Solomon and the temple, see Feldman (1998), 605–610.

20. Jos. *AJ,* 8:55-56. See the comparable statement by Thucydides, 1:21:1, 1:22:4, which Josephus echoes here.

21. Jos. *AJ,* 8:144; cf. 8:324, 9:283. On Menander, of whom we know nothing outside the brief mentions by Josephus, see Wacholder (1974), 219–223; Mendels (1987), 135–138; Barclay (2007), 72–74.

scholar who carefully recorded events in both Hellenic and non-Hellenic nations in systematic fashion, drawing on official records in each nation. As illustration, he cites again Menander's evidence on Hiram and Solomon.[22] To further bolster his status as an authoritative researcher, Josephus cites another pagan author, Dios, whom he describes as a trustworthy historian of Phoenicia and one who confirmed Josephus' own account. The particular quotation concerns a riddling contest between Solomon and Hiram, but the reference serves to validate the Jewish historian's narrative on a broader level through pagan corroboration.[23]

In short, the tale of Solomon and the temple, as retold by Josephus, stands out not so much for deviations from or alterations to the text. Rather, Josephus took the opportunity to display his gifts as a historian and to make a case for thoroughness and scrupulous attention to the evidence. His placement of the temple's founding in chronological context, his reproduction of the process of construction, and the lengthy description of the structure and its furnishings, well beyond the biblical account, produce a richness of detail attesting to the assiduousness of the researcher. Summoning the testimony of non-Jewish sources and official records to supplement or bolster his narrative further exhibited (or was designed to exhibit) his scholarly conscientiousness and skill in reaffirming the Scriptures.

---

22. Jos. *CAp.* 1:116-120.

23. Jos. *AJ*, 8:147-149; *CAp.* 1:112-115: Δῖος μὲν οὖν οὕτω περὶ τῶν προειρημένων ἡμῖν μεμαρτύρηκεν. Of Dios nothing more is known. See the comments of Mendels (1987), 138; Barclay (2007), 70–72.

Chapter 18

THE TRAVAILS OF JOB

The Book of Job possesses a powerful, gripping, unnerving, and terrifying quality unmatched elsewhere in the Hebrew Bible. The inexpressible sufferings of Job, the jolting exchanges between the hero and his flawed friends, and the compelling confrontation with God set this work in a class by itself. The whole issue of what constitutes divine justice and the inadequate ability of humankind to grasp it emerges in most vivid but also most problematic fashion. The perplexity it engenders makes it all the more engrossing, and all the more frustrating.[1]

A brief review of the highlights will be useful—although it does not pretend to convey its poetic impact. The text introduces Job as a man of Uz, wherever that may be, in any case outside of Israel and perhaps in a mythical land, thus apart from the narrative of Israelite history and an entity unto itself. Job receives the most favorable assessment by the author: a man blameless, upright, and God-fearing, innocent of all evil. He had the good fortune of seven sons and three daughters, with abundant flocks of sheep, camels, oxen, and donkeys, as well as numerous servants. God took great pride in Job because of his devoutness, uprightness, and shunning of all evil. But how authentic was it? A heavenly adversary entered the picture to dispute God's assessment of Job, to suggest that Job's exemplary behavior was due only to all the blessings that God bestowed upon him. He challenged the Lord to eradicate all those advantages, thus to see how the bereaved Job would react. The satanic figure declared that Job would revert to hostility and curse God to his face. The Lord readily accepted the challenge, quite confident in Job's rectitude, and proposed that Satan work his will and do his worst, so long as he does not afflict Job himself.[2]

God's antagonist now had free rein and proceeded to lower the boom. His machinations brought about the deaths of all Job's children and servants, the loss of all his livestock, and the destruction of all his property. The brutally bereft Job could only rip apart his garments and throw himself upon the ground, but he would not compromise his faith, and did not attach any blame to God for his

---

1. The bibliography on Job is, of course, vast. No need to register it here. For a selection, see the recent translation, with brief notes, by Greenstein (2019), 189-199.
2. Job, 1:1-12.

misfortunes. Indeed, when God's adversary sought and received permission to torment Job himself, he afflicted him with a fearful rash that covered him from head to toe. Job reacted simply by finding a tool to scrape himself off. His wife, however, was far less steadfast. She pleaded with him to abandon useless reliance on his innocence, to curse God, and thus to die. But Job held firm, rebuked his wife and uttered the arresting line, "shall we accept the good from God and not accept the bad?" The author affirms that he gave God no offense.[3] Yet Job cannot resist a pouring out of grief. He curses the day that he was born in a lengthy and lofty lament with a poignant wish that he had died in the womb.[4]

The bulk of the text is devoted to a painful but absorbing set of dialogues between Job and three friends who sought to provide some consolation. Their modes of comforting, however, rested on conventional pieties and traditional expectations that divine justice will be served. They operated on the presumption that Job must have sinned in some fashion to provoke the punishment inflicted by God; indeed they rebuke Job for dwelling on his virtues and his sufferings instead of acknowledging his transgressions and recognizing that God's judgments exceed human comprehension. The text sets their views out at length.[5] But Job's blistering replies receive even lengthier exposition. He dismisses the rebukes by his would-be consolers and denounces them, insists upon his righteousness, underscores his horrific torments, demands of God the reasons for his suffering, and even pleads for a swift death. Job concedes the immeasurable power of the Lord, his own puny person incapable of contending with him. But he remains defiant, making his case, asserting the exemplary character of his life, and soliciting answers for his plight.[6]

A fourth interlocutor, Elihu, a younger man, speaks up after these electric exchanges. He supplies a sharp reprimand both to the consolers and to Job himself. He expatiates against the three for having failed to identify the sins of Job that triggered divine punishment, and he blasts Job for endeavoring to contend with God and seeking justice in human terms, with no understanding of the vast gap that divides heavenly judgment from the imperfections of humanity.[7] In this Elihu anticipates the thunderous climax of the story: the voice of the Lord from the whirlwind. This terrifying power sweeps all before it with the stupefying and unanswerable question to Job: "Where were you when I founded the earth?" And the voice followed with an awesome list of God's creations and accomplishments that no mere human could even aspire to comprehend.[8] Job, humbled and

3. Job. 2:5-10.
4. Job, 3.
5. The importuning of Job's friends is given at length in Job, 4–5, 8, 11, 15, 18, 20, 22, 25, 27.
6. See, especially, Job. 6:9-13, 6:24-30, 7:16-21, 9:1-4, 9:15-21, 9:32-35, 10:1-2, 10:7-9, 10:15-20, 12:14-15, 13:3, 13:15-16, 13:22-25, 14:14-15, 16:1-2, 16:16-17, 17:8-9, 19:7, 19:25-26, 19:29, 21:34, 23:1-10, 27:1-7, 29:12-17, 30:20-23, 31:6, 31:35.
7. See Job, 32:1-3, 33:12-14, 34:4-9, 34:31-37, 35:36, 37:14-16.
8. Job. 38–41.

thoroughly chastened, could only relapse into recantation and repentance.⁹ The Lord, in his mercy and wisdom at the end, did not direct his anger against the chagrined Job but, rather more meaningfully, against the inept companions whose conventional advice showed a profound ignorance of the ways of the Lord. For Job indeed he provided the restoration of his fortune, his lands, and his flocks, and even bestowed upon him a whole new family that duplicated the previous one—but still more beautiful—and granted a long life that allowed him to enjoy four generations of offspring.¹⁰

For the reader, the reversal of Job's fortune at the conclusion did not eradicate the agony, anguish, and horror to which the bulk of the book is devoted. And any rewritings would have to contend with that forbidding grimness. A creative Hellenistic Jew produced a remarkable version, in full knowledge of the biblical forbear but unhindered in producing a new format. The author set it as a tale told by Job on his death-bed in the form of a testament delivered to his seven sons and three daughters. The testament genre is a familiar one, and the author employed it liberally not only to retell the story but, with his *Testament of Job*, to spice it with additions and revisions.¹¹

The Bible has Job struck with torments out of the blue, in consequence of a challenge by Satan to God of which the innocent Job was completely unaware. The author of the *Testament* preferred a backstory in which the hero himself triggers the events. An angel of the Lord, in the form of a voice in a light, alerts Job to the fact that a shrine to which libations are being made is actually not that of God but of the devil. The pious Job then seeks and receives authorization to raze this idolatrous place of worship. The Lord's messenger, however, warns Job that, if he does so, Satan will inflict monstrous ills upon him and his household. Indeed the forecast includes not only the disasters that will befall him but also the happy ending in which all will be recompensed and divine justice reaffirmed. Job, determined and resolute, expressed himself ready to endure all hardships in the service of God, and proceeded to destroy the satanic shrine, come what may.¹²

The author of the *Testament* has thus supplied a preamble, featuring Job's piety and perseverance, to account for the calamities that followed, no mere wager between Satan and God that victimizes him. But the author does not stop there. He

9. Job. 42:1-6.
10. Job, 42:7-17.
11. For a Greek text of the work, with translation, see Kraft (1974). Haralambakis (2012), 29–75, offers a convenient discussion of the manuscripts and textual traditions. A valuable summary of earlier scholarship can be found in Spittler (1989), 7–32. A more general survey of the scholarship appears in Haralambakis (2012), 9–24. Date and provenance remain uncertain. On the composition of the work, see Schaller (1989), 46–92. On the relationship between this work and the testament genre, see Haralambakis (2012), 100–109. Among many treatments of the work's structure and meaning, see, especially, Philonenko (1968), 1–75; Collins (1974), 35–51; Schaller (1979); Haas (1989), 117–154; Haralambakis (2012), 79–100.
12. *T Job*, 1–5.

inserts an altogether new scenario that animates the narrative, gives it color, liveliness, and even a comic touch. Job, after tearing down the idolatrous temple, raced home immediately, locked his doors tightly, and instructed his doorman not to let anyone enter. He even left word that anyone who sought him should be told that he was busy and could not be disturbed. Satan, of course, was not to be deterred. He appeared in the guise of a beggar and requested some bread. A cat and mouse game played itself out. Job directed his housemaid to provide a burnt loaf as a token of his disdain, but the unfortunate girl, unaware of what was going on, substituted a worthy loaf to maintain the proprieties of hospitality. The devil, however, insisted upon the burnt piece so as to herald the conflagration to come.[13] This little scene, wholly invented by the author, with Job contriving pointless schemes to keep the devil at bay, and the confused servant running back and forth, adds a bit of levity, before reverting to the grisly events drawn from the biblical model.

The text proceeds to delineate Job's impressive generosity and philanthropy, his bounty for the poor, forgiveness of debts, and readiness to give away food to all in need.[14] Yet the inventive author cannot forbear to add a new wrinkle to the tale. The massive charity operation had its price. Job's servants grew weary of preparing endless meals for widows and the poor, even resorting to contemptuous slurs against their master. Job, however, had a novel means of dealing with labor complaints. He picked up his lyre and sang the psalms, a soothing solution to any wage protests.[15] The reader is thus expected to imagine overworked and underpaid servants happily taking recompense for their services in the form of Job's warbling. The *Testament* appears to be leavening misery with a bit of levity.[16]

The horrors imposed upon Job are duly recounted in the text, but the author offers further particulars not found in the Bible that vivify the tale. He has the devil, previously disguised as a beggar, now don the garb of a Persian king and round up all the rascals of the realm to rob Job of his remaining belongings (after his herds and flocks had already been slaughtered).[17] He adds yet another gratuitous scene in which Satan cloaks himself as a bread seller and bargains with Job's wife, exchanging three days' worth of bread for the hair on her head now shorn off.[18] Her despair then transforms itself into an urgent plea to Job to renounce God and die, thus to end their torment, but Job remains adamant. Nothing can bring him to question the Lord's judgment. The author, however, delivers this exchange in innovative fashion. He has Job ascribe his wife's words to Satan himself, who, he claims, had turned her into one of those silly women who lead their husbands' innocence astray. Indeed Satan himself confirms the inference in person by

---

13. *T Job*, 5:3–7.11.
14. *T Job*, 9–12, 15.
15. *T Job*, 13:4–14.5.
16. On comic elements in the *Testament of Job*, see Whedbee (1998), 221–262; Gruen (2002), 193–201.
17. *T Job*, 17.
18. *T Job*. 23–25.

emerging from behind the skirts of Job's wife. No costume this time, just concealment until called out by Job. The direct confrontation, however, fizzled out. Satan meekly conceded the contest, confessing that he had failed to break Job's spirit and thus acknowledged defeat.[19] An unexpected and unexplained twist.

The *Testament*'s author had plainly injected a variety of elements that gave the story more spark and a very different flavor. Satan emerges as a real character in the drama, a presence that drives it in diverse directions, no mere string-puller in the background. Job's determination is undiminished as he resists importuning. And his wife plays a conspicuous role in the narrative, thus adding a dimension muted in the original.

By contrast, the *Testament* muted what was central in the original, the lengthy and compelling interchanges between Job and his four interlocutors. They formed the heart of the biblical grappling with the grave issues of divine justice and human frailty. The author of the *Testament* has little patience with theological argumentation. He cuts the dialogue to a minimum and prefers to concentrate on narrative. The biblical account gives short shrift to the prologue that precedes the meeting between Job and his "consolers": they heard of his plight, came to sympathize with him, could not recognize the man they once knew, and loudly lamented his distress.[20] In the *Testament*, however, this introduction grows substantially, with embellishment and exaggeration. The author sets the stage for an arresting narrative. Job's interlocutors are no mere friends but kings (as in the Septuagint). At first they could not find him, and had to be led to the dunghill on which he now forlornly sat. Their first reaction was, in fact, to deny that this pathetic figure could be Job. Once he identified himself, the three monarchs fell to the ground in a dead faint, and, after recovering, they sat for seven days in a state of disbelief.[21] Nor did that suffice. One of the companions proposed a direct interrogation to make sure that this was the same Job whom they knew. Yet another obstacle emerged. The stench arising from Job's dunghill was so pungent that the three kings (who had arrived with their armies!) had to keep their distance. Only when the soldiers scattered incense everywhere (an operation that took three full days), and the monarchs carried perfume jars which overpowered the stench, could they even approach the dunghill.[22] The whole fumigation scenario, unparalleled in the biblical version, exhibits the imagination of an author intent on placing his own imprint on the saga.

The canonical dialogues between Job and his interlocutors take a very different form in the *Testament*, and markedly transform the character of Job. The defiant figure of the Bible, railing against the stupidity of the friends, cursing the day he was born, demanding redress or explanation from God, and seeking a swift death, has largely disappeared. Instead we get the Job who exemplifies patience and

19. *T Job*, 27.
20. Job, 2:11-12.
21. *T Job*, 28:7-30:5. The seven-day period does occur in the canonical version. The rest is accretion.
22. *T Job*. 31:1-3.

tolerance. The very brief dialogues have the interlocutors lament in condescending fashion or suggest that Job must be mentally unhinged and thus offer to supply medical assistance. It is noteworthy that Job's responses lack the fiery tone of the biblical figure. Instead of fierce indignation, he delivers the serene assurance that his travails on earth only forecast a glorious splendor in the heavens to come, when his kingdom will be eternal, thus surpassing the ephemeral realms of his "consolers."[23] The fourth interlocutor took umbrage at this, but was swiftly silenced by the intervention of the Lord, who rebuked the friends for their ignorant and false claims.[24]

The power and passion of God's voice from the whirlwind disappear in this sequel. The *Testament* refers to the voice in just a single sentence. And God's words are pacific rather than aggressive. He upbraids the kings for their misunderstandings, but offers a ready resolution. They need only ask Job to make sacrifice on their behalf, which he did, and the Lord graciously forgave their transgressions.[25] The bland character of this conclusion stands in stark contrast to the thunderous force of its predecessor and its compelling climax. The re-teller of the tale had little interest in the cosmic resonance for the meaning of divine justice. He found it more attractive to spin smaller tales around the core narrative, to offer a different perspective on Job, to reduce the roles of the consolers, to give some life to the female characters, to add light and amusing touches—and, in a word, to make this story his own.[26]

The *Testament* of Job relied on the Septuagint reproduction of the biblical tale. And that reproduction gave rise to at least one other surviving version—albeit one that was very different in character. A certain Aristeas, otherwise unknown, whose work was picked up by Alexander Polyhistor and preserved by Eusebius, also relied exclusively on the Septuagint. But his text, unlike that of the expansive *Testament of Job*, represents a severe condensation of the original. Aristeas has Job as the son of Esau, thus a man of the patriarchal age, enjoying great wealth, but the very soul of righteousness. God, however, for no ostensible reason, determined to test his fidelity, swamped him with afflictions, the loss of his possessions and his family, and the suffering of bodily ailments. Aristeas further records the names of his consolers, three of them referred to as kings, and has Job claim that his pious

23. *T Job.* 32–38.
24. *T Job.* 42:1-6.
25. *T Job.* 42:5-43:13. Only the fourth of the interlocutors was not forgiven.
26. The author, as we have seen, gives more play to Job's wife, and he appends a concluding episode that involves Job's three daughters who complain of their second-class status by comparison with their brothers but receive final gifts with magical properties that redress the balance; *T Job.* 45-50. On the portraits of women in the *Testament*, see van der Horst (1989), 93-116; Garret (1993), 55-70; Kugler and Rohrbaugh (2004), 43-62. Begg (1994), 435-445, points to a number of specific, but relatively minor differences in portrayals of individuals between the biblical and the testamentary texts. For an analysis of the *Testament of Job* through narratological approaches, see Haralambakis (2012), 110-140, with ample bibliography.

steadfastness is unaffected, thus requiring no encouragement. The Lord was impressed by his fortitude, relieved him of his disease, and restored all his holdings.[27]

Aristeas went no further. This was no rewrite, just a very short précis of the story's frame. He eschews any backstory like that in the *Testament*, and he does not attempt to present the anguish of Job, the profound differences with the consolers, or the questioning of divine justice. Indeed he does away with all details and offers only the bare bones. Nor is there any sense of struggle or grappling with the meaning and implications of the events that assailed Job, who remains unshaken in his conviction and resolute in his piety. Indeed Aristeas alters the story in just one aspect, though quite a telling one. He has God himself marvel at Job's courage and thus lift his travails.[28] Job's unwavering steadfastness, revered by God himself, stands on center stage. God expresses awe at the piety of man. Brief though Aristeas' synopsis is, this conclusion gives it a notable force not present in the original or in the *Testament*.

27. Aristeas, in Euseb. *PE*, 9:25.1-4. The text can be conveniently consulted in Holladay (1983), 268-271. See the analyses of Doran (1987), 253-254; Gruen (1998), 118-120; Collins (2000), 35-37.

28. Aristeas, in Euseb. *PE*, 9:25:4: τὸν δὲ θεὸν ἀγασθέντα τὴν εὐψυχίαν αὐτοῦ τῆς τε νόσου αὐτὸν ἀπολῦσαι καὶ πολλῶν κύριον ὑπάρξεων ποιῆσαι.

Chapter 19

THE ADDITIONS TO ESTHER

A final illustration can extend the picture in a very different direction. The Scroll of Esther is a most familiar text for Jews, recalled annually in the festival of Purim. The famous narrative requires only a brief recapitulation. Its principal figures, the demure Jewess Esther and her cousin (or uncle) Mordecai, are presented as dwelling in Susa, and their adventures take place at the court of the Persian king Ahasuerus. The tableau as a whole ostensibly depicts the experience of the Jews in the realm of Persia under the rule of the Achaemenid monarchy. The story is engaging and uplifting—but largely a comic fantasy.[1] It opens with a fanciful banquet hosted by the king for all the officialdom of his empire lasting for 180 days, at which his queen Vashti was asked to display her charms to the assemblage but refused to do so.[2] As a result Ahasuerus ordered a lengthy contest to choose her successor, from which eventually emerged the beautiful Jewess Esther (though the king did not know that she was Jewish). She would now preside as queen in the royal court—with Mordecai as adviser in the vicinity.[3] They ran into trouble, however, when the monarch's chief vizier, Haman, affronted by the lack of deference shown him by Mordecai, advised the compliant king to order a massacre of all Jews in the empire. The genocide was decreed by a royal edict, and its implementation loomed. But Esther, prodded by Mordecai, overcame initial reluctance, and boldly gained an interview with the king in order to dissuade him from his genocidal path.[4] Through her own machinations, she succeeded in turning the tables on the wicked Haman, whom the king ordered to be hanged on the same gibbet that Haman had prepared for

---

1. It survives in three versions, a complication that need not detain us. The summary here reflects the Masoretic text. Discussions of the variations are numerous; see, e.g., Clines (1984), 9–92; Fox (1991); Jobes (1996); Dorothy (1997), 13–19; Levenson (1997), 27–34; de Troyer (2000); Kossman (2000); a useful summary of opinions by Stone (2018), 5–13. Its comic features are stressed in numerous publications; see, e.g., Whedbee (1998), 171–190; Berlin (2001), xv–xxii; Craig (1995); Radday (1990), 295–313; Gruen (2002), 137–148.
2. Esther, 1:1-12.
3. Esther, 2:1-20.
4. Esther, 3–4.

Mordecai.⁵ Esther then persuaded the ever-accommodating Ahasuerus to rescind his genocidal order and issue another one authorizing the Jews to take whatever murderous actions they wished against their Persian enemies—the clueless king's own people. The Jews took full advantage, slaughtering 75,000 Persians on a single day, and inaugurated a festival to be celebrated annually to commemorate the event.⁶

A remarkable feature makes this tale particularly exceptional. The Scroll of Esther in its Hebrew version conspicuously leaves out God. Esther and Mordecai are on their own against the evil Haman and the buffoonish Ahasuerus. The text makes no allusion to religious tenets, beliefs, or practices. Divine authority is starkly and startlingly absent. When the narrative surfaced in a Greek translation in the late Hellenistic period, however, it contained some quite fascinating and surprising additions. Two of them supplied a dream of Mordecai and its interpretation.⁷ Two others purported to be documents issued by the Persian king, the first authorizing extermination of the Jews, the second rescinding the order.⁸ And there were still two other insertions, one of which supplies the prayers of Mordecai and Esther prior to Esther's audience before the king, and the second records the audience itself.⁹

These fascinating insertions alter the character of the story quite drastically.¹⁰ They convey more than just pious pronouncements. The additions exhibit considerable creativity. The directives of Ahasuerus, first to eradicate, then to spare the Jews, are presented as official documents, but in fact are filled with overblown rhetoric and bombast. Among other things, the king, after the scales fell from his eyes, proceeds to lavish praise upon the Jews, calling them children of the highest and greatest living god, and sanctioning the new festival of Purim as the order of God—the very festival that has virtually no religious overtones.¹¹ The author here not only introduces a religious aura, but makes the Persian monarch its champion, a nice piece of irony. The effusive laudation which no Persian monarch would have bestowed upon Jews suggests mockery by the author. Further, the dream of Mordecai, also an addition to the original, conveys a titanic battle between two

---

5. Esther, 5–7.
6. Esther, 8–9.
7. Esther, Add. A, F.
8. Esther, Add, B, E.
9. Esther, Add, C, D.
10. On the character of the additions, see Moore (1977), 153–168; Wills (1995), 116–131; Koller (2014), 113–123. On their date, probably in the 1st century BCE, see Stone (2018), 14–17, and the bibliography assembled there. Most recently, see the useful comments and notes by Grossman (2020), 125–147.
11. Esther, Add. E, 15–24. Cf. Moore (1977), 232–238. The first edict (Add.B. 1–7), which ordered the persecution, equally bombastic in style, is taken too seriously by Stone (2018), 183–191, as reflection of real persecutions of Jews in Alexandria or Judea. Levenson (1997), 76, recognizes the irony in Esther, Add. B. 3:14.

dragons, with natural and supernatural signs of cosmic clash between the nations, contributing an element of apocalyptic fantasy, quite out of tune with the rest of the text.[12]

The author also has no hesitation in radical refashioning of Esther herself. The celebrated biblical scene in which she finally approaches Ahasuerus in order to save her people gains a drastic revision. Her effort is preceded by pleading prayers to God by Mordecai and Esther praising the Lord's power and authority and begging for divine intervention to protect the nation itself, prayers nowhere evident in the Hebrew version. Whereas the Bible accords Esther the famously courageous statement before confronting the king, "if I perish, I perish,"[13] nothing like that appears in the additions. On the contrary, they have her petrified in the preliminaries to the visit, stripping herself of her splendid garments, covering herself with ashes and dung, and uttering an abject entreaty to God to forgive the sins of his people.[14] She confesses sins of her own but tries, rather clumsily, to explain them away. Yes, she concedes, I slept with the uncircumcised king—but I hated every minute of it. Yes, I wear a crown, but only in public and only because I have to; in fact, I despise it, and never put it on when I am off duty.[15] She plainly protests too much. The author exposes Esther's discomforting compromises and self-consciousness. And when she does finally enter into Ahasuerus' chamber, with proper attire, far from doing so boldly and confidently, she was racked with fear. Indeed, once the king cast an angry glance at her, she passed out on the spot. She had to be revived—only to faint once again.[16] This is not the stuff of which a heroine is made. The interpolator augmented the tale at both Mordecai's and Esther's expense. They are not in control. Only the Lord determines events. The two Jewish characters, who simply outwit Haman through their own resources in the canonical tale, become devotees of the divinity in the Greek additions and owe their success only to his intervention.

12. Esther, Add. A, 4–10. For analysis of the dream and its interpretation in Esther, Add. F. 1–10, see Moore (1977), 174–181, 246–249; Seeman (2011), 3–15. For its relations to apocalyptic literature, see Stone (2018), 88–94.

13. Esther, 4:16.

14. Esther, Add. C, 12–22. The provocative interpretation of Esther's prayer by Stone (2018), 210–226, sees it as a "hidden transcript" and an effort to negotiate with Ahasuerus on behalf of God. The suggestion is a strained one since Esther has debased herself and offers only a plea for divine intervention. Whatever one makes of that idea, however, the notion that Esther could be seen here as reflecting the opposition of some Judeans to the Hasmonean dynasty surely goes too far. For Reinhartz (2017), 9–28, Greek Esther falls into the genre (if it is a genre) of the "revenge fantasy." But why should the Jews of Persia require vengeance?

15. Esther, Add. C, 26–27.

16. Esther, Add. D, 1–15. That this is all sham and performance, as Stone (2018), 227–242, 250–253 suggests, is hard to swallow. A double fainting spell would not easily convince as theater.

The additions accord a very different flavor to the story. The Hebrew version conveyed a straightforward tale of intrigue at the Persian court in which the virtuous Jew and Jewess triumphed over their villainous antagonist, and the God of the Hebrews had no hand in the proceedings. The additions, however, reinstate Yahweh and infuse spirituality into Mordecai and Esther, who possess undeviating devoutness. The Lord intervenes to assure the victory of Jewish piety over its enemies. Perhaps the most arresting feature here, paradoxical though it may be, is that the insertions into the text come from the thoroughly Hellenized Jewish community. It was they who obviously felt that the scriptural text failed to transmit the essential sanctity of the nation. The presumably authoritative Hebrew text, far from being considered sacrosanct, is here indeed subverted. The Greek Esther and its additions turn the whole construct on its head.

CONCLUSION

In all of these rewritings, the elastic and pliable attitude toward Scripture stands out. There is no pattern or formula for the revisions. They sometimes enhance the characters, sometimes diminish them. The stories are occasionally expanded, occasionally contracted. The divinity's role might be increased or decreased. And the narrative is often recast to capture attention or to surprise expectations. Did any of this constitute irreverence? Did it compromise the sacral authority of the ancient source? The question itself may be the wrong one to ask. It presupposes a neat dichotomy that did not exist, namely the idea of a fixed and authoritative Bible on the one hand and a raft of retellings and rewritings that lacked its sanctity on the other. That very presumption is fundamentally misleading. It bears reiterating that in the Second Temple period there was as yet no canonical Bible. To be sure, the Pentateuch in some form commanded sufficient aura to warrant a translation into Greek. But the Scriptures in general were fluid and shifting. Some of what we call "rewritings," in fact, might claim independent authority of their own, like the *Book of Jubilees*, which asserted that its text derived from an angel of the Lord who dictated it to Moses.[1] In that era, with numerous texts and numerous variants floating about, it cannot always have been clear where "authority" lay or even how one identified the "holy Scriptures." Hence the very idea of compromising sanctity, which often worries moderns, may never have been an issue at the time.

What the numerous variations do show is that, insofar as these texts were judged to possess sacred character, that did not require consistent or accurate replication. The adaptation of Jewish legend through different approaches and angles had been an integral part of Jewish culture almost from the start. Nothing suggests that the revivals of scriptural material sought to supersede the biblical account, to substitute for it, or to displace it.[2] That would stand at the furthest remove from the writers' intent. Nor did the authors engage much in exegesis for the purpose of ferreting out hidden meaning, let alone apologia as a response to critics.

1. *Jub.* 1.
2. Petersen (2014), 33–35, endeavors to make the case that *Jubilees* at least did present itself as superseding its scriptural predecessors; cf. Zahn (2010), 331. But see Najman (2003), 44–47; Crawford (2008), 81–82.

Rather, we need to see these revisions as supplements to Scripture, as modifications or adaptations, or simply as a different way of telling the same story, whether for variety or for a deeper understanding, whether to supply a more favorable or a more critical or a more nuanced slant on a particular figure, or even just for purpose of entertainment.

It did not, in any way, compromise the integrity, let alone the sanctity, of scriptural material to provide alternative ways of presenting a narrative or a character. So far as we know, none of the writers who produced these texts was ever excommunicated, censored, or penalized for distorting or disrespecting the sacred Scriptures, any more than Andrew Lloyd Webber would be cited for sacrilege in producing "Joseph and the Amazing Technicolor Dreamcoat" or "Jesus Christ Superstar."

In fact, I would urge, the reverse holds. The variants, perhaps paradoxically, only served to validate the original, even occasionally to elevate it.[3] Indeed they generally took for granted that the readership knew the original or could use it as a check. So, for example, Ps-Philo refers his readers to the Book of Judges for further information on Samson. And Josephus, in discussing Daniel's prophetic interpretation of Nebuchadnezzar's dream, asks his readers, if they wish to know more, to go to the Book of Daniel itself.[4] In this way readers would best appreciate the divergences from and the twists applied to the antecedent text, the expansions and the nuances, even the altogether new renderings that would provide a fresh angle on the earlier text. Far from weakening the force of the precursor, the new compositions called attention to its authority. Variants on scriptural material only reinforced the importance of its inspiration. The relationship was a reciprocal one. The Scriptures stimulated novel variations and the variations validated the source of stimulation.

In this light we can rethink the ostensible paradox with which I began. The claims of an exact duplication of the Pentateuch issued by the *Letter of Aristeas* and by Philo and a similar claim maintained by Josephus about his own reproduction need to be understood and, I believe, were understood in a wider perspective. The practice of retellings had a long literary history. Readers would, for the most part, have a familiarity not only with the Hebrew or Greek bibles but also with some of the many diverse reproductions. They would not have been misled by pronouncements about accurate replication. Those statements carried a broader, non-literal significance. They gave due credit to, indeed honored, the original by reminding readers of the fundamental source. The many variations only underscored the power of the sacred narrative. The rewriting of biblical tales maintained, even strengthened, the authority of those tales, but also found room for creative, inventive, and frequently quite entertaining variations on their rich themes and unforgettable characters.

---

3. Cf. Brooke (2005), 96.
4. *LAB*, 43:4; Jos. *AJ*, 10:210.

Bibliography

Adams, Sean A. "Abraham in Philo of Alexandria," in Sean A. Adams and Zanne Domoney-Lyttle, *Abraham in Jewish and Early Christian Literature* (London, T&T Clark, 2019), 75–92.
Adams, Sean A. *Greek Genres and Jewish Authors: Negotiating Literary Culture in the Greco-Roman Era* (Waco, Baylor University Press, 2020).
Ahearne-Kroll, Patricia D. "Constructing Jewish Identity in Ptolemaic Egypt: The Case of Artapanus," in Daniel C. Harlow et al., *The "Other" in Second Temple Judaism* (Grand Rapids, W.B. Eerdmans Publishing Company, 2011), 434–456.
Ahearne-Kroll, Patricia D. *Aseneth of Egypt: The Composition of a Jewish Narrative* (Atlanta, SBL Press, 2020).
Alexander, Philip S. "Retelling the Old Testament," in D.A. Carson and H.G.M. Williamson, *It is Written: Scripture Citing Scripture* (Cambridge, Cambridge University Press, 1988), 99–121.
Allison, Dale C. *Testament of Abraham* (Berlin, Walter De Gruyter, 2003).
Alter, Robert. *The Art of Biblical Narrative* (New York, Basic Books, 1981).
Amit, Yairah. "Tamar, from Victim to Mother of a Dynasty," in Diana V. Edelman and Ehud Ben Zvi, *Remembering Biblical Figures in the Late Persian and Early Hellenistic Periods: Social Memory and Imagination* (Oxford, Oxford University Press, 2013), 295–305.
Atkinson, Kenneth. *A History of the Hasmonean State: Josephus and Beyond* (London, Bloomsbury, 2016).
Attridge, Harold W. *The Interpretation of Biblical History in the Antiquitates Judaicae of Flavius Josephus* (Missoula, Scholars Press, 1976).
Avioz, Michael. *Josephus' Interpretation of the Books of Samuel* (London, Bloomsbury, 2015).
Baarda, Tjitze. "The Shechem Episode in the Testament of Levi," in J.N. Bremmer and F. García Martínez, *Sacred History and Sacred Texts in Early Judaism* (Kampen, Kok Pharos Publishing House, 1992), 11–73.
Bacchi, Ashley L. *Uncovering Jewish Creativity in Book III of the Sibylline Oracles: Gender, Intertextuality, and Politics* (Leiden, Brill, 2020).
Barclay, John M.G. *Flavius Josephus, Translation and Commentary,* vol 10: *Against Apion* (Leiden, Brill, 2007).
Barraclough, Ray. "Philo's Politics, Roman Rule, and Hellenistic Judaism," *ANRW*, II.21.1 (1984), 417–553.
Begg, Christopher T. "Comparing Characters: The Book of Job and the *Testament of Job*," in W.A.M. Beuken, *The Book of Job* (Leuven, 1994), 435–445.
Begg, Christopher T. *Flavius Josephus, Judean Antiquities 5–7* (Leiden, Brill, 2005).
Bellis, Alice Ogden. *Helpmates, Harlots, Heroes: Women's Stories in the Hebrew Bible* (Louisville, Westminster/John Knox Press, 1994).
Berlin, Adele. *Esther* (Philadelphia, Jewish Publication Society, 2001).
Bernhardt, Johannes Christian. *Die jüdische Revolution: Untersuchungen zu Ursachen, Verlauf, und Folgen der hasmonäischen Erhebung* (Berlin, De Gruyter, 2017).

Bernstein, Moshe J. "Rewritten Bible: A Generic Category Which has Outlived its Usefulness?" *Textus*, 22 (2005), 169–196.
Berthelot, Katell. *In Search of the Promised Land? The Hasmonean Dynasty Between Biblical Models and Hellenistic Diplomacy* (Göttingen, Vandenhoeck & Ruprecht, 2018).
Beuken, W.A.M. *The Book of Job* (Leuven, Leuven University Press, 1994).
Bilde, Per. *Flavius Josephus between Jerusalem and Rome* (Sheffield, Sheffield Academic Press, 1988).
Bloch, René et al. "Les Fragments d'Artapan cités par Alexandre Polyhistor dans la Préparation évangélique d'Eusèbe. Traduction et commentaire, in Ph. Bourgeaud and Th. Römer, *Interprétations de Moïse: Judée, Egypte, Grèce et Rome* (Leiden, Brill, 2010), 25–39.
Bloch, René. *Jüdische Drehbühnen* (Tubingen, 2013).
Bloch, René. "Philo's Struggle with Greek Myth," in Francesca Alesse and Ludovica De Luca, *Philo of Alexandria and Greek Myth* (Leiden, Brill, 2019), 107–128.
Bloch, René. "How Much Hebrew in Jewish Alexandria?" in B. Schliesser et al., *Alexandria: Hub of the Hellenistic World* (Tübingen, Mohr Siebeck, 2021), 261–278.
Bloch, René et al. "Les Fragments d'Artapan cités par Alexandre Polyhistor dans la Préparation évangélique d'Eusèbe. Traduction et commentaire," in Ph. Bourgeaud and Th. Römer, *Interprétations de Moïse: Judée, Egypte, Grèce et Rome* (Leiden, Brill, 2010), 25–39.
Bohak, Gideon. *Joseph and Aseneth and the Jewish Temple in Heliopolis* (Atlanta, Society of Biblical Literature, 1996).
Breed, Brennan W. *Nomadic Text: A Theory of Biblical Reception History* (Bloomington, Indiana University Press, 2014).
Bremmer, Jan N. "Sacrificing a Child in Ancient Greece: The Case of Iphigeneia," in Ed Noort and Eibert J.C. Tigchelaar, *The Sacrifice of Isaac (Genesis 22) and its Interpretations* (Leiden, Brill, 2002), 21–43.
Bremmer, Jan N. "From Holy Books to Holy Bible: An Itinerary from Ancient Greece to Modern Islam via Second Temple Judaism and Early Christianity," in Mladen Popović, *Authoritative Scriptures in Ancient Judaism* (Leiden, Brill, 2010), 327–360.
Brooke, George J. "Between Authority and Canon: The Significance of Reworking the Bible for Understanding the Canonical Process," in Esther G. Chazon et al., *Reworking the Bible: Apocryphal and Related Texts at Qumran* (Leiden, Brill, 2005), 85–104.
Buitenwerf, Rieuwerd. *Book III of the Sibylline Oracles and its Social Setting* (Leiden, Brill, 2003).
Burchard, Christoph. *Untersuchungen zu Joseph und Aseneth* (Tubingen, J.C.B. Mohr, 1965).
Burchard, Christoph. *Joseph und Aseneth* (Leiden, Brill, 2003).
Campbell, Jonathan G. "Rewritten Bible: A Terminological Reassessment," in József Zsengellér, *Rewritten Bible after Fifty Years: Texts, Terms, or Techniques?* (Leiden, Brill, 2014), 49–81.
Cazeaux, J. "Nul n'est prophète en son pays -contribution à l'étude de Joseph après Philon," in John Peter Kenney, *The School of Moses: Studies in Philo and Hellenistic Religion* (Atlanta, Scholars Press, 1995), 41–81.
Charles, Robert Henry. *The Testaments of the Twelve Patriarchs* (London, Adam and Charles Black, 1908).
Chesnutt, Randall D. *From Death to Life: Conversion in Joseph and Aseneth* (Sheffield, Sheffield Academic Press, 1995).
Clines, David J.A. *The Esther Scroll: The Story of the Story* (Sheffield, JSOT Press, 1984).

Cohen, Shaye J.D. *Josephus in Galilee and Rome* (Leiden, Brill, 1979).
Collins, John J. *The Sibylline Oracles of Egyptian Judaism* (Missoula, The Society of Biblical Literature, 1974).
Collins, John J. "Structure and Meaning in the Testament of Job," *SBL Seminar Papers*, 1(1974), 35–51.
Collins, John J. "Sibylline Oracles," in James H. Charlesworth, *The Old Testament Pseudepigrapha* (Garden City, Hendrickson Publishers, 1983), I, 317–472.
Collins, John J. *Between Athens and Jerusalem: Jewish Identity in the Hellenistic Diaspora*, 2nd ed. (Grand Rapids, W.B. Eerdmans, 2000).
Collins, John J. *Jewish Cult and Hellenistic Culture: Essays on the Jewish Encounter with Hellenism and Roman Rule* (Leiden, Brill, 2005).
Craig, Kenneth. *Reading Esther: A Case for the Literary Carnivalesque* (Louisville, Westminster John Knox Press, 1995).
Crawford, Sidnie White. *Rewriting Scripture in Second Temple Times* (Grand Rapids, W.B. Eerdmans, 2008).
Daly, Robert J. "The Soteriological Significance of the Sacrifice of Isaac," *CBQ*, 39 (1977), 45–75.
Davies, Philip R. and Bruce D. Chilton. "The Aqedah: A Revised Tradition History," *CBQ*, 40 (1978), 514–546.
Docherty, Susan. "Abraham in Rewritten Scripture," in Sean A. Adams and Zanne Domoney-Lyttle, *Abraham in Jewish and Early Christian Literature* (London, T&T Clark, 2019), 59–74.
Doran, Robert. "The Jewish Hellenistic Historians before Josephus," *ANRW*, II.20.1 (1987), 246–297.
Dormeyer, Detlev. "The Hellenistic Biographical History of King Saul: Josephus, *A.J.* 6.45–378 and 1 Samuel, 9:1–31:13," in J. Sievers and G. Lembiu, *Josephus and Jewish History in Flavian Rome and Beyond* (Leiden, Brill, 2005), 147–157.
Dorothy, Charles V. *The Books of Esther: Structure, Genre, and Textual Integrity* (Sheffield, Sheffield Academic Press, 1997).
Droge, Arthur J. *Homer or Moses? Early Christian Interpretations of the History of Culture* (Tübingen, J.C.B. Mohr, 1989).
Emerton, John Adney. "Judah and Tamar," *VT*, 29 (1979), 403–415.
Endres, John C. *Biblical Interpretation in the Book of Jubilees* (Washington, Pickwick Publications, 1987).
Eshel, Hanan. *The Dead Sea Scrolls and the Hasmonean State* (Grand Rapids, W.B. Eerdmans, 2008).
Feeley, Jacob. "Josephus as a Political Philosopher: His Concept of Kingship" (unpublished PhD dissertation, University of Pennsylvania, 2017).
Feldman, Louis H. "Prolegomenon," in Montague Rhodes James, *The Biblical Antiquities of Philo* (New York, 1971), vii–clxix.
Feldman, Louis H. "Josephus' Portrait of Balaam," *Studia Philonica Annual*, 5 (1993), 48–83.
Feldman, Louis H. *Jew and Gentile in the Ancient World* (Princeton, Princeton University Press, 1998a).
Feldman, Louis H. *Josephus' Interpretation of the Bible* (Berkeley, University of California Press, 1998b).
Feldman, Louis H. *Studies in Josephus' Rewritten Bible* (Leiden, Brill, 1998c).
Feldman, Louis H. *Flavius Josephus, Translation and Commentary*, Vol. 3: *Judaean Antiquities, 1–4* (Leiden, Brill, 2000).

Feldman, Louis H. "Philo, Pseudo-Philo, Josephus, and Theodotus on the Rape of Dinah," *JQR,* 94 (2004), 253–277.
Fishbane, Michael. *Biblical Interpretation in Ancient Israel* (Oxford, Clarendon Press, 1985).
Fitzmyer, Joseph A. *The Genesis Apocryphon of Qumran Cave I, A Commentary* (Rome, Biblical Institute Press, 2nd rev. edition, 1971).
Fox, Michael V. *The Redaction of the Books of Esther* (Atlanta, Society of Biblical Literature, 1991).
Franxman, Thomas W. *Genesis and the "Jewish Antiquities" of Flavius Josephus* (Rome, Biblical Institute Press, 1979).
Freudenthal, Jacob. *Alexander Polyhistor* (Breslau, Wentworth Press, 1874/5).
Gambetti, Sandra. "Some Considerations on Ezekiel's Exagoge," *JAJ*, 8 (2017), 188–207.
García Martíinez, Florentino. "The Sacrifice of Isaac in 4Q225," in Ed Noort and Eibert Tigchelaar, *The Sacrifice of Isaac: The Aqedah (Genesis 22) and its Interpretations* (Leiden, Brill, 2002), 44–57.
Garret, Susan R. "'The Weaker Sex' in the Testament of Job," *JBL*, 112 (1993), 55–70.
Gera, Deborah Levine. *Judith* (Berlin, De Gruyter, 2014).
Gnuse, Robert Karl. *Hellenism and the Primary History* (London, Routledge, 2021).
Goldstein, Jonathan. "Jewish Acceptance and Rejection of Hellenism," in E.P. Sanders, *Jewish and Christian Self-Definition* (Philadelphia, SCM Press, 1981), 64–87.
Goodman, Martin. "Jewish Literature Composed in Greek," in Emil Schürer, *The History of the Jewish People in the Age of Jesus Christ*, rev. ed. by Geza Vermes, Fergus Millar, and Martin Goodman, III.1 (Edinburgh, T&T Clark, 1986), 467–704.
Greene, John T. *Balaam and his Interpreters: A Hermeneutical History of the Balaam Traditions* (Atlanta, Scholars Press, 1992).
Greenstein, Edward L. *Job: A New Translation* (New Haven, Yale University Press, 2019).
Grossman, Maxine. "Expanded (Greek) Esther," in Jonathan Klawans and Lawrence M. Wills, *The Jewish Annotated Apocrypha* (Oxford, Oxford University Press, 2020), 125–147.
Gruen, Erich S. *Heritage and Hellenism: The Reinvention of Jewish Tradition* (Berkeley, University of California Press, 1998).
Gruen, Erich S. *Diaspora: Jews Amidst Greeks and Romans* (Cambridge, Mass., Harvard University Press, 2002).
Gruen, Erich S. "The Twisted Tales of Artapanus: Biblical Rewritings as Novelistic Narrative," in Ilaria Ramelli and Judith Perkins, *Early Christian and Jewish Narrative: The Role of Religion in Shaping Narrative Forms* (Tübingen, Mohr Siebeck, 2015), 31–44.
Gruen, Erich S. *The Construct of Identity in Hellenistic Judaism: Essays on Early Jewish Literature and History* (Berlin, De Gruyter, 2016a).
Gruen, Erich S. "Sibylline Oracles," *Oxford Classical Dictionary* (2016b).
Haas, Cees. "Job's Perseverance in the Testament of Job," in Michael A. Knibb and Pieter W. van der Horst, *Studies on the Testament of Job* (Cambridge, Cambridge University Press, 1989), 117–154.
Halpern-Amaru, Betsy. *Rewriting the Bible: Land and Covenant in Postbiblical Literature* (Valley Forge, Trinity Press International, 1994).
Hamerton-Kelly, Robert. "Sources and Traditions in Philo Judaeus: Prolegomena to an Analysis of his Writings," *Studia Philonica*, 1 (1972), 3–26.
Haralambakis, Maria. *The Testament of Job: Text, Narrative, and Reception History* (London, Bloomsbury, 2012).
Harrington, Daniel J. "Palestinian Adaptations of Biblical Narratives," in Robert A. Kraft and George W.E. Nickelsburg, *Early Judaism and its Modern Interpreters* (Atlanta, Scholars Press, 1986), 239–247.

Hay, D.M. "Philo's References to Other Allegorists," *Studia Philonica*, 6 (1979–80), 41–75.
Heinsch, Ryan. *The Figure of Hagar in Ancient Judaism and Galatians* (Tübingen, Mohr Siebeck, 2022).
Hengel, Martin. *Judaism and Hellenism* (London, SCM-Canterbury Press, 1974).
Henten, Jan Willem van. "Noble Death in Josephus: Just Rhetoric?" in Zuleika Rodgers, *Making History: Josephus and Historical Method* (Leiden, Brill, 2007), 195–218.
Henten, Jan Willem van. "Balaam in Revelation 2:14," in George H. van Kooten and Jacques van Ruiten, *The Prestige of the Pagan Prophet Balaam in Judaism, Early Christianity, and Islam* (Leiden, Brill, 2008), 247–263.
Hicks-Keeton, Jill. *Arguing with Aseneth: Gentile Access to Israel's Living God in Jewish Antiquity* (Oxford, Oxford University Press, 2018).
Hilgert, Earle. "The Dual Image of Joseph in Hebrew and Early Jewish Literature," *Biblical Research*, 30 (1985), 5–21.
Holladay, Carl R. *Theios Aner in Hellenistic Judaism* (Missoula, Society of Biblical Literature, 1977).
Holladay, Carl R. *Fragments from Hellenistic Jewish Authors,* vol. I: *Historians* (Chico, Society of Biblical Literature, 1983).
Holladay, Carl R. *Fragments from Hellenistic Jewish Authors*, vol. II: *Poets* (Atlanta, Society of Biblical Literature, 1989).
Holladay, Carl R. *Fragments from Hellenistic Jewish Authors,* vol. III: *Aristobulus* (Atlanta, Society of Biblical Literature, 1995).
Hollander, Harm W. and M. De Jonge. *The Testaments of the Twelve Patriarchs* (Leiden, Brill, 1985).
Hollander, Harm W. "The Portrayal of Joseph in Hellenistic Jewish and Early Christian Literature," in Michael E. Stone and Theodore A. Bergren, *Biblical Figures Outside the Bible* (Harrisburg, Trinity Press International, 1998), 237–263.
Honigman, Sylvie. *The Septuagint and Homeric Scholarship in Alexandria: A Study in the Narrative of the Letter of Aristeas* (London, Routledge, 2003).
Horst, van der, Pieter. "The Image of Women in the Testament of Job," in Michael A. Knibb and Pieter van der Horst, *Studies on the Testament of Job* (Society for New Testament Studies Monograph Series, 66, 1989), 93–116.
Inowlocki, Sabrina. "Neither Adding nor Omitting Anything: Josephus' Promise not to Modify the Scriptures in Greek and Latin Context," *JJS*, 56 (2005), 48–65.
Jackson, Melissa A. *Comedy and Feminist Interpretation of the Hebrew Bible: A Subversive Collaboration* (Oxford, Oxford University Press, 2012).
Jacobson, Howard. *The Exagoge of Ezekiel* (Cambridge, Cambridge University Press, 1983).
Jacobson, Howard. *A Commentary on Pseudo-Philo's Liber Antiquitatum Biblicarum*, 2 vols. (Leiden, Brill, 1996).
Jobes, Karen. *The Alpha-Text of Esther: Its Character and Relationship to the Masoretic Text* (Atlanta, Scholars Press, 1996).
Johnson, Howard. "Artapanus Judaeus," *JJS*, 57 (2006), 210–221.
Johnson, Sara Raup. *Historical Fictions and Hellenistic Jewish Identity* (Berkeley, University of California Press, 2004).
Keddie, G. Anthony. "Solomon to his Friends: The Role of Epistolarity in Eupolemos," *JSP,* 22 (2013), 201–237.
Koller, Aaron. *Esther in Ancient Jewish Thought* (Cambridge, Cambridge University Press, 2014).

Konstan, David. "The Testament of Abraham and Greek Romance," in Ilaria Ramelli and Judith Perkins, *Early Christian and Jewish Narrative* (Tübingen, Mohr Siebeck, 2015), 45–51.

Kooten, George H. van. "Balaam as the Sophist *par excellence* in Philo of Alexandria: Philo's Projection of an Urgent Contemporary Debate into Moses' Pentateuchal Narratives," in George H. van Kooten, *The Prestige of the Pagan Prophet Balaam in Judaism, Early Christianity, and Islam* (Leiden, Brill, 2008), 131–161.

Koskenniemi, Erkki. "Greeks, Egyptians, and Jews in the Fragments of Artapanus," *JSP*, 13 (2002), 17–31.

Kossman, Ruth. *Die Esthernovelle vom Erzählen zur Erzählung* (Leiden, Brill, 2000).

Kraemer, Ross Shepard. *When Aseneth Met Joseph: A Late Antique Tale of the Biblical Patriarch and his Egyptian Wife, Reconsidered* (Oxford, Oxford University Press, 1998).

Kraft, Robert A. *The Testament of Job According to the SV Text* (Missoula, University of Montana, 1974).

Kugel, James L. *In Potiphar's House: The Interpretive Life of Biblical Texts* (Cambridge, Mass., Harvard University Press, 1990).

Kugel, James L. "The Story of Dinah in the *Testament of Levi*," *HTR*, 85 (1992), 1–34.

Kugel, James L. *The Bible As It Was* (Cambridge, Mass., Harvard University Press, 1997).

Kugel, James L. *Traditions of the Bible: A Guide to the Bible as it Was at the Start of the Common Era* (Cambridge, Mass., Harvard University Press, 1998).

Kugel, James L. "Early Jewish Biblical Interpretation," in John J. Collins and Daniel C. Harlow, *Early Judaism: A Comprehensive Overview* (Grand Rapids, W.B. Eerdmans, 2012), 151–178.

Kugel, James L. "The Beginnings of Biblical Interpretation," in Matthias Henze, *A Companion to Biblical Interpretation* (Grand Rapids, W.B. Eerdmans, 2012), 3–23.

Kugel, James L. "Jubilees," in Louis H. Feldman, James L. Kugel, and Lawrence H. Schiffman, *Outside the Bible* (Lincoln, Jewish Publication Society, 2013), 272–465.

Kugler, Robert A. *The Testaments of the Twelve Patriarchs* (Sheffield, Sheffield Academic Press, 2001).

Kugler, Robert A. and Richard L. Rohrbaugh, "On Women and Honor in the Testament of Job," *JSP*, 14 (2004,), 43–62.

Lanfranchi, Pierluigi. *L'Exagoge d'Ezéchiel le Tragedien* (SVTP 21) (Leiden, Brill, 2006).

Lans, Birgit van der. "Hagar, Ishmael, and Abraham's Household in Josephus' *Antiquitates Judaicae*," in M. Goodman, et al. *Abraham, the Nations, and the Hagarites: Jewish, Christian, and Islamic Perspectives on Kinship with Abraham* (Leiden, Brill, 2010), 185–199.

Lester, Olivia Stewart. *Prophetic Rivalry, Gender, and Economics* (Tübingen, Mohr Siebeck, 2018).

Leveen, Adriane. *Biblical Narratives of Israelites and their Neighbors: Strangers at the Gate* (London, Routledge, 2017).

Levenson, Jon D. *Esther: A Commentary* (Louisville, Westminster John Knox Press, 1997).

Levine, Baruch A. *Numbers, 21–36* (New York, Doubleday, 2000).

Levine, Lee I. *Judaism and Hellenism in Antiquity: Conflict or Confluence* (Seattle, University of Washington Press, 1998).

Lloyd-Jones, Hugh and Peter Parsons. *Supplementum Hellenisticum* (Berlin, Walter De Gruyter, 1983).

Lightfoot, Jane L. *The Sibylline Oracles: With Introduction, Translation, and Commentary on the First and Second Books* (Oxford, Oxford University Press, 2007).

Ludlow, Jared. *Abraham Meets Death: Narrative Humor in the Testament of Abraham* (Sheffield, Continuum-3PL, 2002).
Machiela, Daniel A. "Once More with Feeling: Rewritten Scripture in Ancient Judaism—A Review of Recent Developments," *JJS*, 61 (2010), 308–320.
Margalith, Othniel. "The Legends of Samson/Heracles," *VT*, 37 (1987), 63–70.
Mason, Steve. "Josephus and his Twenty Book Canon," in Lee McDonald and James A. Sanders, *The Canon Debate* (Peabody, Mass., 2002), 110–127.
Mason, Steve. "Introduction to the *Judean Antiquities*," in Louis H. Feldman, *Flavius Josephus, Translation and Commentary*, Vol. 3: *Judean Antiquities, 1–4* (Leiden, Brill, 2000), xiii–xxxvi.
McCarter, P. Kyle. *I Samuel* (New Haven: Yale University Press, 1980).
McDonald, Joseph. *Searching for Sarah in the Second Temple Era* (London, T&T Clark, 2020).
McDonald, Lee Martin and James A. Sanders. *The Canon Debate* (Peabody, Mass., Hendrickson Publishers, 2002).
Mendels, Doron. *The Land of Israel as a Political Concept in Hasmonean Literature* (Tübingen, Mohr Siebeck, 1987).
Menn, Esther Marie. *Judah and Tamar (Genesis 38) in Ancient Jewish Exegesis* (Leiden, Brill, 1997).
Milgrom, Jacob. *Numbers* (Philadelphia, Jewish Publication Society, 1990).
Moore, Carey A. *Daniel, Esther and Jeremiah: The Additions* (Garden City, Anchor Bible, 1977).
Moore, Michael S. *The Balaam Traditions: Their Character and Development* (Atlanta, Scholars Press, 1990).
Mroczek, Eva. *The Literary Imagination in Jewish Antiquity* (Oxford, Oxford University Press, 2016).
Mroczek, Eva. "The Hegemony of the Biblical in the Study of Second Temple Literature," *JAJ*, 6 (2015), 2–35.
Murphy, Frederick James. *Pseudo-Philo: Rewriting the Bible* (Oxford, Oxford University Press, 1993)
Najman, Hindy. *Seconding Sinai: The Development of Mosaic Discourse in Second Temple Judaism* (Leiden, Brill, 2003).
Nati, James. *Textual Criticism and the Ontology of Literature in Early Judaism* (Leiden, Brill, 2022).
Nickelsburg, George W.E. "The Bible Rewritten and Expanded," in Michael E. Stone, *Jewish Writings of the Second Temple Period* (Philadelphia, Fortress Press, 1984), 89–156.
Niditch, Susan. "Eroticism and Death in the Tale of Jael," in Alice Bach, *Women in the Hebrew Bible* (New York, Routledge, 1999), 305–315.
Niehoff, Maren. *The Figure of Joseph in the Post-Biblical Literature* (Leiden, Brill, 1992).
Nikiprowetzky, Valentin. *La Troisieme Sibylle* (Paris, De Gruyter Mouton, 1970).
Noort, Ed. "Balaam the Villain: The History of Reception of the Balaam Narrative in the Pentateuch and the Former Prophets," in George H. van Kooten and Jacques van Ruiten, *The Prestige of the Pagan Prophet in Judaism, Early Christianity, and Islam* (Leiden, Brill, 2008), 3–23.
Noort, Ed. and Eibert Tigchelaar. *The Sacrifice of Isaac: The Aqedah (Genesis, 22) and its Interpretations* (Leiden, Brill, 2002).
Parke, Herbert W. *Sibyls and Sibylline Prophecy in Classical Antiquity* (London, Routledge, 1988).
Petersen, Anders K. "Reflections on the Phenomenon of Rewritten Scripture," in József Zsengellér, *Rewritten Bible after Fifty Years: Texts, Terms, or Techniques?* (Leiden, Brill, 2014).

Philonenko, Marc. *Joseph et Aséneth* (Leiden, Brill, 1968).
Philonenko, Marc. "Le Testament de Job: Introduction, traduction et notes," *Semitica*, 18 (1968), 1–75.
Pritchett, W. Kendrick. *Dionysius of Halicarnassus: On Thucydides* (Berkeley, University of California Press, 1975).
Puech, Émile. "Bala'am and Deir 'Alla," in George H. van Kooten and Jacques van Ruiten, *The Prestige of the Pagan Prophet Balaam in Judaism, Early Christianity, and Islam* (Leiden, Brill, 2008), 25–47.
Pummer, Reinhard. "Genesis 34 in Jewish Writings of the Hellenistic and Roman Periods," *Harvard Theological Review*, 75 (1982), 177–188.
Rad von, Gerhard. *Genesis: A Commentary* (Philadelphia, Westminster John Knox Press, 1961).
Radday, Yehuda T. "Esther with Humour," in Yehuda T. Radday and Athalya Brenner, *On Humour and the Comic in the Hebrew Bible* (Sheffield, Sheffield Academic Press, 1990), 295–313.
Rajak, Tessa. "Moses in Ethiopia: Legend and Literature," *JJS*, 29 (1978), 111–122.
Rajak, Tessa. *The Jewish Dialogue with Greece and Rome: Studies in Cultural and Social Interaction* (Leiden, Brill, 2000).
Rajak, Tessa. *Translation and Survival: The Greek Bible of the Ancient Jewish Diaspora* (Oxford, Oxford University Press, 2009).
Regev, Eyal. *The Hasmoneans: Ideology, Anthropology, Identity* (Göttingen, V&R Academic, 2013).
Reinhartz, Adele. "LXX Esther: A Hellenistic Jewish Revenge Fantasy," in Eileen Schuller and Marie-Theres Wacker, *Early Jewish Writings* (Atlanta, Society of Biblical Literature, 2017), 9–28.
Reinmuth, Eckart. *Joseph und Aseneth* (Tübingen, Mohr Siebeck, 2009).
Ribary, Marton. "Josephus' 'Rewritten Bible' as a Non-Apologetic Work," in József Zsengellér, *Rewritten Bible after Fifty Years: Texts, Terms, or Techniques?* (Leiden, Brill, 2014), 249–266.
Robker, Jonathan Miles. *Balaam in Text and Tradition* (Tübingen, Mohr Siebeck, 2019).
Römer, Thomas C. "Why Would the Deuteronomists Tell About the Sacrifice of Jephthah's Daughter?," *JSOT*, 77 (1998), 27–38.
Römer, Thomas C. "Les Guerres de Moïse," in Thomas C. Römer, *La Construction de la figure de Moïse* (Paris, Gabalda, 2007), 169–193.
Roncace, Mark. "Another Portrait of Josephus' Portrait of Samson," *JSJ*, 35 (2004), 185–207.
Ruiten, Jacques T.A.G.M. van. "The Rewriting of Numbers 22-24 in Pseudo-Philo, *Liber Antiquitatum Biblicarum* 18," in George H. van Kooten and Jacques T.A.G.M. van Ruiten, *The Prestige of the Pagan Prophet Balaam in Judaism, Early Christianity, and Islam* (Leiden, Brill, 2008), 101–130.
Ruiten, Jacques T.A.G.M. van. *Abraham in the Book of Jubilees* (Leiden, Brill, 2012).
Runnalls, Donna. "Moses' Ethiopian Campaign," *JSJ*, 14 (1983), 135–156.
Satlow, Michael L. *How the Bible Became Holy* (New Haven, Yale University Press, 2014).
Schaller, Berndt. *Das Testament Hiobs* (JHRZ, III.3) (Gütersloh, Gütersloher Verlagshaus, 1976).
Schaller, Berndt. "Zur Komposition und Konzeption," in Michael A. Knibb and Pieter van der Horst, *Studies on the Testament of Job* (Cambridge, Cambridge University Press, 1989), 46–92.
Schürer, Emil. *The History of the Jewish People in the Age of Jesus Christ*, III.1 rev. ed. by Geza Vermes, Fergus Millar, and Martin Goodman (Edinburgh, T&T Clark, 1986).

Schwartz, Daniel R. "Josephus on Jewish Constitutions and Community," *SCI*, 7 (1983-4), 30-52.
Seeman, Chris. "Enter the Dragon: Mordecai as Agonistic Combatant in Greek Esther," *BTB*, 41 (2011), 3-15.
Seeman, Chris. *Rome and Judea in Transition: Hasmonean Relations with the Roman Republic and the Evolution of the High Priesthood* (New York, Peter Lang Inc., 2013).
Segal, Michael. *The Book of Jubilees: Rewritten Bible, Redaction, Ideology, and Theology* (Leiden, Brill, 2007).
Shields, Mary E. "'More Righteous than I': The Comeuppance of the Trickster in Genesis 38," in Athalya Brenner, *Are We Amused? Humour About Women in the Biblical World* (London, Continuum, 2003), 31-51.
Simkovich, Malka Z. *Discovering Second Temple Literature* (Philadelphia, The Jewish Publication Society, 2018).
Slingerland, H. Dixon. *The Testaments of the Twelve Patriarchs: A Critical History of Research* (Missoula, Scholars Press, 1977).
Spencer, F. Scott. "Those Riotous—Yet Righteous—Foremothers of Jesus: Exploring Matthew's Comic Genealogy," in Athalya Brenner, *Are We Amused? Humour About Women in the Biblical World* (London, Continuum, 2003), 7-30.
Spilsbury, Paul. *The Image of the Jew in Flavius Josephus' Paraphrase of the Bible.* (Tübingen, Mohr Siebeck, 1998).
Spittler, Russell P. "The Testament of Job: A History of Research and Interpretation," in Michael A. Knibb and Pieter W. van der Horst, *Studies on the Testament of Job* (Cambridge, Cambridge University Press, 1989), 7-32.
Standhartinger, Angela. *Das Frauenbild im Judentum der hellenistischen Zeit: Ein Beitrag anhand von Joseph & Aseneth* (Leiden, Brill, 1995).
Standhartinger, Angela. "Recent Scholarship on Joseph and Aseneth (1988-2013)," *Currents in Biblical Research*, 12 (2014), 353-406.
Sterling, Gregory E. *Historiography and Self-Definition: Josephus, Luke-Acts, and Apologetic Historiography* (Leiden, Brill, 1992).
Stewart, Edmund James. "Ezekiel's *Exagoge*: A Typical Hellenistic Tragedy?," *GRBS*, 58 (2018), 223-252.
Stone, Meredith J. *Empire and Gender in LXX Esther* (Atlanta, Society of Biblical Literature, 2018).
Tarlin, J.W. "Tamar's Veil: Ideology at the Entrance to Enaim," in George Aichele, *Culture, Entertainment, and the Bible* (Sheffield, Sheffield Academic Press, 2000), 174-181.
Thiessen, Matthew. "Protecting the Holy Race and Holy Space: Judith's Reenactment of the Slaughter of Shechem," *JAJ*, 49 (2018), 165-188.
Troyer, Kristin de. *The End of the Alpha Text of Esther* (Atlanta, Society of Biblical Literature, 2000).
Toorn, Karel van der and Pieter van der Horst. "Nimrod before and after the Bible," *HTR*, 83 (1990), 1-29.
Tov, Emanuel. *Textual Criticism of the Hebrew Bible* (Minneapolis, Fortress Press, 2002).
Unnik, Willem Cornelis van. "Josephus' Account of the Story of Israel's Sin with Alien Women in the Country of Midian (Num. 25.1ff)," in M.A. Beek, Matthieu Sybrand, Huibert Gerard Heerma van Voss, Ph H. J. Houwink ten Cate, N. A. van Uchelen, *Travels in the World of the Old Testament* (Assen, Van Gorcum, 1974), 241-261.
VanderKam, James C. "Mastema in the Qumran Literature and the Book of Jubilees," in Joel Baden, Hindy Najman, and Eibert J.C. Tigchelaar, *Sibyls, Scriptures, and Scrolls: John Collins at Seventy* (Leiden, Brill, 2017), 1346-1360.

VanderKam, James C. *Jubilees*, 2 vols. (Minneapolis, Fortress Press, 2018).
Vermes, Geza. *Scripture and Tradition in Judaism* (Leiden, Brill, 1961).
Wacholder, Ben Zion. *Eupolemus: A Study of Judaeo-Greek Literature* (Cincinnati, Jewish Institution of Religion, 1974).
Wassén, Cecilia. "The Story of Judah and Tamar in the Eyes of the Earliest Interpreters," *Literature and Theology*, 8 (1994), 354–366.
Weisberg, Dvora E. "The Widow of our Discontent: Levirate Marriage in the Bible and Ancient Israel," *JSOT*, 28 (2004), 403–429.
Welles, C. Bradford. *Royal Correspondence in the Hellenistic Period: A Study in Greek Epigraphy* (Chicago, Ares Publishers, 1974).
Werman, Cana. "Jubilees 30: Building A Paradigm for the Ban on Intermarriage," *HTR*, 90 (1997), 1–22.
West, Stephanie. "*Joseph and Aseneth*: A Neglected Greek Romance," *CQ*, 24 (1974), 70–81.
Whedbee, J. William. *The Bible and the Comic Vision* (Cambridge, Cambridge University Press, 1998).
White, L. Michael and G. Anthony Keddie. *Jewish Fictional Letters from Hellenistic Egypt: The Epistle of Aristeas and Related Literature* (Atlanta, Society of Biblical Literature, 2018).
Whitmarsh, Tim. *Beyond the Second Sophistic: Adventures in Greek Postclassicism* (Berkeley, University of California Press, 2013).
Whitmarsh, Tim. *Dirty Love: The Genealogy of the Ancient Greek Novel* (Oxford, Oxford University Press, 2018).
Will, Edouard and Claude Orrieux. *Ioudaismos-Hellènismos: Essai sur judaisme judéen à l'époque hellénistique* (Nancy, Année, 1986).
Wills, Lawrence M. *The Jewish Novel in the Ancient World* (Ithaca, Wipf and Stock, 1995).
Wills, Lawrence M. "Jewish Novellas in a Greek and Roman Age: Fiction and Identity," *JSJ*, 42 (2011), 141–165.
Wills, Lawrence M. *Judith* (Minneapolis, Fortress Press, 2019).
Wright, Benjamin G. *The Letter of Aristeas: Aristeas to Philocrates or On the Translation of the Law of the Jews* (Berlin, De Gruyter, 2015).
Zahn, Molly M. "Rewritten Scripture," in Timothy H. Lim and J.J. Collins, *The Oxford Handbook of the Dead Sea Scrolls*. (Oxford, Oxford University Press, 2010), 323–336.
Zahn, Molly M. "Genre and Rewritten Scripture: A Reassessment," *JBL*, 131 (2012), 271–288.
Zahn, Molly M. *Genres of Rewriting in Second Temple Judaism: Scribal Composition and Transmission* (Cambridge, Cambridge University Press, 2020).
Zakovitch, Yair. "Inner-Biblical Interpretation," in Matthias Henze, *A Companion to Biblical Interpretation in Early Judaism* (Grand Rapids, W.B. Eerdmans, 2012), 27–63.
Zellentin, Holger. "The End of Jewish Egypt: Artapanus and the Second Exodus," in Gregg Gardner and Kevin Osterloh, *Antiquity in Antiquity: Jewish and Christian Pasts in the Greco-Roman World* (Tübingen, Mohr Siebeck, 2008), 27–73.

Primary Sources Index

HEBREW BIBLE

Genesis
10	14
10.8-9	15
10.8-10	15
11.1-9	13
11.4	14
11.5	14
12.10-20	21
15.18-21	46
16.1-2	29
16.1-5	25
16.1-16	27
16.4-6	29
16.6-9	29
16.6-12	25
17.17	26
18.10-15	26, 29
20.1-18	21
20.12	21
21.1-7	26
21.8-20	26, 28
22	102
22.1-2	31
22.3-6	31
22.7-9	31
22.10-12	31
22.13-18	31
24	97
26.6-11	21
33.18-34.12	43
34.7	43, 51
34.13-17	43
34.18-24	44
34.25-30	44
34.31	44
37.3	53
37.5-11	53
37.12-24	53
37.21-22	55
38.1-5	63
38.2	65
38.6-9	63
38.9-11	64
38.12-18	64, 66
38.19-23	64
38.24-26	64
38.26	66
38.27-30	65
39-41	53
39.6	55
41.45	59
41.50	59
42.1-43.14	56
43.15-44.34	56
45.1-15	56
46.20	59
47.13-26	53, 57, 58
49.5-7	44

Exodus
14	73
14.21-22	80
20.22-23	5
20.33	5
31.1-10	80
32	72
34.16	47

Leviticus
18	47
18.16	63, 65
20	47
20.21	63, 65

Numbers
12.1	75
22.1-7	83
22.7	87
22.7-22	88
22.8-20	84
22.9	89
22.21-33	84
22.36-24.19	85
23.13-14	89
24.25	86
24.2	92
25.1-9	86
25.1-18	90
25.1	90
31.8	86
31.16	86

Deuteronomy
1.28	14
4.2	4
7.3-4a	47
12.32	4
23.4-6	93
25.5-10	63
31-34	73

Joshua
13.22	93
23.9-10	93

Judges
4.1-9	95, 98
4.10-22	96
4.23-24	99
5.24-30	96
5.27	96
11.1-40	101
11.25	93
13	109
13.3-7	107
14.1-4	107, 110
14.5-6	110
14.5-14	108
14.15-20	108
14.19	110
15.1-17	108
15.14	110
15.18	111
16.1-3	108
16.4-17	109
16.18-30	109
16.20	109
16.21	110
16.28	109, 110

Primary Sources Index

Ruth				2 Chronicles	
4.12-22	65	15.21	118	2.1-17	131
		15.24-35	118	2.1-2	132
		15.29	121	2.10-11	133
1 Samuel		15.35	117, 121	2.10-15	132
1-3	115	16.1	118, 121	3-4	135
3.1	120	16.3	121		
3.4-21	120	16.12-13	117	Nehemiah	
4-7	115	16.12-14	121	13.2	93
8.1-6	115	16.13-15	118		
8.4-22	129	16.21-22	118	Esther	
8.5-6	123	17.11	118	1.1-12	145
8.7	116	17.33	118	2.1-20	145
8.7-9	116, 122	18.7-9	118	3-4	145
8.7-22	120	18.10-11	119	4.16	147
8.11-18	115	18.17-21	119	5-7	146
8.19-22	116	18.21	119	8-9	146
9.2	117	18.25	119		
9.15-17	116, 121	19.1-8	119	Job	
9.16-17	117	19.9-10	119	1.1-12	137
9.21	117	19.14-16	119	2.5-10	138
10.1-2	116, 121	20.30-33	119	2.11-12	141
10.8	118	22.11-19	119	3	138
10.9	121	23.2-4	122	4-5	138
10.14-16	116	23.7-14	119	6.9-13	138
10.16-17	117	23.10-13	122	6.24-30	138
10.17	125	24.5-23	119	7.16-21	138
10.23-25	116, 121	24.13-16	122	8	138
10.24	117, 121	26.1-11	119	9.1-4	138
10.27	117	26.17-25	119	9.15-21	138
11.6	121	28	120	9.32-35	138
11.11-15	116, 117, 121	30.6-8	122	10.1-2	138
		31	120	10.7-9	138
12.12-13	121	62.1	123	10.15-20	138
12.12-24	121, 125	62.3-6	123	11	138
12.12-25	117	63.2	123	12.14-15	138
12.13-17	121	63.5	123	13.3	138
13.7-14	118			13.15-16	138
13.13	121	1 Kings		13.22-25	138
14.2	121	5.15-32	131	14.14-15	138
14.23	121	5.15	132	15	138
14.35	121	5.21	133	16.1-2	138
14.37	121	5.21-24	132	16.16-17	138
14.41	121	6	135	17.8-9	138
14.45	121	9.10-15	131	18	138
15.1	116, 121	11.1-6	134	19.7	138
15.1-19	118			19.25-26	138
15.10-11	121			19.29	138
15.15	118	1 Chronicles		20	138
15.17	116	2.4-15	65		

21.34	138	*Joseph and Aseneth*		41.7	66	
22	138	1-4	59	41.11-12	66	
23.1-10	138	5-6	59	41.19-20	66	
25	138	6.2	61	41.23	67	
27	138	7-8	59	41.23-24	67	
27.1-7	138	7.1-5	61	41.25-28	67	
29.12-17	138	7.13	60	42.25	54	
30.20-23	138	8.4-5	61	43.14	54	
31.6	138	9-13	60	48.2	32	
31.35	138	13.11	61	48.9	32	
32.1-3	138	14-21	60	48.12	32	
33.12-14	138	20.6-21.5	61	48.15	32	
34.4-9	138	22-29	60			
34.31-37	138	23.13	48, 51	*Judith*		
35.36	138	29.10-11	61	8.25-26	37	
37.14-16	138			9.2	50, 51	
38-41	138	*Jubilees*		9.2-4	50	
42.1-6	139	1	149	9.4	50	
42.7-17	139	1.27-29	5	9.24	48	
		2.1	5			
Micah		10.8	32	*Letter of Aristeas*		
6.5	93	10.18-19	14	3	3	
		10.22	14	31	3	
APOCRYPHA AND		10.22-26	14	308-311	2	
PSEUDEPIGRAPHA		11.5	32	313	3	
		11.11	32			
Additions to Esther, A	146	13.13-15	22	*1 Maccabees*		
Additions to		14.21-24	27	2.52	37	
Esther, A. 4-10	147	16.1-2	28	3.48	3	
Additions to Esther, B	146	17.4	28	12.9	3	
Additions to		17.15-16	32			
Esther, C	146	17.17-18	32	*2 Maccabees*		
Additions to		18.1-8	33	8.23	3	
Esther, C. 12-22	147	18.8	35			
Additions to *Esther*,		18.9-12	33	*4 Maccabees*		
C. 26-27	147	18.13-16	33	2.18-21	51	
Additions to		30.2-4	46			
Esther, D	146	30.5	48	*Sibylline Oracles*		
Additions to Esther,		30.5-6	47	3.99-100	15	
D. 1-15	147	30.7-10	47	3.101-107	15	
Additions to Esther, E	146	30.11-17	47	11.6-13	15	
Additions to Esther,		30.18-20	47			
E. 15-24	146	30.23	47	*Testament of Abraham*		
Additions to Esther, F	146	30.25	47	1-15	40	
Additions to Esther,		34.20-21	65	16-18	40	
F.1-10	147	39.5-8	54	17-20	41	
		40.6-7	54			
Ben Sira		41.1	65	*Testament of Job*		
Prol.	9	41.2	66, 67	1-5	139	
44.20	37					

5.3-7.11	140	167-177	33	2.38-40	2
9-12	140	176	35	2.45	3
13.4-14.5	140	112	26		
15	140	178-183	33	*De Mutatione Nominum*	
17	140	184-190	33	*(Mut.)*	
23-25	140	193	34	89-90	57
27	141	196	34	134-136	64
28.7-30.5	141	206	26	193-200	50, 51
31.1-3	141			202-203	87
32-38	142	*Legum Allegoria (Leg. All.)*			
42.1-6	142	217-219	30	*Quaestiones et*	
42.5-43.13	142			*Solutiones in Genesin*	
45-50	142	*De Cherubim (Cher.)*		*(Quaest. Gen.)*	
		31-35	87	2.82	19
Testament of Judah				4.68	21
10.1-3	68	*De Confusione Linguarum*			
10.4-5	68	*(Conf. Ling.)*		*Quod Deterius Potiori*	
10.6	68	1-13	19	*insidiari solis*	
11.1-2	68	14-15	19	*(Quod Deter.)*	
11.3-5	68	150-158	19	71	87
12.1-3	69	159-160	87		
12.4	69	168	19	*Quod Deus Immutabilis*	
12.5	69	196	19	*sit (Quod Deus Imm.)*	
12.6-11	69			180-183	87
13.4-7	68	*De Fuga et Inventione*			
14.6	68	*(Fug.)*		*De Sobrietate (Sobr.)*	
17.1	68	149-153	64	17	3
Testament of Levi		*De Josepho (Jos.)*		*De Somniis (Somn.)*	
2.1-10	48	4-5	54	1.219-220	57
5.1-4	48	37-39	54	2.15-16	57
6.3	49	232	56	2.42-47	57
6.6-7	49	257-260	55	2.44	64
6.8-11	49	268-270	55	2.63	57
7.3	49			2.93-113	57
		De Migratione Abrahami			
Wisdom of Solomon		*(Migr.)*		*De Virtute (Virt.)*	
10.5	37	113-114	87	95	3
		203-204	57		
DEAD SEA SCROLLS		223-224	51		
		253-255	50	JOSEPHUS	
Genesis Apocryphon,					
col. XXI.1-33	22	*De Vita Mosis (Mos.)*		*Antiquitates Judaicae*	
4Q225, col. I	32	1.264-265	85	*(AJ)*	
4Q225, col. II	36	1.266	85	1.5	3
		1.272-274	85	1.17	3
PHILO OF ALEXANDRIA		1.281-284	86	1.107	17
		1.286	86	1.112	16
De Abrahamo (Abr.)		1.289-291	86	1.113-114	16
92-98	23	1.294-304	86	1.114	17

1.115	17	4.158	90	6.268	125		
1.118	17	4.196	3	6.290-291	127		
1.119	17	4.223	125	6.291	125		
1.161-168	23	5.135	125	6.310-318	127		
1.187	29	5.202-203	98	6.335-336	125, 129		
1.188	29	5.204	98	6.343	126		
1.188-189	29	5.205-206	99	6.343-350	127		
1.198	29	5.207-208	99	6.344	126		
1.213	29	5.209	99	6.346	127		
1.214-215	29	5.264	102	6.349	126		
1.216-217	29	5.265	102	6.349-350	127, 128		
1.222-223	34	5.276-285	109	6.368-372	127		
1.224	35	5.286	110	6.378	129		
1.225	35	5.287	110	8.55-56	135		
1.228-231	36	5.294	110	8.61-62	135		
1.232	36	5.300	110	8.63-98	135		
1.233-235	36	5.301	110	8.144	135		
1.337-338	51	5.301-303	111	8.147-149	136		
1.339-341	51	5.306	110	8.324	135		
2.9-10	55	5.312	110	9.208	3		
2.14	55	5.314-316	110	9.283	135		
2.20-28	55	5.317	111	10.210	150		
2.41-59	55	6.25-28	128	10.218	3		
2.50-52	55	6.35-44	124	11.111	125		
2.97	56	6.36	125	12.113	3		
2.105	56	6.38-39	128	14.1	3		
2.125	56	6.40-42	129	16.164	3		
2.189-193	57	6.51	126	20.261	3		
2.238-242	75	6.58-59	126	20.229	125		
2.243	75	6.60-61	125, 129				
2.244-248	75	6.63	116	*Bellum Judaicum (BJ)*			
2.252-253	76	6.80-82	126	2.159	3		
2.347	3	6.83	125				
4.102-104	87	6.84-85	125	*Contra Apionem (CAp)*			
4.103	89	6.88-91	125	1.42	3, 4		
4.105	88, 89	6.116-119	126	1.37-41	9		
4.106	88	6.137-138	126, 129	1.112-115	136		
4.107	88, 89	6.138	129	1.116-120	136		
4.107-111	89	6.142	129	1.118	134		
4.113	88	6.142-151	129	1.215-216	134		
4.114-122	89	6.150	129				
4.118	89	6.151	126	*Vita*			
4.120-121	89	6.168-169	126	418	3		
4.123	88, 89	6.181	126				
4.126-127	89	6.193-198	126	Pseudo-Philo			
4.127	88	6.205	126				
4.126-130	90	6.211-214	126	*Liber Antiquitatum*			
4.126-158	90	6.237	126	*Judaicarum (LAB)*			
4.131-155	90	6.255-262	126	4.7	18		
4.157	90	6.262-268	127	6.1	17		

6.3-12	17	56.1-3	122	9.22.9b	45, 46
6.14	18	56.3	124	9.22.10-11	45
7.1	17	56.5	124	9.23.1	58
7.2	18	56.5-7	122	9.23.2	58
7.3	18	56.6	123	9.25.1-4	143
7.4	17, 18	57.3	122, 124	9.25.4	143
7.5	18	57.4	123	9.26.1	81
8.1	30	58.2-3	123	9.27.3	79
8.7	50, 51	58.4	122, 124	9.27.3-4	79
9.5	65, 67	59.1	124	9.27.4	79
10.3-4	73	59.5	124	9.27.4-10	76
12.9	72	61.3	124	9.27.4-6	79
18.3	91	61.5-8	124	9.27.19	80
18.4	91	63.5	123	9.27.21-22	80
18.5	36	65.4	124	9.27.23-26	80
18.5-6	91	65.5	123	9.27.28-33	80
18.8	92			9.27.35	80
18.9	92	CHRISTIAN SOURCES		9.27.37	80
18.10-11	92			9.29.1	3
18.11-12	92	*2 Peter*		9.29.4-6	71
18.13-14	93	2.15-16	94	9.29.15	3
19.9	73			9.30.4	133
31.1	96, 97	*Jude*		9.31.1-32.1	133
31.1-2	97	11	94	9.32.1	133
31.3-5	97			9.33.1	132
31.6	97	*Revelation*		9.34.3	133
31.7	98	2.14	93	9.34.18	134
31.8-9	98	22.18-19	4	9.34.19	134
32.1-2	36, 37				
32.11-12	97	CLEMENT OF		GREEK AND LATIN	
32.3	37	ALEXANDRIA		AUTHORS	
32.4	37	*Stromata*			
39.1-5	103	1.23.153.4	81	DIONYSIUS OF	
39.6-7	103			HALICARNASSUS	
39.11	103	EUSEBIUS		*On Thucydides*	
40.1	103	*Praeparatio Evangelica*		5.331	4
40.2	36, 104	*(PE)*			
40.3	104	9.17.2-3	16	EURIPIDES	
40.4	104	9.17.6-7	22	*Iphigeneia in Aulis*	34, 102
40.5	104	9.17.8	23		
40.6-7	104	9.18.1	23	*Hippolytus*	55
40.8	105	9.18.2	16		
42	112	9.20.1	37	THUCYDIDES	
43.2-3	113	9.21.9	51	1.21.1	135
43.4	112, 150	9.22.2	44	1.22.4	135
43.5	113	9.22.3-4	45		
43.6-7	113	9.22.5	45	VERGIL	
43.7-8	113, 114	9.22.7	45	*Eclogues*	
55.2	124	9.22.8-9a	46	10.50-69	104

AUTHOR INDEX

Adams, S.A. 7, 23, 44, 58, 60, 71, 132
Ahearne-Kroll, P.D. 60, 81
Alexander, P.S. 6, 7, 10, 102
Allison, D.C. 39
Alter, R. 63
Amit, Y. 63
Attridge, H. W. 4, 23, 125
Avioz, M. 126, 128, 129

Baarda, T. 48, 49, 50
Bacchi, A. 15
Barclay, J.M.G. 4, 135, 136
Barraclough, R. 57
Begg, C.T. 110, 111, 125, 129, 142
Bellis, A.O. 96
Berlin, A. 145
Bernstein, M.J. 7, 10
Berthelot, K. 132
Bilde, P. 23
Bloch, R. et al. 76
Bloch, R. 3, 19, 60
Bohak, G. 60
Breed, B. W. 8
Bremmer, J. N. 3, 34
Brooke, G. J. 150
Buitenwerf, R. 15
Burchard, C. 60

Campbell, J.G. 7, 8
Cazeaux, J. 57
Charles, R. H. 48
Chesnutt, R.D. 60
Clines, D.J.A. 145
Cohen, S.J.D. 23
Collins, J.J. 14, 15, 81, 139, 143
Craig, K. 145
Crawford, S.W. 6, 7, 8, 22, 149

Daly, R. J. 32
Davies, P.R. and Chilton, B.D. 32
Docherty, S. 22
Doran. R. 143

Dormeyer, D. 128
Dorothy, C.V. 145
Droge, A.J. 81

Emerton, J.A. 63
Endres, J.C. 46, 66

Feeley, J. 125
Feldman, L.H. 3, 4, 10, 17, 23, 29, 34, 35, 36, 46, 50, 52, 55, 57, 76, 77, 87, 90, 93, 110, 111, 112, 125, 126, 135
Fishbane, M. 5
Fitzmyer, J.A. 6, 22
Fox, M.V. 145
Franxman, T. W. 34
Freudenthal, J. 6

Gambetti, S. 71
Garcia Martinez, F. 32, 36
Garret, S.R. 142
Gera, D. L. 50, 51
Gnuse, R.K. 102, 107
Goodman, M. 14, 15
Greene, J.T. 83
Greenstein, E.L. 137
Grossman, M. 146
Gruen, E.S. 11, 14, 15, 39, 44, 53, 58, 60, 62, 63, 81, 132, 140, 143, 145

Haas, C. 139
Halpern-Amaru, B. 7
Hamerton-Kelly, R. 57
Haralambakis, M. 139, 142
Harrington, D.J. 7, 8
Hay, D.M. 33
Heinsch, R. 27, 29, 30
Henten, J.W. van 94, 127
Hicks-Keeton, J. 60
Hilgert, E. 57
Holladay, C.R. 6, 15, 23, 44, 45, 58, 76, 132, 143
Hollander, H.W. and De Jonge, M. 48

Hollander, H. W. 53
Honigman, S. 2
Horst, P. van der 142

Inowlocki, S. 4

Jackson, M.A. 65, 96
Jacobson, H. 17, 18, 36, 37, 71, 72, 73, 81, 91, 92, 93, 97, 102, 104, 112, 123, 124
Jobes, K. 145
Johnson, S.R. 81

Keddie, G.A. 132, 133
Koller, A. 146
Konstan, D. 39
Kooten, G.H. van 87
Koskenniemi, E. 81
Kossman, R. 145
Kraemer, R.S. 60
Kraft, R.A. 139
Kugel, J.L. 7, 10, 14, 16, 23, 32, 45, 46, 47, 48, 49, 56, 67, 69, 83
Kugler, R.A. 48
Kugler, R.A. and Rohrbaugh, R. L. 142

Lanfranchi, P. 71
Lans, B. van der 29
Lester, O.S. 87, 90, 94
Leveen, A. 108
Levenson, J.D. 145, 146
Levine, B.A. 83, 84, 85
Lightfoot, J. L. 14
Lloyd-Jones, H. and Parsons, P. 44
Ludlow, J. 39

Machiela, D.A. 7, 8
Margalith, O. 107
Mason, S. 9, 23, 111, 125
McCarter, P.K. 116, 121
McDonald, J. 23
McDonald, L.M. and Sanders, J.A. 9
Mendels, D. 7, 132, 133, 135, 136
Menn, E.M. 63, 65, 67, 68,
Milgrom, J. 83
Moore, C.A. 146, 147
Moore, M.S. 83
Mroczek, E. 9, 10
Murphy, F.J. 17, 37, 72, 93, 98, 102, 123, 124

Najman, H. 7, 10, 149
Nati, J. 8
Nickelsburg, G.W.E. 7
Niditch, S. 96
Niehoff, M. 57
Nikiprowetzky, V. 15
Noort, E. 93
Noort, E. and Tigchelaar, E. 32

Parke, H.W. 14
Petersen, A.K. 7, 8, 149
Philonenko, M. 60, 139
Pritchett, W.K. 4
Puech, E. 83
Pummer, R. 44

Rad, G. von 14, 25, 26, 32
Radday, Y. T. 145
Rajak, T. 2, 77
Reinhartz, A. 147
Reinmuth, E. 60
Robker, J.M. 83, 93
Römer, T. C. 76, 77, 102
Roncace, M. 111
Ruiten, J.T.A.G.M. van 22, 27, 28, 83, 91
Runnalls, D. 77

Satlow, M.L. 8
Schaller, B. 139
Schurer, E. 10, 81
Schwartz, D.R. 125
Seeman, C. 147
Segal, M. 67
Shields, M.E. 65
Simkovich, M.Z. 9
Slingerland, H.D. 48
Spencer, F.S. 65
Spilsbury, P. 125
Spittler, R. P. 139
Standhartinger, A. 51, 60
Sterling, G. E. 4, 23, 76, 81, 132
Stewart, E.J. 71
Stone, M. J. 145, 146, 147

Tarlin, J.W. 65
Thiessen, M. 50
Troyer, K. de 145
Toorn, K. van der and Horst, P. van der 15
Tov, E. 8

Unnik, W.C. van 90

VanderKam, J.C. 5, 13, 14, 27, 28, 32, 46, 47, 66, 67
Vermes, G. 7, 83, 93

Wacholder, B.Z. 7, 132, 134, 135
Wassen, C. 65, 66, 68
Weisberg, D.E. 63
Welles, C.B. 132
Werman, C. 46, 47

West, S. 60
Whedbee, J.W. 65, 140, 145
White, L.M. and Keddie, G.A. 132
Whitmarsh, T. 60, 72
Wills, L.M. 11, 39, 50, 146
Wright, B.G. 2

Zahn, M.M. 7, 9, 10, 149
Zakovitch, Y. 5
Zellentin, H. 81

SUBJECT INDEX

Abraham 6, 15, 17, 18, 21–24, 25–30, 31–37, 39–41, 45, 49, 53, 54, 91, 102
Agag 118, 123, 124
Ahasuerus 145, 146, 147
Alexander Polyhistor 6, 44, 132, 142
Alexandria 9, 146
Amalekites 118, 123, 129
Ammonites 101, 103
Amorites 83, 95
apologia 10, 52, 149
Aqedah 31–38
Aristeas (historian) 142–143
Artapanos 23, 58, 76, 77, 79, 80–81
Aseneth 59–61
Astarte 134

Babel, tower of 13–19
Babylon 15, 16, 17
Balaam 83–94
Balak 83–93
Barak 95, 96, 98, 99
Belus 16
Benjamin 55–56
Ben Sira 9
biblical text, sacredness of 1, 3, 4, 5, 9, 34, 112, 149, 150

Canaanites 63–69, 95, 96, 97, 98
circumcision 45, 46, 48, 49, 51, 52, 79
Clement of Alexandria 6, 132

Dagon 109, 110, 113
David 1, 6, 17, 65, 67, 87, 118–128, 131, 133
Dead Sea Scrolls 6, 8, 22, 36
Death 40, 41
Deborah 95–99
Delilah 108, 109, 110, 113, 114
Diaspora 2, 3
Dinah 43–52
Dios 134, 136

Egypt 1, 6, 7, 21, 23, 39, 53–58, 59–62, 72–75, 79, 80, 133, 134, 135
Elihu 138
Er 63, 66
Esau 142
Esther 145–148
Ethiopia 4, 12, 75, 76, 79, 80
Eupolemos 6–7, 15, 81, 131–135
Eusebius 6, 22, 44, 132, 142
Exagoge 71–72
Exegesis 10, 149

Gaza 108, 113
Genesis Apocryphon 6, 22
Gilead 101, 132
God/the Lord/Yahweh
    and Abraham, 21–24
    and the Aqedah, 31–38
    and Babel, 13–19
    and Balaam, 84–86, 87–94
    and Dinah, 45, 47, 48, 49, 50–52
    and Esther, 146–148
    and Jephthah, 101–105
    and Job, 137–143
    in *Joseph and Aseneth*, 59–61
    and Moses, 71–73, 80
    and Samson, 107–114
    and Sarah and Hagar, 25–30
    and Saul, 115–118, 119, 120–122, 123–124, 125, 126, 128–129
    and Solomon, 132, 133, 134
    in the *Testament of Abraham*, 40–41
    and Tamar and Judah, 63, 65, 67
    and Yael, 95, 97–99
golden calf 1, 4, 5, 11, 72
Goliath 1, 118, 123, 124

Hagar 1, 25–30, 32, 107
Haman 145, 146, 147
Hamor 43, 44, 45, 46, 48, 50, 51
Hercules 107

Hesiod 11
Hestiaios 17
Hiram 131–136
Homer 11

Isaac 1, 4, 21, 26, 28, 29, 31–37, 102, 104
Ishmael 25, 26, 27, 28, 29, 30, 31, 32

Jacob 4, 43, 44, 45, 46, 47, 48, 49, 51, 52, 54, 55, 63, 64, 91
Jephthah 34, 101–103
Job 32, 137–143
Jonathan 119, 120, 121
Joseph 1, 53–62, 63, 113
Joseph and Aseneth 12, 59–62
Josephus
   on Abraham in Egypt, 23–24
   on adherence to Scripture, 3–5, 11, 150
   on the Aqedah, 34–36
   on Balaam, 87–91, 93, 94
   on Barak and Deborah, 98–99
   on Jephthah, 102, 105
   on Joseph, 55–57
   on Moses, 75–76, 77
   on Nimrod, 16–17
   on rape of Dinah, 51–52
   on Samson, 109–112, 114
   on Sarah and Hagar, 28–30
   on Saul, 124–129
   on Solomon, 135–136
Jubilees 5, 13, 14–15, 21, 27, 28, 30, 32–33, 35, 36, 37, 46–49, 50, 54, 56, 65–68, 69, 149
Judah 63–70
Judith 50–51, 97

Letter of Aristeas 1, 2, 150
Levi 44, 45, 46, 47, 48, 49, 50, 51
Lloyd Webber, Andrew 53, 150

masoretic text 12, 145
Mastema 32, 33, 37
Menander of Ephesus 135, 136
Michael 40, 41
Midianites 86, 87, 88, 89
mixed marriages 43, 45, 46, 47, 48, 50–51, 52
Moabites 86, 87

monarchy 115–117, 120–125, 126, 128–129
Mordecai 146–148
Moses 1, 3, 4, 5, 6, 7, 9, 12, 18, 54, 71–73, 75–77, 78–81, 85, 86, 90, 122, 125, 149

Nimrod 15–17, 18, 19
Noah 6, 13, 14, 15
Nob 126, 127

Onan 63, 68

Palestine 2
Pentephres 59–61
Perez 64
Pharaoh 21, 22, 23, 24, 32, 53, 55, 56, 57, 58, 59, 60, 61, 75, 76, 80
Philistines 7, 107–115, 117–124, 126–128
Philo of Alexandria 2, 10, 18–19, 22–23, 30, 33–35, 37, 50, 54–55, 56, 57–58, 85–88, 90, 91, 93, 94, 150
Phinehas 86, 90
Phoenicia 6, 7, 81, 131–134, 135, 136
Potiphar's wife 53, 54, 55, 58, 59, 113
Pseudo-Eupolemos 15, 16, 22
Pseudo-Philo 17, 18, 30, 36, 50, 65, 67, 72–73, 91–94, 96–98, 99, 102–105, 112–114, 122–124, 126, 128, 129, 150
Purim 145, 146

Rachel 59
Rebecca 49, 59, 107
Reuben 55
"rewritten Bible" 7, 8, 10

Samson 1, 107–114, 150
Samuel 115–125, 128, 129
Sarah 1, 21–23, 24, 25–30, 35, 39, 49, 59, 107
Satan 32, 137, 139, 140, 141
Saul 115, 116–129
Seila 103, 104, 105
Septuagint 2, 3, 4, 6, 12, 15, 141, 142
Shechem/Shechemites 43–52
Shelah 64, 66, 68, 69
Sibylline Oracles 14, 17
Simeon 44, 45, 46, 50, 51
Sisera 95–99
Solomon 7, 131–136

talking donkey 84–85, 87, 88, 92, 94
Tamar 63–70
Temple of Jerusalem 7, 131–136
Testament of Abraham 12, 39–41, 59
Testament of Job 139–143
Testament of Judah 67–69
Testament of Levi 48–50, 51
Theodotus 44–46, 47, 48, 50, 51
Tyre 7, 131, 134, 135

Uz 137

Vaphres 133, 135
Vashti 145

witch of Endor 119–120

Yael 95–99

Zambrias 90

www.ingramcontent.com/pod-product-compliance
Lightning Source LLC
Chambersburg PA
CBHW052125300426
44116CB00010B/1792